Reflections on the Gospel of John

VOLUME 1
The Word Was Made Flesh
John 1–5

Leon Morris

BAKER BOOK HOUSE
Grand Rapids, Michigan 49506

1986

ISBN: 0–8010–6202–0

Library of Congress
Catalog Card Number: 85–73360

Unless indicated otherwise, Old Testament quotations are from the *Holy Bible: New International Version* © 1978 by the New York International Bible Society, used by permission of Zondervan Bible Publishers. New Testament quotations are the author's translation.

Printed in the United States of America

Contents

Preface

For some years I have been very much occupied with John's Gospel. I have lectured on it, preached on it, written on it, thought about it, endeavored to live out its teachings. To audiences of various kinds, I have often tried to convey its message as I see it. This series of studies arises out of such ventures. It is an attempt to convey to today's reader the meaning of some of the great things John is saying to us. The tone is devotional, for I think that is the way John should be read. There is profound theology in this Gospel, and there are critical questions that have preoccupied the scholars through the centuries and still keep them busy. But we must always bear in mind that John wrote so that we might believe and in believing might have life (John 20:31). Some of the things he says are easier to grasp in the original Greek than in our translations, and I have tried to bring out some of these points, but I trust in such a way that the believer who has no Greek will not be at a disadvantage. Indeed one of my aims has been to make the meaning of such passages as clear as I can for the non-Greek reader. These, then, are some of the things John is saying to me as I read what he has written, and they are sent forth in the hope that they will also be of interest to others.

I have made my own translation from the New Testament. Though not a particularly good translation, it will help the reader to understand what the Greek text is saying to me. When quoting from the Old Testament, I have normally used the New International Version. My former secretary, Mrs. Dora Wellington, typed the manuscript, and I express my appreciation for her help.

Leon Morris

1

The Word

In the beginning was the Word, and the Word was with God, and the Word was God. He was in the beginning with God (John 1:1–2).

It was the end of a very hot day. I was leaning against a stockyard fence, talking to the overseer on a sheep station in the Australian outback. Suddenly and without anything that led up to it as far as I could see, he said, "You know, there's one thing in the Bible I don't understand."

"You're a lucky man," I said. "There are many things in the Bible I don't understand. But tell me, what is it?"

And while I was expecting a hoary old chestnut like "Where did Cain get his wife?" he replied, " 'In the beginning was the Word'—what could that mean?"

If he was going to have just one biblical passage he could not understand, I think he chose well. These words from the opening of John's Gospel are certainly difficult. We often read them without giving them much thought. Exactly what do they mean? There is no obvious answer. The basic problem is that the expression comes from a way of thinking that we do not share. We must thus make a special effort and do a little digging if we are to overcome our problem and enter into the writer's meaning.

To us a "word" is a unit of language, the shortest thing we say or write. But people in antiquity sometimes used the term in ways different from ours. They could, of course, use it in much the same way we do, and they often did. But the Greeks in particular had other ways of using the term *logos* ("word"). To get technical for a moment, they spoke of the *logos prophorikos* and the *logos endiathetos*. (They also spoke of the *logos spermatikos*, but that expression we can afford to ignore in this inquiry.) The *logos prophorikos* was the word going out from someone, the uttered word, the word spoken or written with a view to communicating with others. Since this is substantially the way we use the term, it gives us no problems.

But we have nothing corresponding to the *logos endiathetos*. This was the word that was not spoken or written, not uttered in any way. It was the word that remained in the mind. It was something like our "reason," signifying what is rational, intelligible. Used in this way it stood for a most important part of any person.

This *logos* might also be used of what lay beyond man. As the Greeks looked out at the universe, they saw order. They did not live in a gigantic and frightening chaos. The sun rose and set predictably every day. The stars moved with regularity in their orbits and appeared when the mathematicians said they should. The seasons came and went in an orderly manner. What the farmer sowed, that (and not something else) was what he reaped. The Greeks found order everywhere.

Why? Why an orderly universe, not a chaos? When they thought about such questions, some of their philosophers said, "Because there is a *logos*, a 'word,' in the universe. Just as there is a *logos* ('reason') within a person, so there is a *logos* in this mighty universe." They conceived of a rationality, an ordering principle, effective throughout all that there is. It was only this, they thought, that makes sense of it all. Their "word" was something like a "soul" in the universe. It was infinitely wise, and now and then the thought appears that it was from this wise principle that wise men derive their wisdom.

Heraclitus, a philosopher of the sixth century b.c., could speak of the "Word" as God. He seems not to have put much difference between God, Fire, and Word. When he thought of God as the Word, he thought of him (in the words of James Adam) as "the omnipresent Wisdom by which all things are steered." But before we get to thinking that Heraclitus was thinking along lines similar to those we might use, we should notice that he had some curious things to say about God. For example, "God is day and night, winter and summer, war and peace, satiety and hunger. But he is changed, just as fire, when mingled with different kinds of incense, is named after the flavor of each." What are we to make of this?

Fortunately, our concern is not with the complexities of Heraclitus's thought. Since he is far from easy to understand, it is well that we are not called upon to make the attempt. We simply notice that Heraclitus thought highly of the *logos* and could even speak of the *logos* as God. For the most part, those who came after him did not use this terminology. Perhaps they were deterred by his abstruse way of putting things. For whatever reason, they spoke little of the *logos*. The term occurs now and then, but not often until we come to the Stoics, who made a good deal of use of the concept. They saw the universe as pervaded by reason and called this reason the *logos*. The terminology gave expression to their deep conviction that the universe is rational. The Stoics did not think of the *logos* as a person, but as a principle, a force. They thought of this principle as one that runs right through the universe. It originated everything and directs all things. Everything acts in accordance with it.

John, of course, was neither a disciple of Heraclitus nor a follower of the Stoics. Nor were those for whom he wrote his Gospel, though all of them knew that the philosophers who used the term thought highly of the *logos*. The prevailing attitude toward philosophers was not unlike the normal way of regarding scientists today. Ordinary people do not understand them, but they do realize that what they are saying is important. Most of us have learned a few scientific terms and use them now and then, terms like "evolution" or "bromide." Most of us could not give an accurate definition of such terms, certainly not in a form that would be acceptable to the scientists. But we know that these are scientific terms and that if a scientist speaks highly of anything, that thing is important.

It was something like this, I think, with the term *logos* in the first century. People did not understand exactly what the philosophers meant when they used the term. But they did understand that the philosophers used it of someone or something that was very important. So when non-Christian Greeks came across John's Gospel and read it for the first time, they would not have found his reference to "the Word" very strange. Certainly it would not have puzzled them as it did my overseer friend. They would not have understood all that John meant by it, but they would have recognized that he was referring to a being or a principle of the greatest importance.

The Jews

The Greeks were not the only people who read John's Gospel. Jews read it, too, and their background differed widely from that of the Greeks. Among other things, that meant that their understanding of "the Word" differed from that of the Greeks. For some Jews this came about as the result of speculation on certain Old Testament passages that speak of "the Word" or of "Wisdom" as being active. For example, they read: "By the word of the LORD were the heavens made" (Ps. 33:6).

Sometimes they read that the word of the Lord "came" to the prophets (Jer. 1:2; 34:1; Ezek. 34:1), or that the prophets "saw" the word (Isa. 2:1), or that the word was active in doing God's will: "So is my word that goes out from my mouth: It will not return to me empty, but will accomplish what I desire and achieve the purpose for which I sent it" (Isa. 55:11). We would not normally use the term *word* in this way, but the Jews found no difficulty in understanding "word" in a dynamic fashion. And they associated it with the activity of God.

The Jews had similar ideas about wisdom. There is a vivid personalization of wisdom in Proverbs 8:

> "The Lord possessed me at the beginning of his work, before his deeds of old; I was appointed from eternity, from the beginning, before the world began. . . . Before the hills, I was given birth, before he made the earth or its fields or any of the dust of the world. I was there when he set the heavens in place. . . . I was the craftsman at his side. I was filled with delight day after day, rejoicing always in his presence, rejoicing in his whole world and delighting in mankind" (Prov. 8:22–31).

This is a vivid picture of wisdom as in one sense separate from God and in another sense one with him. The Jews did not define this very closely. It is not unlikely that they had no precise idea in mind. But they were certainly fond of using this symbolism.

The Law was also highly esteemed and came in for this kind of semipersonalization. Sometimes it was thought of as very close to "the word," a development encouraged by some passages in Scripture. Thus we read, "The law will go out from Zion, the word of the LORD from Jerusalem" (Isa. 2:3; Mic. 4:2). In such a passage the parallelism shows that "the law" and "the word" mean much the same. As the Law was the most significant part of Scripture for the Jew, this put "the word" in a very significant place indeed.

Another interesting use of the term is found in the Targums, the name given to translations of the Bible as it was read in public. The Old Testament was written for the most part in Hebrew, and it was held that the Bible should always be read in the original language when used in worship, even when most Jews had ceased to speak the beautiful tongue. But, as a concession to the weakness of the flesh, the custom arose of giving a running translation into the language the worshipers spoke. Such a translation was called a Targum. At first the Targums were all oral, but in time some of them came to be written down. Those that survive give us some interesting insights into the way the Jews of the time understood the Bible.

Our concern is with the way they approached the divine name. They read in Scripture, "You shall not misuse the name of the LORD your

God, for the LORD will not hold anyone guiltless who misuses his name" (Exod. 20:7). At the time of which we are thinking, pious Jews had developed the custom of "putting a fence around the law." When God's law said, "You must not cross this line," they drew a line of their own well inside that specified limit. Then if in a bad moment they broke their own rule, they were still a long way from breaking God's rule.

The commandment about God's name was obviously one to be taken very seriously indeed. So the Jews put their fence about it with some care. In effect they said, "It would be a terrible thing to misuse God's name. Let us make sure that we never do this. Let us not speak God's name at all. If we never use the name, we will not misuse it!" So they never did.

But what were they to do when they came to God's name in the public reading of Scripture? They could scarcely pass it by. So they used some reverent alternative. They might say "the Lord" or "the Blessed One" or "the Holy One." And the Targums show that they sometimes said "the Word." For example, in Exodus 19:17 a Targum reads, "Moses brought forth the people out of the camp to meet the Word of God." This kind of thing is found frequently. William Barclay says that it occurs about 320 times in one Targum, the *Targum of Jonathan*. This, of course, is different from the Old Testament use of "the Word" to denote a separate entity working with God. But it is relevant to our study because it shows that where the Targums were in use, "the Word" was a well-known way of referring to deity.

The dynamic use of "wisdom" and "word" that we saw in the Old Testament continued in the period between the Old and New Testaments. For example, in the book entitled the *Wisdom of Solomon* there is a little prayer: "O God of the fathers, and Lord of mercy, who has made all things by your word and formed man by your wisdom . . ." (Wisdom 9:1–2). Clearly the writer used "wisdom" and "word" in much the same way, and equally clearly he conceived of both terms in dynamic fashion. Later he has a vivid passage that reads: "While gentle silence enwrapped all things, and night in its swift course was at mid point, your all-powerful Word leaped from heaven, from the royal throne." It goes on to speak of the Word as "a relentless warrior" and to say that the Word "touched heaven, while standing on earth" (Wisdom 18:14–16).

There were other usages of the term *word* among the Jews. The Alexandrian Jew, Philo, is said to have used the term thirteen hundred times and more. Sometimes he used it as a way of referring to God in action; sometimes he seems to be talking about a being separate from God. We need not go deeply into his usage. It is enough to notice that here once more we find "the word" used in close connection with God.

All this means that whether John's first readers were Greeks or Jews they would immediately perceive that the "Word" was very important. William Temple put it this way: The Word "alike for Jew and Gentile represents the ruling fact of the universe, and represents that fact as the self-expression of God. The Jew will remember that 'by the Word of the Lord were the heavens made'; the Greek will think of the rational principle of which all natural laws are particular expressions. Both will agree that this Logos is the starting-point of all things."

Christian Usage

But all this is background. We must bear in mind that John was writing as a Christian. His thought was essentially Christian. And while the other New Testament writers do not speak of Jesus as "the Word," they sometimes come very close to it. Thus Luke speaks of people who were "eyewitnesses and servants of the word" (Luke 1:2). Obviously it is difficult to be an "eyewitness" of a "word" in the way we use the term, and it is not easy to be its "servant." It seems that Luke has in mind the very close connection between Jesus and the Christian message. We see this also in the fact that he seems to view preaching the word (Acts 8:4) and preaching Jesus (Acts 11:20) as meaning much the same thing.

Paul is another to speak of preaching Christ: "We preach Christ crucified" (1 Cor. 1:23; 2 Cor. 4:5; cf. also Gal. 3:1). And he has a very interesting section in Colossians 1:25–27, where he writes of "the word of God," which is "the mystery," and proceeds to explain the mystery as "Christ in you" (i.e., the word of God = the mystery = Christ). Paul does not take the step of actually calling Christ "the Word," but he comes very close. He has the essential thought.

We should probably also notice the way Paul writes about Christ in passages like Philippians 2:5–11 and Colossians 1:15–20. These passages are not unlike those in which Jewish writers wrote about "the word" or about "wisdom." There was thus a preparation for John's use of the expression.

John's Climax

It is important to see that while John was using a term that would be widely recognized, he was not simply reproducing Greek or Jewish usage. Both Greek and Jew would be able to put meaning into what he was saying, but he was also going to surprise them. It is impossible for us to put completely out of our minds the thought that by "the Word" John means Jesus, but let us make the attempt. Let us try to read the opening to his Gospel as a non-Christian Greek or Hebrew might have read it in the first century. Bear in mind that Logos or Word meant some great rational principle running through the universe, or perhaps it was a poetical way of referring to God or one of God's attributes. We will not be precise, but just think of the Word in terms of undefined greatness and majesty.

"In the beginning was the Word," we read, "and the Word was with God, and the Word was God. He [or It, and so throughout] was in the beginning with God." So far, no problem. We recognize that the Word points to greatness and are not surprised to find this new writer linking the Word with deity. "All things were made through him," he proceeds, "and apart from him not one thing came into being that came into being. In him was life, and the life was the light of men. And the light shines in the darkness, and the darkness did not overcome it" (vv. 3–5). So far, so good. The Word, we see, is being pictured as active in creation. This is not greatly different from the cosmological speculations of which the reader had undoubtedly heard (whether or not he understood them is another matter).

Now comes a little interlude. "There was a man sent from God, whose name was John. This man came for witness, to bear witness to the light so that all should believe through him. He was not the light, but came to bear witness to the light" (vv. 6–8). Since this has to do with John the Baptist and not the Word, we pass it by.

Then we are back with the Word: "That was the true light that gives light to every man, and he was coming into the world" (v. 9). Our reader can understand this. Divine illumination is channeled through the Word. And there is no great problem with the great principle or spirit or whatever it was that was coming into the world. How else would illumination come to men?

"He was in the world, and the world was made through him, and the world did not know him" (v. 10). There was always a problem with people who did not recognize divine leading. "He came to his home and the home folk did not receive him" (v. 11). This brings out an all too common tragedy. Those who might have been expected to welcome the divine illumination have, regrettably, all too often turned away from it.

But this is not the whole story. There were some who responded: "But as many as received him, to them he gave the right to become children of God, even to those that believe on his name, who were born, not of blood nor of the will of the flesh nor of the will of man, but of God" (vv. 12–13). When people open their hearts to divine illumination, they are transformed.

Up to this point the intelligent first-century reader with no knowledge of Christianity has no real problem. He might not have chosen to

7

express himself in this way and certainly does not understand John's full meaning. But what he reads makes sense to him.

The next words do not: "And the Word became flesh" (v. 14). This is staggering, unbelievable. It is a difficult line, something that the average intelligent first-century reader simply could not accept. "Flesh" is a strong term, almost a crude word in such a context. John does not say, "The Word became human," or "The Word took a body"; he says, "The Word became *flesh*"! This is a strongly emphatic way of saying that the Word entered this physical, human life. He came right where we are. He became one of us. How could the mighty principle of reason that runs through the universe ever become human? How could the God of Abraham, or any "Word" that stood close to him, ever become "flesh"? It made no sense.

When John starts his Gospel, then, by saying that this happened, he is not mouthing a commonplace. He is not repeating Greek or Jewish platitudes. His book is not to be about the kind of thing that was familiar to thinkers throughout the world of the day. He is writing about sheer miracle, about "incarnation." This familiar word derives from the Latin *carnis* ("flesh"). It means "enfleshment." "The Word became flesh." The One who was truly and fully God (v. 1) was so truly and fully man that the word *flesh* may be used of him.

It has been suggested that John may have been writing these words with people called Docetists in mind. ("Docetist" derives from a Greek word that means "to seem.") These were people who were so sure of the deity of Christ that they thought he only "seemed" to be man. They thought that he had no real physical body, but only "seemed" to have one. He did not eat and drink, but "seemed" to do these things. In the end he did not die on the cross to put away sin, but only "seemed" to die. In this way the Docetists preserved the deity of Christ but at a terrible cost. They lost the humanity altogether. So, some scholars think, John uses the strong word *flesh* to make sure that his readers have no doubt about the reality of the humanness of Jesus.

Whatever be the truth of this, we should be clear that right at the outset of his Gospel John makes two points and makes them emphatically: Jesus was God and Jesus was man. The Word of whom John writes was God. He leaves us in no doubt about that. He says plainly, "The Word was God." But at the same time he insists on the true humanity of the Word: "The Word became flesh." We will not make sense of John's Gospel unless we constantly keep in mind these two truths which he sets before us so emphatically at the beginning.

John is going to tell us what God has done for our salvation. He will devote a good deal of space to the events surrounding the crucifixion. Chapters 13–21, which represent a considerable proportion of his Gospel, are taken up entirely with Jesus' last night with his disciples, the crucifixion, and the resurrection. This is the heart of John's message. God took action in Christ to bring salvation to sinners.

Right at the beginning John makes it clear that Jesus can indeed do all this. He is nothing less than the Word, with everything that means for divinity. And the Word did nothing less than become flesh, with everything that means for humanity. Until we have grasped this we cannot begin to understand what John is saying in his Gospel. We must be clear about the person of Jesus Christ or we misunderstand his whole message. John is going to write about God, but his God is not some remote being living on the top of Mount Olympus (or, for that matter, hidden behind the curtain that screened the Holy of Holies). His God is love, and in love for sinful people he came to this earth. The true Godhead and the true manhood of Jesus Christ constitute the necessary preliminary to all that John has to say to us.

2

The Family of God

He was the true light that gives light to every man, and he was coming into the world. He was in the world, and the world was made through him, and the world did not know him. He came to his own, and his own people did not receive him. But as many as received him, to them he gave the right to become God's children, even to those who believe in his name, who were born, not of blood nor of the will of the flesh nor of the will of man, but of God (John 1:9–13).

John is writing about the incarnation. He is bringing to his readers' attention something of the significance of Jesus' coming into the world. He tells us that Jesus is the true light and that all who are enlightened get their enlightenment from him. John goes on to say that Jesus came into the world. "He was in the world," John writes, "and the world was made through him." This prepares us to hear something about a warm response to the coming of one who was God. But no. "The world did not know him."

John writes of the greatest of tragedies: "He came to his own, and his own people did not receive him." Here the tragedy of the rejection is put before us in stark simplicity.

"He came to his own" is a translation that we might perhaps put a little differently. The expression occurs again in John's Gospel, namely, when Jesus is hanging on the cross. Before him is his mother, Mary, and with her the beloved disciple. Jesus says to her, "Behold, your son," and to him, "Behold, your mother." The writer goes on, "And from that hour the disciple took her into his home" (19:26–27). "Into his home" is exactly the same expression as that used here. It means, literally, "into (the) one's own things." It was an ordinary expression people used to refer to home.

So we could translate John's words in this place, "He went home"; "He went home, and the home folk did not receive him." It might not have been so bad, we imagine John thinking, if Jesus had gone to the Romans or the Greeks or the barbarians and had had a bad reception. That might even have been expected. But he did not go to any such place. He went home. He went to God's own people, to those who had the Scriptures explaining how God had constantly dealt with his own people and worked out his plan for mankind through them. He went to those who had the message of the prophets. He went to those who had in the Psalms a priceless treasure of devotion and a continuing revelation of God's love for people and his dealings with them. He went to those who had been delivered by the Lord at the time of the exodus from Egypt and again in the return from the exile in Babylon. These were people who might be expected to know something of the ways of God. Would they not welcome God's Messiah? As it happens, no, they would not. When God's own Son came to them, his very own people did not receive him.

From my early days as a Christian I recall the way S. D. Gordon brought this out. When I was an undergraduate it was the fashion of the young Christians among whom I moved to read books by Gordon. This very popular writer had a series entitled *Quiet Talks: Quiet Talks on Prayer, Quiet Talks on Power, Quiet Talks on Service,* and so on. He seems to have spent quite a lot of time talking quietly. One of his books is called *Quiet Talks on John's Gospel,* and I have always found it very helpful.

When Gordon comes to this passage, he pictures someone coming home at the end of a hard day's toil. He is worn out by the exertions of the day, glad to be finished with his work, and looking forward to being at home with his family. His step quickens as he gets near his home. He feels in his pocket for his key, but it is not there; somehow he has misplaced it. But that does not matter; the family is at home. So he goes up to the front door and rings the bell. And nothing happens. No one opens to him. They are there and they know that he is there. The curtain at the window is drawn back a little, and eyes that he knows so well look out and see him. But they leave him standing there.

A silly illustration? Our immediate reaction is to say, "That's stupid. It isn't an illustration at all. It could not happen." No, it could not happen.

But it did happen to Jesus. He went home. He did not go to strangers. He went home. And it was the home folk—those who, above all people, might be expected to welcome him in—who did not receive him.

And the tragedy has been repeated again and again. Jesus continually comes to us who are his own, to us who have received so many blessings at his hand, to us who have the Scriptures so full of the revelation of his love and of what his loving purpose has done for us and expects from us. He comes to us whom he has created, whom he loves, and for whom he died. And all too often it is still true that his own people do not receive him. The tragedy of rejection is as much a part of our world as it was of the world of the New Testament.

The Children of God

Though the tragedy of rejection happened and thus must be mentioned, it is not John's theme. He knows that rejection is far from being inevitable. He goes on immediately to say, "But as many as received him, to them he gave the right to become God's children, even to those who believe in his name" (v. 12). There *are* people of faith, men and women who believe. There are people who receive Christ. That is what matters, and that is what John is writing about.

There are three important words here: "gave," "right," and "children." John is writing about God's gift. He is not writing about the tragedy of rejection but about the grace of acceptance. God accepts those who respond to Christ. To them he "gives." Entrance into the heavenly family is not achieved by human effort; it is always the gift of God. To those who receive Christ he gave (and he still gives) the gift of membership in the family of God.

The second great word is "right." Many translations have "power" or the like. We must be careful here, because there is power in the gospel message. Paul, for instance, frequently emphasizes this (for example, when he speaks of the gospel as "the power of God unto salvation" [Rom. 1:16]). All who have received Christ can testify to the power that has come into their lives. God does give power, but at this point that is not John's concern. He is talking about the "right" to membership in the family. He is saying that, of themselves, people have no right to a place in God's family. That is beyond any human achievement. John does not say that they achieve or attain or merit membership in God's family, as though they make their own way in. He says that they are given the right. The right is God's gift. Receiving this gift, they "become" members of the family. They were outside the family; they did not belong. Now they have been given the right to become members; they do belong.

The third word is "children." Those in the family can call God "Father." Here let us take notice of an interesting piece of Johannine terminology. John never calls men "sons" of God; his word is always "children." This is not the case with other New Testament writers; Paul, for example, cheerfully uses both words of believers. Thus he can say, "As many as are led by the Spirit of God, these are the sons of God" (Rom. 8:14), just as he can also say that the Spirit bears witness that we are "God's children" (Rom. 8:16). But for some reason John reserves the word *son* for Jesus Christ (unless, of course, he is referring to an ordinary human family; there he uses the term in the same way as anyone else; his distinctiveness is in the way he refers to people as members of the heavenly family). This seems to be part of the way in which he brings out the uniqueness of our Lord. He is the Son of God in a way that nobody else is, and John's language points to this truth.

The word *children* indicates those who share a common nature. That is what we expect in a family; it is what makes a family. A family is a group of people linked by ties of kinship; they share a common nature derived from their parents. John has the thought that believers are people whose essential nature comes from God. In chapter 3 of his Gospel he speaks of being reborn. The thought is that a divine miracle takes place whereby people are reborn into the heavenly family. Elsewhere we read of people becoming "partakers of the divine nature" (2 Peter 1:4), and it is something like that of which John is speaking here. Believers have the right to a place in the heavenly family because of what God has done in them.

John proceeds to bring this out by telling us how they get into that family (v. 13). He has three negatives and one positive. Three times he shows how people do not get in (no matter how strongly they feel that they do), and then he tells us of the one way in which they do get in. First, the negatives. Believers are born, John says, "not of blood nor of the will of the flesh nor of the will of man." "Not of blood" is actually a plural ("not of bloods"), which is puzzling. Some point out that there was an idea held by some people in antiquity that in the process of reproduction the father contributes seed and the mother blood. But though this would explain why blood is specifically mentioned (it points to the process of natural birth), it does not explain the plural. Some think that the reference is to the many drops that make up blood, or that it somehow refers to both parents, but neither suggestion carries conviction. Sir Edmund Hoskyns in his commentary holds that John could not have used the singular. He could not have said that Christians are not born "of blood," because in fact they *are* born of blood, the blood of Christ. That is true, but is it what John is saying here? It is not easy to think so. In the end I fear that we must content ourselves with remaining in some uncertainty about this point. That John means that we are not born into the heavenly family by any such process as natural birth is clear. Precisely why he uses the plural *bloods* to bring this out is not.

"Nor of the will of the flesh" continues the thought. Perhaps we should notice that John does not use the term *flesh* in quite the same way as does Paul. Paul often uses the word to bring out the inherent sinfulness of human nature. He says, for instance, "The mind of the flesh is death" (Rom. 8:6). When John uses this term he is usually thinking of the weakness of our nature rather than its sinfulness. That is the way it is here. The flesh is limited; its best efforts cannot secure entrance into the heavenly family. It is impossible for us to work ourselves up into such a state that we become fit for membership in the family of God. "Flesh" is not the way at all. As John tells us later in his Gospel, "What is born of the flesh is flesh" (3:6). It cannot be otherwise; "flesh" is not the way into the family of God.

Nor does one enter that family by "the will of man." The word John uses for "man" is often used in the sense of "husband" (John uses it this way, for example, in the story of the woman of Samaria [4:16–18]). If we insist on the meaning "husband" here, it will be taken as standing over against an implied reference to a wife in the use of the term *bloods*. But it may mean no more than simply a member of the human race. Our interpretation will depend on whether or not we think that John is making sharp distinctions. If he is, then at this point the meaning is that the husband in an earthly family cannot get the other members into God's family. His influence will help them in many areas but not in this one. We might also reflect that if a father wished to adopt a child into his earthly family, there was nothing to stop him. In that sphere what he said was law. But not so in the heavenly family; he has no jurisdiction there.

But it is perhaps more likely that John is not making such sharp distinctions. It seems to me that he is simply piling up one expression on top of another to bring out his point that entrance into the heavenly family is not the result of anything human. It is not what we do nor where we stand in the human scale of importance that effects our entrance. We can do a good deal for ourselves and for one another in the here and now, but membership in God's family is quite another thing.

S. D. Gordon, in the book to which I referred earlier (p. 11), makes the point that an earthly family has its limitations. He tells us that he knew people who had great pride in their families. Aristocrats the world over tend to boast of their ancient lineage and see themselves as important because of the families to which they belong. Gordon is not impressed. He says: "I come of a rather old family myself. It runs clear back without break or slip to Adam in Eden." This is a nice, humorous way of debunking pride in one's family. Our human family, after all, is something for which we can take no credit, however much we may appreciate it. We did not bring it about. John is saying that nothing of this sort counts. We do not get into the family of God because we happen to belong to some fine aristocratic earthly family. That is not the way.

We have a slightly ungrammatical saying, "It's not what you know, it's who you know," cynical words that point to the power of human influence. In this life it often matters to have the right connections, to know people who can pull strings for us. But however that may help in the furthering of human ambition, it does not help with the heavenly family.

John is saying that no human effort of any sort will get us into the family of God. Consider what people can do for themselves and for one another any way you will. That is not the way into God's family. Nothing human can bring it about.

Born of God

Now we come to John's positive. Believers, he says, "were born . . . of God." I guess "were born" is quite a reasonable translation, but the verb in Greek is one that is properly used of the action of the male parent rather than of the female parent. In old-fashioned language it means "were begotten." John is saying that membership in the heavenly family comes about because of the action of the Father, of God the heavenly Father. He does what must be done to make us "children of God."

John is saying with some emphasis that to get into the family of God there must be a miracle. It can be explained by no merely human mechanism. It is not in the control of men. It is what God does, sheer miracle.

As we shall see, John brings out a little more of his meaning when he comes to chapter 3. There he speaks of the necessity of being born all over again, of being reborn from above. To become a member of God's family does not mean to make the best of the ordinary human life. It is not a matter of dusting off a few of the worst habits of our present life to make it somewhat better. It is not a matter of a little moral improvement. It means a radical revolution. It means such a drastic change that it cannot be brought about by anything that we do, but only by what God does. It is not the way of human excellence, nor the result of some human philosophy; it is the way of God.

God's Action in Christ

A little later in the prologue, John speaks of the Word as becoming flesh and dwelling among men (v. 14). That is the way God began the

15

process of bringing about the adoption of people into his family. In their natural state they are not fit to be members of the family, for they are sinners. None of their puny efforts can make them fit for membership in the family. For that a great divine action is needed, and that action began with the sending of the Son of God to become man.

It continued when the Son of God laid down his perfect life on Calvary's cross. John tells of this in the best-known words in the whole of Scripture: "God so loved the world that he gave his only Son, so that everyone who believes in him should not perish, but have life eternal" (3:16). That is the great divine action that puts away our sin and opens up the way into everlasting life, the life of the children of God.

John is not saying that everyone is saved. It is the person who believes who does not perish. Believing and eternal life go hand in hand. And not just believing as though it does not matter what one believes as long as one is sincere. This passage makes it clear that the saved are those who believe in Jesus' name.

When people trust God in this way, God acts within them. God takes them, transforms them, fills them with his Spirit, enables them to be the kind of people they could never be in their own strength or by their own wisdom or ability. John is saying that God's love for us is so great that he makes provision for us to leave the old self-centered way, the way that concentrates on our own success and our own happiness. He enables us to leave that way and to enter the new way, the way of membership in the family of God.

John is saying that God will take over our lives and put order into them. He will make them rich and full and significant. He will set us on the right way. John is putting before us early in his Gospel the possibility of living in the fullness of all that is involved in being able to call God "our Father."

3

We Saw His Glory

And the Word became flesh and lived among us, and we saw his glory, glory as that of the only Son from the Father, full of grace and truth (John 1:14).

One of the surprising things about the Fourth Gospel is that it does not mention the transfiguration of Jesus. All the other three Gospels do (Matt. 17:1–8; Mark 9:2–8; Luke 9:28–36). We might have expected John to emphasize this narrative because he is very interested in the idea of glory. He uses the noun *glory* eighteen times, which is nowhere near Paul's total of seventy-seven, but is more than that in any of the other Gospels (Luke is next with thirteen). John uses the verb *to glorify* twenty-three times, while no other New Testament writing has it more than nine times (Luke). These statistics show that John sees "glory" as one of the important elements in the life of Jesus. We might reason that it would be intelligible if John had included the transfiguration story with its revelation of Jesus' glory, and the other three had omitted it. But in fact it is the other way around. They tell us about it; and John, for all his emphasis on glory, omits it.

Some, it is true, see a reference to the transfiguration in the words "we saw his glory." They understand this to mean, "we saw his glory when it was revealed on the Mount of Transfiguration." But that is more than John actually says. In the light of the fact that he does not tell the story of what happened on that mountain, I do not see how we can find here a reference to that intriguing incident. If John meant us to

17

see it in this verse, he would surely have said something specific about the mountaintop experience, either here or elsewhere. But he does not.

It seems to me that John has no intention of referring to the glorious transformation of Jesus before his disciples at any point in his Gospel. It simply would not fit into what he is saying. His idea of glory cannot be concentrated into any one incident. He has the distinctive idea of seeing glory everywhere in Jesus' life.

The Reality of the Incarnation

Let us begin with the fact that John tells us that "the Word became flesh." He is writing about One who is supremely great. He has already said that the Word was "in the beginning," that the Word was "with God," and that the Word "was God." He has used "the Word" as a name for One who is as great as can possibly be imagined. There is no way of thinking of anyone or anything as being greater than the Word. The Word is true God.

But John is saying also that Jesus is true man: "The Word became flesh." He came right where we are. He took our nature upon him. He underwent all that being human means. He did not play at being a man.

There is plenty of playing at being man in the legends of the Greeks. They would picture some god or goddess coming down from the lofty heights of Mount Olympus and looking just like an ordinary man or woman. The divine one would have all sorts of adventures. But in due course, when the situation became a trifle sticky, the deity would get tired of it all, throw off the disguise, perhaps perform a miracle or two to get out of whatever difficulty had arisen, and then return to the abode of the gods. That is all good clean fun. But it is not incarnation. Those gods are not really human, but only look that way. They do not undergo any real limitations, but simply disguise themselves. They do not put up with the trials and chances of a normal human lot, but are merely playing a game and doing so by their own rules.

John is writing about a genuine incarnation. The Word took upon himself our flesh, with all that that means. He accepted the limitations that are part and parcel of human existence. John does not spell out what those limitations are, but his choice of word leaves his readers in no doubt about the real humanity of the Word. He became *flesh*.

Not only so, but he "lived among us." John's verb *(skēnoō)* is connected with the Greek word for "tent" *(skēnē)* or, as some prefer to put it, "tabernacle." Some people think, accordingly, that John means "lived among us for a short time." Reasoning that people normally do not live in tents permanently, they understand John to mean "he pitched his tent among us for a while." They see the picturesque phrase as pointing to a temporary dwelling.

Of course, the incarnation was a temporary thing. Jesus did not live on earth as a man forever. But we cannot get that out of John's verb. While it referred initially to living in a tent, it came to be used of permanent dwelling. For example, it is used of those who dwell in heaven (Rev. 12:12), and there is nothing more permanent than that!

The Shekinah

If from the term John uses we cannot argue the temporary character of the incarnation, we can point to something else of great importance. To Jewish minds the reference to "tent" brings the thought, not of *a* tent, but of *the* tent, the tent or tabernacle of which they read in their Bible. In the wilderness wanderings of their ancestors, the place of worship was a tent called "the tent of meeting" or "the tabernacle of the congregation" (Exod. 33:7). It was a very holy place, and quite plainly the Israelites in the wilderness looked on it as a very significant place, a place where they could meet God.

Now when the tabernacle was first set up and was ready for worship, a wonderful thing happened: "Then the cloud covered the Tent of Meeting, and the glory of the LORD filled the tabernacle. Moses could not enter the Tent of Meeting because the cloud had settled upon it, and the glory of the LORD filled the tabernacle" (Exod. 40:34–35). That the Lord put his seal of approval (so to speak) on the place of worship meant a great deal to the Israelites, and subsequent generations loved to dwell on the way the "glory" came down. Nor was this only a kind of opening-day celebration, for at a later time "the glory of the LORD" appeared to all the people at this same tabernacle (Lev. 9:23).

The Hebrew word for "tent" is *mishkān*, which is related to *shekīnāh*. For later generations of Israelites, this term *shekīnāh* often referred to the glory of God as it is manifested to men. They saw it as bringing out the truth that God gloriously dwells among his people. At any time that he chose to make that truth manifest, he might do so by some public showing of his glory. This happened at other times than the setting up of the tabernacle. It happened, for example, on Mount Sinai, where "the glory of the LORD settled on Mount Sinai. For six days the cloud covered the mountain. . . . To the Israelites the glory of the LORD looked like a consuming fire on top of the mountain" (Exod. 24:16–17). It happened again during the wilderness wanderings. At a time when the people were ready to stone Joshua and Caleb, "the glory of the LORD appeared at the Tent of Meeting to all the Israelites" (Num. 14:10). This, of course, put a stop to the murderous enterprise. And it led on to the revelation that "the glory of the LORD fills the whole earth" (Num. 14:21).

John is saying to his readers, then, that the glory that had been manifested in one way or another in the wilderness wanderings and later, as at the dedication of Solomon's temple (1 Kings 8:10–11), was manifested in its fullness in the life of Jesus of Nazareth. All the previous manifestations had been partial. Now came that manifestation that was appropriate for the only Son from the Father.

A. M. Ramsey says of the use of the term here: "We are reminded both of the tabernacle in the wilderness, and of the prophetic imagery of Yahweh tabernacling in the midst of His people, and of the Shekinah which He causes to dwell among them. . . . The place of His dwelling is the *flesh* of Jesus." He goes on to say, "*All* the ways of tabernacling of God in Israel had been transitory or incomplete: *all* are fulfilled and superseded by the Word-made-flesh and dwelling among us."

The Place of Worship

The setup of the tabernacle and later of the temple tells us something about the glory of God as the Jews understood it. The architecture of the temple taught them something about the greatness and unapproachableness of God. There was first the outer court. There was no problem about that. Anyone could go there, even the Gentiles; indeed, it was called the Court of the Gentiles (each court was named for the people who could enter it, but go no farther). Then came the Court of the Women, which marked the farthest point the ladies might approach. The Court of Israel likewise stood for the limit beyond which the gentlemen of Israel might not go. It seems that in the wilderness tabernacle these distinctions were not made, but that the outer court was open to all Israelites in a ceremonially clean condition.

However, a common feature of the tabernacle and the temple was the Court of the Priests, into which no lay person might go. It was set apart for those who had been admitted to the sacred priesthood. It was "the Holy Place" (Heb. 9:2).

Finally, further on there was a place too sacred even for the priests to enter, "the Holy of Holies" (Heb. 9:3). This was entered on only one day in the year and by one man alone. On the great Day of Atonement, when suitable sacrifices had been offered, the high priest entered this very holy place and carried out prescribed rituals. Even so it was required that he take a censer and incense, and when he came inside the curtain that marked the Holy of Holies, he was "to put the incense on the fire before the LORD, and the smoke of the incense [would] conceal the atonement cover above the Testimony, so that he [would] not die" (Lev. 16:13).

The way the place of worship was constructed and the restrictions placed on access to the Holy Place and to the Holy of Holies emphasized the greatness and the majesty of God. The worshipers must not presume that they had the right to approach God when and how they pleased. Even the priests were limited and, of course, lay people even more so. That God's presence was among the people was not in doubt. That people could approach that presence as they chose was not a possibility.

Perhaps this is a lesson that we need to relearn. God is a great God. Man, as such, has no rights in God's presence. We often behave as though we can do as we like with God. I read about a church that had a sign outside: "The church is open. Come in. Sit, pray. It is never too late to talk to God." But underneath there was inscribed in smaller letters: "Hours: 9 A.M. to 12 noon." We do that with God. We say wonderful things about him. We say that he is great and wonderful and mighty. But then we act as though he were subject to our control. We even determine how he is to be approached and, of course, arrange things so that he is not going to be too hard to get along with.

But we cannot do that with God. The Old Testament teaching about God's glory should warn us away from our common approach. God is wonderful, majestic, a glorious being. He may choose to manifest himself to men, even to dwell among them. But that is for him to say, not for us to decide. There was a glory associated with the awe-inspiring spectacle of Mount Sinai that impressed on the people who saw it their own littleness (Deut. 5:24–25). There was a glory associated with the tabernacle that could even restrain a murderous impulse (Num. 14:10; 16:41–42). God is glorious. But men may not presume on that glory just because God is pleased to manifest it to them. They must retain a proper awe.

Humble Glory

John is well aware of what the Old Testament says about God's glory, but he is not simply repeating what the Old Testament says. He is saying something new. He says not only, "The Word became flesh and lived among us," but also, "we saw his glory."

What, then, did they see?

They saw the Carpenter of Nazareth. They saw a man who brought cheer to some lowly people at a wedding in an obscure Galilean village. They saw one whom Nicodemus thought he could patronize. They saw one with whom an unimportant Samaritan woman argued, as, for that matter, did many Jews in Jerusalem. They saw one who healed a lame man by the pool of Bethesda and was promptly denounced by the same man to his enemies. They saw him defend himself and his attitude toward the Sabbath.

They saw him feed a multitude of people with a few loaves of barley bread and some small fishes, and go on to be quizzed by an ignorant crowd of people who challenged him because he had not brought the manna from heaven as Moses did. They heard him speak at the Feast of Tabernacles and were interested spectators of the controversy that resulted. He healed a man blind from birth and stirred up more controversy. He raised Lazarus from the dead and stirred up yet more controversy.

And as John comes to the climax of his narrative, he tells of a long talk Jesus had with his disciples in the upper room, a talk that they clearly did not understand as they should have. Then he was betrayed into the hands of his enemies by one of his followers and disowned publicly three times by another. Finally he was tried before the Roman authorities, with his own people bringing the accusation. He was nailed to a cross and left to die.

John goes on to God's vindication in the resurrection and tells of how some of Jesus' followers saw him again. He relates a moving story of the way in which Peter was restored to his place of leadership and then of how that apostle immediately presumed on his place to poke his nose into the affairs of another follower of Jesus.

The Gospel of John is an interesting account with many ups and downs. It certainly is a long way from being a straightforward account of "glory" in anything like its Old Testament sense. Jesus does not appear as a lofty, unapproachable person, secure in his majesty from all assaults of his enemies. On the contrary. He is despised and opposed, and in the end his enemies get him. They crucify him.

This is not the way we understand glory. We can make sense of glory in the way we see it at the transfiguration. There we have Jesus overshadowed by the bright cloud and with his face shining like the sun. His clothing was white as the light, white as no one on earth could make it white. There were the heavenly visitants, Moses and Elijah, and the voice from heaven saying, "This is my beloved Son." That is glory that we can understand.

But a carpenter using a hammer and a chisel and a saw? What is glorious about that? That is no more than ordinary, everyday stuff. It happens all the time.

It is the same with Jesus' entire life. We can pick out a few glorious moments, but for the most part we would not call that life glorious. What, after all, did he do? He preached to a few people in an outlying province of an ancient, long since vanished empire. Even there he was not often in the capital, the center of affairs, but in a remote country area. He taught a few people, gathered a few disciples, did an uncertain number of miracles, aroused a great number of enemies, was betrayed by one close follower and disowned by another, and died on a cross. Where is the glory?

Centuries before, the prophet said of him: "He was despised and rejected by men, a man of sorrows, and familiar with suffering. Like one from whom men hide their faces he was despised, and we esteemed him not" (Isa. 53:3). That is the kind of life John is writing about. "Word become flesh" as he was, that is the kind of life he lived. And yet John says, "We saw his glory."

John is telling us that God does not need tinsel. There is no need for the outward trappings of majesty and pomp for God's purposes to be carried out. God does not see things as we see them.

The trouble with our vision is that we instinctively look for the glitter and the show. Public recognition and praise are important to us. We expect people to bolster their egos with claims to magnificence. We are a little like the opera singer Jan Klepura. It is said that on one occasion he complained to his publicity agent that another singer was getting much more publicity than he was. He did not want to be robbed of his share of glory. His agent said mildly, "The trouble is that the gentlemen of the press think that you are conceited and therefore they do not care to write about you." The singer was incredulous. He exclaimed, "Conceited? Me? The great Klepura?"

That's the way it is. We do not want people to miss our greatness. Even though our circle be a lowly one, we want all the kudos and the credit to which we are entitled, and a bit more if we can get it. We insist on being recognized and are upset when people do not accept us for what we think we are.

John is saying that God is not like that. Real greatness does not need to assert itself. Real glory is not to be found in pomp and circumstance and pageantry and show. That is just so much glitter. It does not matter. Real glory is different.

Real glory is to be seen in lowly service. When something must be done and someone so great and high that he need not do it nonetheless leaves his exalted place and does the lowly thing, that, John is saying, is glory indeed.

That is the kind of glory that the Fourth Gospel describes. It is that glory that we see on every page. Right at the beginning, John has left us in no doubt about the greatness of his Lord. The Word was in the beginning, he was with God, he was God. And it was that Word, that supremely great Word, who lived on earth in lowliness.

Where people needed help, he helped them. Where there were sick, he healed them. Where there were ignorant folk, he taught them. Where there were hungry people, he fed them. All the time he was seeking the needy. He did not haunt the palaces of kings and governors.

He was not found in the high places of the earth. Perhaps we may fairly say that people in such places felt that they had sufficient resource and could cope on their own. It was not to such that the Word came. All his life he was among God's little people, those who in one way or another felt their need. And wherever there was need, he was found doing lowly service. That is what Christ came to do. And that is glory.

Do you see why it would have been difficult for John to have included the story of the transfiguration? I do not say that it could not have been done, but in this Gospel it would have been difficult. It would have represented an attempt to concentrate in one incident the glory that John sees as spread out through a whole life. And it might have given a picture of glory in the sense of majesty and splendor. While John is not denying that there is a certain truth in the traditional understanding of the term as applied to Jesus, he is saying that real glory is not to be found in splendor but in humility. True glory is seen in lowly service, and John sees it in every moment of Jesus' lowly life.

Glory in the Cross

Particularly does John see glory in the cross. That was very hard for first-century people to take. For them the cross was an instrument of shame. There was nothing glorious about it. We Christians do not easily see the cross their way, because from early days we have been conditioned to see it as wonderful. We have made out of it an ornament. We work it into wonderful designs on the exterior and the interior of our places of worship. We wear it on our persons. We see it as a proper object of art, and innumerable artists have painted the crucifixion. The Red Cross is a symbol of humanitarianism. To make the sign of the cross is for many a pious religious act. Others of us reject this kind of symbolism, but we accept as our basic truth that it is the cross alone that gives us hope for time and for eternity. It was on the cross that our salvation was wrought. Piety, art, and humanitarianism combine to make the cross a valuable symbol.

But people in the first century did not see the cross that way. To die on a cross was painful, so painful that someone has called it "the acme of the torturer's art." The weight of the body on the arms, the pain of the wounds, the constriction of the lungs, the flies, the thirst—all these combined to make crucifixion one of the most uncomfortable ways of dying that man has ever devised. The pain of it all is obvious.

But many saw the humiliation involved as even worse. Crucifixion was considered by the Romans the most shameful way of dying. It was reserved for criminals and provincials and defeated enemies. A Roman citizen might not be crucified, no matter what he had done. That law was occasionally broken, but its force was clear. This was not a noble way to die. A Roman might be executed, but it would be in some honorable manner, say, by the sword. There was no honor in a cross. Crucifixion was for slaves and outcasts. It was not for good, honorable people like Roman citizens.

Yet John saw the cross of Jesus as glory. He tells us that Jesus introduced a teaching on his death with the words, "The hour has come for the Son of man to be glorified" (12:23), on which William Barclay comments, "Jesus did not mean by *glorified* what they meant. By *glorified* they meant that the subjected kingdoms of the earth would grovel before the conqueror's feet; by *glorified* He meant *crucified*." They defined glory as triumph; Jesus defined it as service. So for John the cross was not shame. It was glory. It was the glorious way in which God's Son brought life to people in darkness and death.

It was glory because it was the way in which the ultimate service was given to sinners. John reports the words of John the Baptist: "Look, the Lamb of God, who takes away the sin of the world" (1:29). By his lowly death Jesus dealt with the problem of the world's sin. John does not tell us why this should be the way that sin is dealt with, nor how the death of the Lamb of God takes away sin. It is enough for him that this *is* the way. Jesus must die to put away sin. John tells us that Jesus spoke of being "lifted up from the earth" and adds, "This he spoke signifying by what death he would die" (12:32–33). It may be that he has the same idea as Paul, that death by crucifixion meant bearing the curse spoken of in Deuteronomy 21:23 (see Gal. 3:13).

But whether or not this is the way John is thinking, it is not the central point. The central point is that he saw the death of Jesus on the cross as the supreme example of glory, not as the shameful thing his contemporaries thought it was. Jesus lived a life of humility, of lowliness, of rejection; then he accepted the most shameful of deaths. In that way he performed the ultimate service: he took away the sin of the world.

John is saying that this is what real glory means. Jesus had no need to come to earth. He might have retained all the joy and splendor of heaven. But he left it. And when he came to earth there was no necessity for him to live in poverty and rejection. But he did it. And when he came to the end of his life he was not compelled to die the painful and shameful death of the cross. But he did.

Could anything be more glorious? John speaks of this glory as "full of grace and truth." Perhaps a better understanding of his words is that the Word is full of grace and truth. But this is the Word in the capacity of which John has just spoken, and that means his taking the lowly way, the way of real glory. It is in that way that grace becomes a reality for mankind.

25

John is here putting before us a tremendous concept, one which is at the heart of the Christian faith. It is at the heart of the faith because it is by this glorious act of Christ that people are brought into salvation.

Perhaps we should also observe as a final note that this concept is at the center of Christian living. When we have entered into the meaning of the death of Jesus, we see that for us, as for him, real glory is in lowly service. The Christian way is not a way in which we look for people to praise us, to recognize us for what we think is the full extent of our merit. Real glory rather is finding some useful piece of service, no matter how lowly, and doing it as well as we can. Unless we see that, we do not understand what Christian service is. The call to Christian service is not a call to occupy some comfortable and eminent place. It is not the suggestion that if we go along in the right way, everyone will speak well of us. The call to Christian service is a call to take up our cross daily and to walk in the steps of him who for our sake took up his cross.

4

Who Are You?

And this is the testimony of John when the Jews of Jerusalem sent priests and Levites to ask him, "Who are you?" And he confessed and did not deny; he confessed, "I am not the Christ." They asked him, "What then? Are you Elijah?" And he says, "I am not." "Are you the prophet?" and he replied, "No." They said to him therefore, "Who are you? so that we may give an answer to them that sent us. What do you say about yourself?" He said, "I am a voice of one crying in the wilderness, 'Prepare the way of the Lord,' as the prophet Isaiah said" (John 1:19–23).

John the Baptist was preaching in the wilderness. The Fourth Gospel does not tell us, as the others do, that he was preaching a baptism of repentance, nor that the crowds were flocking to hear him. But it does tell us of the deep concern that John's preaching aroused among the official religious leaders in Jerusalem, for they sent a mission of inquiry. Here was a man claiming to speak in the name of God. This was doubly dangerous. In the first place, he should not have been speaking at all. They were the religious experts. If anyone was to speak in the name of God it was they. It would never do for people to get the impression that others could do the job as well! And in the second place, he might be the kind of man that would arouse enthusiasm. Then the multitudes would be stirred up, and who could tell what that would lead to? There might be riots or other behavior of the kind that would lead the Romans to intervene. And then where would the Jewish nation be? So the officials had to know all about it. They had to satisfy themselves that the Baptist was harmless.

The delegation was made up of "priests and Levites," suitably accredited religious men (incidentally, this is the only New Testament passage where the two groups are linked). They asked simply, "Who are you?"

The writer introduces John's reply with a solemn rigmarole: "And he confessed and did not deny; he confessed. . . ." He need have said no more than "He replied." This solemn, emphatic introduction to the Baptist's answer shows that it is important; the words should be listened to carefully. John's reply is, "I am not the Christ." The word *Christ* is our transliteration of a Greek word meaning "anointed." It is also the translation into Greek of a Hebrew word (which we transliterate as "Messiah") that has the same meaning. The words *Christ* and *Messiah*, then, both mean "the anointed one." John is denying that he is "the anointed one." Old Testament kings were anointed; hence the repeated expression "the Lord's anointed." Sometimes we read of "the anointed priest" (e.g., Lev. 4:3), and now and then a prophet was anointed (1 Kings 19:16). Anointing signified the setting apart of a person for the service of God; it was a solemn act of consecration. The Old Testament looks for the coming in God's good time of a special servant of God, one who would be not simply *an* anointed one, but *the* Anointed One, the Messiah. He would be God's agent in a very special way and accomplish some important service for the salvation of God's people.

John the Baptist's answer, then, is an emphatic denial that he was this special servant of God, the Messiah. We might ask, "Who said he was?" Well, no one had actually said this as far as we know (though some had wondered about the possibility [Luke 3:15]). John, being as perceptive as most, discerned what the mission of inquiry was all about. His questioners did not want people to be caught up in messianic speculations. They must have been wondering whether John would claim to be the Messiah. The inquiry cleared the ground for him to dispose of this possibility straightaway.

That led to a second question, "Are you Elijah?" This was not an easy question to answer. There was a sense in which the Baptist was Elijah; Jesus said that he was (Matt. 11:14). Jesus said that the Baptist fulfilled the prophecy that Elijah would come before the "great and dreadful day of the Lord" (Mal. 4:5). But the Jews were not looking for the Elijah of the prophecy ("He will turn the hearts of the fathers to their children, and the hearts of the children to their fathers"). They remembered only that Elijah had not died; he had been taken up to heaven in a chariot of fire (2 Kings 2:11). Maybe they did not expect the same chariot to bring him back, but they did expect that the same physical

Elijah would return. Since John was not Elijah in the sense in which the question was asked, he simply said, "I am not."

It is sometimes objected that if John was Elijah in one sense but not in another, he should have said so plainly instead of making this blank denial. There are two things to be said in answer to this objection. The first is that John may not have known that he was Elijah. Jesus' teaching that he was did not come until later. No man is what he thinks he is. He is what God knows him to be. John was a humble man and may well have refused to claim this exalted function for himself.

The other response is that to imagine the Baptist as going into a detailed explanation of the sense in which he was Elijah and the sense in which he was not is to miss the important thing that the Fourth Gospel is saying about him. In this Gospel the Baptist does one thing only: he bears his witness to Jesus.

We read in the other Gospels that John the Baptist called people to repentance. We read there that when they repented he baptized them. We read something of John's teaching to people like the tax collectors and the soldiers and the multitudes generally (Luke 3:10–14). For John's deeds and his teaching and his baptism and his imprisonment and his death we must look elsewhere. The writer of this Gospel is interested in only one thing about John—his witness. There can be little doubt that this Gospel does make reference to the occasion when Jesus came to the Baptist and was baptized by him (1:29–34). But it does not say so explicitly. It says only that the Baptist bore his witness to Jesus.

Witness

Quite apart from the activity of John the Baptist, our author is interested in witness. He stresses the idea in a way that none of the other Evangelists does. He uses the noun *witness* (or *testimony*) fourteen times, whereas Mark has it only three times, Luke once, and Matthew not at all. He uses the corresponding verb *to witness* thirty-three times, while Matthew and Luke each have it once, and it is absent from Mark. In both cases John uses the word more often than does anyone else in the New Testament.

I think he is saying two especially important things with his stress on this concept. The first is that what he tells us about Jesus is well grounded. He is aware that "witness" is a legal concept. The witness of at least two people is required to prove anything according to the law (8:17). He insists that there is not simply the testimony of two people to Jesus, though there is that (8:18); there is other testimony as well. There is the testimony of the works of Jesus (5:36; 10:25). There is the testimony of sacred Scripture (5:39). There is the testimony of each of the persons of the Trinity—of the Father (5:31–32, 37, etc.), of the Son (8:14, 18), and of the Spirit (15:26). There is the testimony of a variety of human witnesses, such as the disciples (15:27), the woman of Samaria (4:39), the multitude (12:17). And, of course, there is the testimony of John the Baptist. With all this weight of testimony, the writer seems to be saying that there should not be any doubt about Jesus; his attestation is formidable. Witness is a way of showing what the truth is, and in this case there is plenty of evidence as to what the truth about Jesus is.

The other thing John is saying arises from the nature of "witness." Witness commits. Suppose that you have seen an accident. Two cars have been involved in a collision. As long as you keep silent, you preserve all your options. You are free to come down on either side. As the protagonists argue and seek your support, both you and they know that you are uncommitted and may support either of them. But the moment you bear your witness the situation is different. You may say, "The Ford ran through a red light and crashed into the Chevy." Now everybody knows where you stand. You cannot afterwards say, "It was really the fault of the driver in the Chevrolet," without discrediting yourself. Witness commits.

So it is a striking thought that the Father has borne witness to Jesus. The Evangelist is saying that God has committed himself in Jesus. In the life and the teaching and the death and the resurrection of Jesus, he has said in effect, "This is what I am like." God has committed himself in Jesus. That is a staggering thought. It is important to this gospel writer, and, indeed, to the whole church of God.

But at the moment our concern is with the witness of John the Baptist. John told what he knew. That is the function of a witness. A witness is not there to give a beautiful oration adorned with magnificent periods and scintillating phrases. He is there to tell plainly and clearly what he knows. John was well aware of what was required of him: he was to bear witness to Jesus Christ.

But here were these wretched people from Jerusalem asking him about himself. He was not there to talk about himself. He was there to bear witness to Jesus. Notice how his answers get progressively more terse. To the first question he replies, "I am not the Christ." It may not be eloquent, but at least it is a decent sentence. It has a subject, a verb, and a predicate. The second time he is shorter: "I am not." The third time he is monosyllabic: "No." Since his interest is in Jesus, not in himself, he has no intention of being sidetracked into a discussion about himself. He does not matter. Jesus does.

The third question asks, "Are you the prophet?" Though not defined, this is plainly the prophet spoken of in Deuteronomy 18:15–19, the prophet like Moses that the Lord would raise up in due time. It is not clear why the Jews expected this prophet in connection with the Messiah. But the Messiah would be a wonderful person; he would come in splendor and be attended by many. They expected, for example, that Jeremiah would be there (Matt. 16:14), and "a prophet like one of the prophets" (Mark 6:15). So it is not really surprising that some of them thought of the prophet of Deuteronomy as well. But John was not this prophet either, so he simply answered "No."

A Voice Crying

So far the delegation had not done very well. They had been asked to get some information about John the Baptist, and all that they had was a string of negatives. Since they had to go back to Jerusalem saying who he was, not who he was not, they turned directly to the subject of their inquisition. They asked John, "Who are you?" and added, "so that we may give an answer to them that sent us." They had to take back some answer. Would John be helpful?

John told them how he saw himself. He quoted Isaiah 40:3, saying, "I am a voice of one crying in the wilderness, 'Prepare the way of the Lord.'"

It is interesting that the community responsible for the Dead Sea Scrolls took this same passage of Isaiah and found its fulfillment in what they were doing. But they understood the words differently, the difference depending on punctuation. In the very old manuscripts there is little or no punctuation and we must supply it. This is usually not too difficult. In this case we put a comma after "wilderness" (as in the way I have just quoted the passage).

But the men of Qumran put their equivalent of the comma earlier. They understood the words in the sense, "The voice of one crying, 'In the wilderness prepare the way of the Lord.'" Where were they? In the wilderness. What were they doing? Preparing the way of the Lord. How were they doing it? Sitting down and quietly reading their Bibles. Their whole emphasis was on looking after themselves and their own salvation. They had little thought for the multitudes outside.

John the Baptist was different. He was not primarily concerned with the salvation of his own soul. He was concerned for the needs of others. He was only a voice. But he kept on with his "crying in the wilderness." For him to prepare the way of the Lord meant getting out among the people and warning them so that they might be ready when the Lord came. He did not, it is true, go into the cities. His place was far from the big centers of population. But he did preach at a ford of the Jordan where many were coming and going. Crowds came to him. What he said would inevitably be widely known. So he called on people to be ready, because the Messiah was coming. It would not do for them to be found with all their sins about them. They must repent and accept his cleansing baptism, so that they would be ready.

Why Baptize?

John's questioners had elicited the fact that he made no claim to being the Messiah or a messianic personage. He was no more than a voice calling on people to repent. Why then, they asked, did he baptize? First-century Jews understood and practiced baptism. It was the proper thing for people who needed spiritual and ceremonial cleansing. It was used, for example, in the reception of proselytes (converts) to the Jewish faith from among the Gentiles. When a Gentile decided to become a Jew, he and all his family were baptized and all the males were circumcised. Baptism was necessary because during their life in the Gentile world they had picked up all manner of defilement. They had to be cleansed before they could begin their new lives as members of the people of God. So they were baptized. Their defilements were washed away in the waters of baptism.

The sting in John's practice lay in the fact that he was applying to Jews, members of the people of God, the very rite that they saw as appropriate for defiled people coming from the outside world into their number. Had John been the Messiah or someone closely associated with the Messiah, they might have seen some justification for the practice. Who could tell what the Messiah would do? But John had firmly denied being either the Christ or a prophet. It was all very puzzling. So they asked, "Why then do you baptize if you are neither the Christ, nor Elijah, nor the prophet?" (1:25).

Characteristically John answers in his own way. We have already seen that his interest was in Christ, not himself. So he says, "I baptize in water; in the middle of you there stands someone whom you do not know, he who comes after me and whose sandal-thong I am not worthy to unloose" (1:26–27). The question gave him the opportunity to speak about Christ.

His "I" is emphatic. It sets him in strong contrast with someone else. He does not name the other, but the comparison is plain. John acknowledges that he baptizes in water, but that is all that he can do.

What is important is that he is to be followed by someone far greater. The assertion that the someone greater will come after John is noteworthy. People in those days took it for granted that the ancients were the wise ones. Incredible as it sounds to the youth of today, young men then believed that their fathers were wiser than they. They really believed it. With us "Pop" is often a figure of fun. Our notions of progress tend to see the aged and those of previous generations as not attaining to our own achievements. "The good old days" are good for a laugh at any time. We simply do not believe that the old days could possibly compare with the present. But in the first century, most people the world over thought that there had been a golden age earlier in the history of the race, and that subsequent generations had not been able to reach that standard again. How could they? They were younger, and an ingrained respect for age forbade the thought.

So it would be expected that Jesus would be less than John. Coming later, he would look up to the older man, people would think. Not so, says the Baptist. Jesus came later into Judea, it is true, but that is not the whole story. In a more significant sense he was actually before John (vv. 15, 30). His essential being is such that he is far greater than John. In the sense that matters he existed long before John did.

The Sandal-Thong

John's humility comes to expression again when he says that he is not worthy to untie the thong of Christ's sandal. This takes us back into travel on the hot and dusty paths of Palestine. As one walked in the heat and the dust, one's feet inevitably became hot and dirty and smelly. When one came to a friend's house, the first courtesy provided was water to wash the guest's feet. But the host would not normally do this himself. To attend to the feet was a task fit for a slave, and it would be a slave who was expected to do the actual washing of the feet.

We may get a little help in appreciating the significance of John's words if we reflect on customs among students and rabbis. Rabbis were not paid for teaching their disciples. Their teaching was always in one way or another instruction in the Bible, and they held that it would be a dreadful thing to take money for teaching God's Word. So a rabbi's needs had to be met in some other way.

It was the custom for every Jewish boy to learn a trade. Sometimes we are told that this arose out of some grand notion of the dignity of labor. I greatly doubt this. In the case of people like rabbis it was sheer economic necessity. If the rabbi could not be paid for teaching, it was obviously important that he get a little money in some other way (cf. Paul and his tentmaking [Acts 18:3]).

But that was not the whole story. The rabbi could not work a full day and still have time to devote to his studies. Here the students could help. They were expected to perform all manner of little duties that freed their rabbi from preoccupation with the minor chores of life and gave him time to put into his books. There is a pertinent regulation which in its present form is dated about A.D. 250 but is probably much older. In view of John's words it is not unlikely that it went back to New Testament times. It reads: "Every service which a slave performs for his master shall a disciple do for his teacher, except the loosing of his sandal-thong."

The feet of even godly and learned rabbis got hot and dusty and smelly. It would be most unpleasant to perform the office of taking off the sandals and washing those feet. It was just too much to expect of a student. Anything else he would do. Cheerfully. But, please, not the sandal-thong!

It is fascinating that John selects precisely this duty which the student would not do for his rabbi and says of it, "I am not worthy."

I was reading of an airman in World War II who was a fine fighter pilot, but unfortunately a very obnoxious person. In his preoccupation with his own success, he got on well with nobody. It happened that he was transferred to another unit. His commanding officer passed on the message, "Splendid officer at 5,000 feet. Should never come lower."

John the Baptist was not like this. John knew how to take the lowly place. It was not for him to parade his own virtues. He came to bear witness to Jesus and never ceased to do so.

Later in chapter 1 we read of the time when Jesus appeared. John directed some of his own disciples to Jesus (vv. 35–37). Here we see the real greatness of this man. It is not easy in this life to gather followers around oneself in a good cause. But once they have been gathered, it is infinitely harder to say to them, "I have taken you as far as I can. Leave me and follow him." But this the Baptist did.

It is all summed up in words of his a little later in this Gospel: "He [i.e., Jesus] must increase, I must decrease" (3:30). That was John the Baptist. He was not the Savior and knew it. He was simply a voice, a witness. Consistently he called on his followers to follow Jesus instead. That was why he came. And those who were faithful to his teaching went after Jesus. Mission accomplished.

5

The Lamb of God

"Look, the Lamb of God that takes away the sin of the world. . . . Look, the Lamb of God" (John 1:29, 36).

T he Lamb of God" is an expression that has come to mean much to Christian people. It is embodied in some of the ancient liturgies of the church, and people still pray fervently, "O Lamb of God that takest away the sins of the world, have mercy upon us." Even where people do not use liturgical forms, they often find that "Lamb of God" comes easily to their lips. It is a meaningful way of speaking about (and to) Christ.

In view of its widespread use among Christians, it is all the more curious that no one knows exactly what it means. Of course, we are not lacking in suggestions. Many have pointed confidently to one meaning or another. The trouble is that there is no proof that any such suggestion is what the Baptist had in mind when he spoke the words, or what the writer of the Fourth Gospel meant when he recorded them.

For all the research that has gone into it, there is no agreement as to what the term originally meant. Some curious statements are made. One scholar thinks it "likely that the Evangelist is throwing back into John's words a title which, as applied to Christ, had in his own day become stereotyped." This conveys the impression that lots of people talked about "the Lamb of God." It suggests that at the time this Gospel was written this was a common title ("stereotyped"), and that the writer, with scant regard to what had actually happened, put it on the

35

lips of John the Baptist. But if this is what happened, we have no way of knowing it. The difficulty with the expression is that far from its being stereotyped in the church before this Gospel was written, we have no knowledge of anyone at all, inside or outside the church, ever using it before John did. It is a standard method of procedure when we meet an expression like this to look back at those who used it previously. It generally happens that there is a clue to its meaning in the way people had employed the words. But with "Lamb of God" the trouble is that there is no previous example of its use. We cannot even take later examples and say, "Perhaps these are independent of the use in John and will help." The later examples, as so far known, all depend on this Gospel. Christians found the expression a meaningful one, so they took it from John and used it in their prayers and in other ways. To this day we know of no example of this expression that does not depend on John's Gospel.

It is true that Jesus is elsewhere referred to as a "Lamb." But he is said to be "like a lamb" or else a different Greek word is used, and in those examples the words "of God" are not added. We are left with a mystery. And while it is unlikely that with the evidence at our disposal we will be able to solve the puzzle, it may be profitable to consider some of the suggestions that have been offered. They may not clear up the problem, but they will teach us some important things about our Savior.

1. The Passover Lamb. Some of my friends are surprised that I find a problem here. To them it is plain that what John means is what they call "the Passover Lamb." They sometimes point out that, as John describes it, Jesus died at the time the Passover sacrifices were being offered. Further, this Gospel writer applies to Jesus as he died the words, "Not a bone of him will be broken" (19:36). This appears to be a reference to the regulation that the bones of the Passover victim should not be broken (Exod. 12:46; Num. 9:12), though we should notice that there are some who think the words refer to a passage in the Psalms that has nothing to do with the Passover (Ps. 34:20). On the whole the reference to the Passover seems probable. The argument then runs that John is using here at the beginning of his Gospel words which bring the Passover to mind, and then in his account of the crucifixion he quotes a Scripture passage which clinches the matter. It is John's way of saying what Paul put in these words: "Christ, our Passover, was sacrificed for us" (1 Cor. 5:7).

This suggestion can be made to sound convincing. But there are objections. One of them is that the animal offered in sacrifice at Passover was not necessarily a lamb at all; it might be a kid. Some retort, "But the use of a kid was exceptional; the victim was normally a lamb." As to that, I do not know. Nor do I know why those who put the suggestion forward are so confident. I have never seen it proved and do not know how anyone could possibly prove it. Scripture certainly allows for the use of either a kid or a lamb: "The animals you choose must be year-old males without defect, and you may take them from the sheep or the goats" (Exod. 12:5). It is perhaps worth noticing that a goat was offered at Passover time for a sin offering (Num. 28:16–22).

But in any case, whatever animal was offered, it was not called "the Passover Lamb." It was called simply "the Passover." Paul uses precisely this term when he writes, "Christ, our Passover, was sacrificed for us" (1 Cor. 5:7; his exact expression is "the Passover of us"). If that is what John means, there seems no reason why he does not use the term. Modern-day Christians often speak of "the Passover Lamb" or "the Paschal Lamb," but we should be clear that this is our contemporary way of speaking. It is not found anywhere in the Bible or in early literature.

A further objection is that John in fact says "Lamb of God." There seems no reason why we should take the words "of God" to mean "Passover." There are many things besides the Passover which connect with God (including all the sacrifices), and we need something more than a bare assertion that this is how we should interpret the expression.

Another objection sometimes made is that the Passover was not a sacrifice that took away sin; it was a memorial of a great deliverance. This may perhaps have been so when the Passover was instituted, but by the time the New Testament was written every sacrifice was held to put away sin, at least in some measure. Specifically this is said of the Passover, both in rabbinic writings and by the historian Josephus. So this objection has no real weight.

But the other objections remain and in my opinion are decisive. I cannot feel that it was the Passover that was in mind when the words were originally spoken or first recorded. Nevertheless it is profitable to reflect that the Passover commemorated a great deliverance. A slave rabble was taken out of Egypt and began the long road that would make them into a nation and that nation the people of God. And in Jesus there is also a great deliverance. People who were slaves to sin are set free. As John Bunyan put it in a memorable expression: "One day as I was passing in the field . . . suddenly this sentence fell upon my soul, Thy righteousness is in heaven. Now did my chains fall off my legs indeed." And by virtue of Christ's atoning work the chains have fallen off the legs of countless believers ever since.

While we cannot say that John's words are meant to point us to the Passover, we can say that there is at any rate one aspect in which Passover and "Lamb of God" come together. There is deliverance in both, and the deliverance from sin that Christ accomplished is a mighty deliverance indeed.

2. The Lamb Led to the Slaughter. In words that Christians have always seen as applying to Christ, Isaiah prophesies, "He was led like a lamb to the slaughter, and as a sheep before her shearers is silent, so he did not open his mouth" (Isa. 53:7). Clearly Isaiah is referring to a lamb's lack of resistance when it is brought to the place where it will be killed. This has some obvious links with the way Christ met death. Jesus made no resistance. When Peter struck out with the sword, Jesus told him to put it away, and Matthew adds that he asked, "Do you think that I am unable to petition my Father, and he will provide me with more than twelve legions of angels?" (Matt. 26:53). But Jesus did not make any such petition to his Father. He chose not to resist those who put him to death.

There is nothing to indicate that this is what John had in mind. The unresisting lamb of Isaiah 53 is not called the lamb "of God," and this seems to be a fatal objection to the proposal. This objection might possibly be overturned if it could be shown that there was a widespread belief that Isaiah 53 referred to the Messiah. In that case we could reason that the chapter would have been studied closely for every messianic application, and that accordingly the reference to the lamb would immediately have been seen as a reference to the Messiah. We could argue that, since the chapter refers to the Messiah, who is closely related to God, it would not be too difficult to understand the words "of God" in connection with "lamb." But there are too many assumptions along this line of reasoning. There is no real reason to hold that first-century Jews understood the passage in this way. H. H. Rowley seems to have shown conclusively that the Suffering Servant and the Davidic Messiah were not identified in pre-Christian times. Christians, it is true, have interpreted Isaiah 53 messianically, but it must have taken a little time for this interpretation to become widely accepted. It has not been shown that widespread acceptance was early enough to explain John's reference. There is no real evidence, then, that this is what he had in mind.

3. The Servant of the Lord. A very interesting suggestion put forward confidently by some scholars is that the expression is a mistranslation. John the Baptist spoke in Aramaic, they say, and he used an expression that means "the Servant of God." But he used a word for "Servant," namely *talyā*, that has two meanings. It means "lamb" and it also means "boy"; and "boy," of course, in many languages is used in the sense of "servant." So the thought is that John the Baptist called Jesus "God's Servant" but was misunderstood; *talyā* was meant as "servant" but was misunderstood as "lamb." If this is the explanation, John would have had in mind the Servant spoken of in a number of passages in Isaiah. When he added "that takes away the sin of the world," he had in mind more particularly Isaiah 53, with its statements like "Surely he took up our infirmities and carried our sorrows . . . he was pierced for our transgressions, he was crushed for our iniquities; the punishment that brought us peace was upon him, and by his wounds we are healed . . . the LORD has laid on him the iniquity of us all" (Isa. 53:4–6).

If this suggestion could be shown to be true, it would help us understand John 1. But unfortunately the linguistic basis is far from sound. In the Greek translation of the Old Testament, *taleh*, the Hebrew equivalent of *talyā*, is never translated by a word meaning "lamb." Nor is the Aramaic word used as the equivalent of the Hebrew word for "Servant" in Isaiah 53 (one Palestinian Syriac text is known to use the term in this way; but this is all the evidence there is in support and comes a long way short of proof).

The suggestion, then, lacks support. Though it remains just barely possible, the way people used the words in question in the first century makes it a highly unlikely explanation. Despite what is said in its favor, it seems that we should see the expression John used as referring in some way to a lamb, not to a servant.

4. The Lamb of the Daily Offerings. Every morning and every evening a lamb was offered in sacrifice in the temple (Exod. 29:38–42). It has been argued that everyone who was acquainted with the temple knew that this regular sacrifice was offered and would immediately think of this lamb upon hearing the words "the Lamb of God." And it has also been argued that there is nothing unlikely in the suggestion that this lamb of the daily sacrifices was called "the lamb of God."

It is true that the daily sacrifice would have been well known and that it was associated with God. But precisely because it was so well known we would expect that, if the sacrificed animal was indeed called "the lamb of God," there would be a record of this somewhere. But as far as our information goes, there is not one example of the use of the term "lamb of God" anywhere with respect to this sacrifice. Neither before nor after John's usage do we find the lamb in the temple called by this name. In any case, as it was a different lamb each time, it seems that it would have been called *a* lamb of God rather than *the* lamb of God if this expression was used of it.

We may fruitfully reflect that the temple sacrifices were a continual reminder of sin and of the necessity for doing something about it. We may go on to the thought that it is only the sacrifice of Christ that really puts away sin. But we cannot say that we have any real reason for holding that John had the daily sacrifices in the temple in mind when he used this expression.

5. The Lamb That God Provides. When Abraham took Isaac up the mountain to sacrifice him in accordance with the command of God

(Gen. 22:2), the lad asked a question: "'The fire and wood are here,' Isaac said, 'but where is the lamb for the burnt offering?'" To this Abraham replied, "God himself will provide the lamb for the burnt offering, my son" (vv. 7–8). Some suggest that John was drawing attention to this passage and to this lamb. He had in mind, it is said, the thought that the one sacrifice that really puts away sin would be that which God himself provided. It is the divine initiative in dealing with the problem of sin that is in mind.

This is supported by some considerations taken from Jewish thought about Genesis 22. That passage does not tell us how old Isaac was, but it speaks of him several times as a "lad." This word was used of Joseph when he was seventeen (Gen. 37:2), and while it may also be used of people somewhat younger and for that matter somewhat older, it does not suggest a small boy. Nor does the fact that on the trip up the mountain it was Isaac who carried the wood that was to be used for the fire in which the sacrifice would be offered (Gen. 22:6). The Jews in fact held that Isaac was a mature man at this time (one suggestion they made was that he was twenty-five years old, another that he was thirty-seven). Now Abraham was very old; he was a hundred years old when Isaac was born (Gen. 21:5). Add a few more years for Isaac to become a "lad" and it is plain that the old man could not have overcome the husky youth had he resisted being bound and placed on the altar (Gen. 22:9). The inference the Jews drew from this was that Isaac had consented to be offered, and they saw the submission of the young man as being just as important as the obedience of the old one. They dwelt so lovingly on this narrative that "the Binding" became a very familiar term. When they used this term, everyone knew what was meant; there was no need to add "of Isaac."

Since this was so well known and so well loved a story among the Jews, it is suggested that "the Lamb of God" is simply an allusion to it, pointing us to the fact that God would provide what is needed in sacrifice, just as he had provided so long ago in the case of Abraham and Isaac. In the end, of course, it was not Isaac who was offered on the altar, but a victim God provided, "a ram caught by its horns" in a thicket (Gen. 22:13).

One cannot but be respectful to this suggestion. It might just possibly be the answer to our quest. But difficulties remain. One is that, as far as we know, the term "Lamb of God" was never applied to "the Binding." Neither in Genesis 22, nor in the relevant Jewish literature about it, do we find the term used. Moreover, when the sacrifice was eventually offered in that incident, it proved to be not a God-provided lamb but a God-provided ram. It may also be relevant that in the many references to "the Binding" there is no indication that the attitude of Isaac (or, for that matter, of Abraham) or the offering of the ram was held to signify such a far-reaching atonement that it could be said to be the pattern for the taking away of the sins of the world. The suggestion is intriguing and opens up before us some profitable lines of thought. But we have no real reason for thinking that it was what John had in mind.

6. *The Triumphant Lamb of the Apocalypses.* In the last couple of centuries B.C. and the first couple A.D., there are several examples of a class of literature that the scholars call "apocalyptic." They make use of vivid symbolism of the kind we see in the canonical book Revelation. The exact meaning of this symbolism is not always clear, nor is the reason it was employed. But it is at least a reasonable suggestion that it was used so that enemies would not be able to get the meaning if by any chance the books fell into their hands. One surprising thing that emerges from a close study of this literature is the curious nature of the lamb symbolism. We would expect a lamb to stand for someone meek or gentle or lowly. Instead, a lamb, and especially a horned lamb, stood for a mighty conqueror. We see this in such passages as Revelation 5:8; 7:9–10, and indeed in the general picture of the Lamb throughout that book. Such symbolism is found in a number of other places. We can imagine that it would not have been easy for an uninitiated enemy to have made sense of it.

Some have thought that, since this use of "the Lamb" is so clear in Revelation, we should understand the same use in the Gospel of John. Why should there be a variation? This argument can be made to sound very convincing.

But there are a few difficulties. The first is the one we have been meeting all the way through: neither in Revelation nor in any other literature of the kind do we find the Lamb called "the Lamb of God." It is this linking of the Lamb with God that is so distinctive in John and so hard to find elsewhere. But without it we do not know whether we are dealing with the same imagery.

Another objection concerns the meaning. In apocalyptic literature the lamb, as we have seen, is a mighty conqueror. But there is no suggestion of conquest in John. There the thought is that of atonement for sin, not victory over enemies. It is true that in Revelation the Lamb that is so powerful is "the Lamb that was slain" (Rev. 5:12), but the problem remains. John's Gospel is not dealing with triumph but with sacrifice for sin. The two thoughts may be connected, but they are not the same.

7. *Other Suggestions.* Other suggestions are sometimes made. It scarcely seems necessary to try to canvass them all. But we should at least notice one or two of them. Some students see an allusion to the "gentle lamb" of Jeremiah 11:19. This lamb is a symbol of a righteous person being killed by the unrighteous. It stresses his harmlessness; he

does not resist. We are reminded of the attitude of Jesus toward those who arrested him. But the parallel stops there. John is concerned with putting away sin. There is no such suggestion in the passage in Jeremiah. Nor, of course, is there the use of the words "of God."

A suggestion difficult to take seriously is that it is the scapegoat of Leviticus 16 that is in mind. This would fit in quite well with the idea of taking away sin. But it suffers from the obvious and fatal objection that a goat is not a lamb, let alone "the Lamb of God."

Yet another idea is that there is a reference to the guilt offering. In support of this is the fact that on some occasions a lamb was offered as a guilt offering (e.g., Lev. 14:12, 21, 24; notice the expression "the lamb for the guilt offering"). But once again we have no reference to such an animal as being "of God." And further, while a lamb was sometimes offered in this way, more often the victim was not a lamb but some other animal. It is not likely that anyone hearing the expression "the Lamb of God" would think of the guilt offering.

It thus appears that there are objections to all of the suggestions that have been made. We cannot have full confidence in any one of them. But we can see points of truth in several.

Perhaps the best understanding is that the term is used with a general meaning. That is to say, it does not refer to any one specific lamb, but to the lamb as the sacrificial animal *par excellence*. A lamb was offered in many sacrifices; it was almost certainly the most common sacrificial animal. To the people of the first century, a lamb that takes away sin meant sacrifice. In what other way could a lamb take away sin? Our failure to tie down the expression to any one sacrificial offering may be due to the fact that it was intended to point in a general way to all that the sacrifices meant. If this is so, John is saying that in Jesus we find that divine victim who would perfectly fulfill all that the entire sacrificial system foreshadowed. That this Lamb is the "Lamb of God" means that he is closely related to God (John has just told us that he is with God and is God [1:1]). It also points to the divine initiative in bringing about the atonement for the world's sins.

Thus we may continue to use the expression meaningfully even if we cannot claim that we know exactly what John meant by it originally. At the very least it speaks to us of that divine sacrifice that put our sins away forever, a sacrifice that God provided and that we could never have found for ourselves.

When the two disciples of John the Baptist heard him say, "Look, the Lamb of God," they immediately followed Jesus (1:37). May our study of the expression do the same for us!

6

The First Disciples: Andrew

The next day again John was standing and two of his disciples. He looked at Jesus as he walked, and says, "Look, the Lamb of God." And the two disciples heard him speaking and they followed Jesus. . . . Andrew, the brother of Simon Peter, was one of the two who heard from John and followed him. This man first finds his own brother Simon and says to him, "We have found the Messiah" (which, being interpreted, is "the Christ"). He brought him to Jesus (John 1:35–42).

Of those who followed Jesus, Andrew is the first whose name we know. He came with a companion who is often thought to have been John, the beloved disciple. There seems little to be said against this, but on the other hand there is nothing to show conclusively that it was John. The name is not given and the man is not identified with the beloved disciple or with anyone else. But the beloved disciple was the author of this Gospel (21:24), and the story of the coming to Jesus has touches that many have thought indicate an eyewitness. It may be significant that no name is given to this man and that the same is true of the beloved disciple. Another question arises: Why should the author of the Gospel include this man if he is to play no further part? Be all that as it may, there is no doubt about Andrew. He is named, and there is no one known to have come to Jesus before him.

The name is a Greek one, with the meaning "manly." We do not read much about Andrew in the other Gospels, though we know from Mark that he and Peter had a house in Capernaum (Mark 1:29). Interestingly

43

Matthew and Luke speak of the house as Peter's and say nothing about Andrew's ownership (Matt. 8:14; Luke 4:38). Even in John, where we are told more about Andrew than anywhere else, Andrew is rather in the shadow of his brother Simon; the incidental notice about the house fits in with this fact. Andrew was not one for taking the center of the stage. We learn that he was a fisherman and that Jesus called him and Peter to become "fishers of men" (Matt. 4:18–20; Mark 1:16–18).

The only other information we get about Andrew in the synoptic Gospels is Mark's recording of the fact that he joined with his brother Simon and the sons of Zebedee in asking Jesus the question that touched off his apocalyptic discourse on the Mount of Olives (Mark 13:3). Neither of the other Evangelists specifies who asked the question: Matthew has "the disciples" and Luke simply "some" (Matt. 24:3; Luke 21:5).

Andrew Could Adapt

Most of our information about Andrew, then, comes from John's Gospel. There is a certain consistency about the references to this man that enables us to build up something of a picture of him. It is far from complete, and in the end there is much that we do not know about Andrew. But we know enough to see him as an individual, one who still teaches us important lessons.

The first thing we learn about him is that he was flexible; he could adapt. That he had been one of the disciples of John the Baptist indicates that he was not content with run-of-the-mill first-century Judaism. John the Baptist was preaching a baptism of repentance for the forgiveness of sins and announcing that the coming of the Messiah was near. For Andrew this was good news, so he attached himself wholeheartedly to John and accepted his preaching.

We do not know as much as we would like about the Baptist's preaching, but we do know that he was concerned to say a good deal about the one who would come after him, the Messiah. We know little about the terminology he employed, but it is plain that he told his disciples that it was the Great One to come who was important. When he came they should attach themselves to him.

He did his work so well that when the time came, Andrew and his friend knew what to do. When Jesus came along the Baptist did not say anything like "Follow this man." He said no more than "Look, the Lamb of God." We see Andrew's adaptability in that this was all he needed. He had learned from John so well that he simply left his teacher and followed Jesus.

Our interest in Andrew must not result in our overlooking the important thing that all of this tells us about John the Baptist. He had

44

preached effectively and had gathered around him a group of people who wanted more than the conventional Judaism of the day. They were ready to repent and be baptized as a sign of their repentance, or at least many of them were. It must have been a source of great satisfaction to John to see so many attach themselves to him. But now he pointed them away from himself and directed them to Jesus. It is always a difficult thing for a preacher to direct people away from himself and to someone else, even when he knows that the other person can help them more. But this is what John did. The figure left by Andrew and his friend was a lonely one, but he was a figure of solitary splendor. It was a great thing that John did.

It is tempting to speculate on what meaning "the Lamb of God" had for Andrew. As we saw in our previous chapter, it is impossible for us at this distance in time to be sure of exactly what John had in mind. Presumably Andrew understood the expression far better than we do. But unfortunately he has not left a record of what he thought about it.

We have seen that at the very least a Lamb that takes away sin means sacrifice. It means rejection and suffering and death. Andrew could not have foreseen Calvary with all its horror, but he must have seen that John was pointing to a concept of messiahship far different from the one normally accepted in contemporary Judaism. The Jews were looking for a Messiah who would deal with the pressing problem of the Roman occupation. He would raise an army and drive the hated conquerors into the sea.

Now we cannot be sure how far Andrew had accepted such an understanding of the Messiah before he attached himself to John the Baptist. But it is not unreasonable to hold that his basic way of thinking was something like the contemporary understanding. It was not difficult to interpret the messianic prophecies of the Old Testament in terms of triumph, and in the first century over whom would the Messiah triumph if not the Romans?

It means a great deal that a man brought up with such an understanding of the Messiah came, as Andrew did, to such a fresh understanding that he was ready to attach himself immediately to one whose designation was "Lamb of God" and whose future was bound up with sacrifice. Obviously Andrew was not a mass of hardened prejudices. He could accept new thinking and act on it.

I do not mean that Andrew saw at once all the implications of "Lamb of God." No one could have done so at that time. Like the others who followed Jesus, he had a good deal of unlearning to do, and it must have taken time. But at least he was ready to make a beginning. He was not so set in his old ways that he could not change his thinking. Though "the Lamb of God" did not fit into the conventional understanding of

45

the Messiah, that did not stop Andrew from accepting what it meant, as far as he could understand it.

Not only was he ready, then, to accept a sacrificial Messiah, but the words to which he responded spoke of the Lamb of God as taking away the sin of the world. This was something no political or military Messiah could do or would want to do. It was much more important, but it was not the kind of thing most people had in mind. Once more we see Andrew's readiness to adapt. He was not in a rut. He had learned many things from John the Baptist and responded to them. He learned from Jesus, too, and it is fitting that the last thing we hear about him in the Gospels is that he is asking Jesus a question (Mark 13:3).

Andrew the Evangelist

Andrew was not slow to bring his brother Simon to Jesus. There is a minor uncertainty about the Gospel writer's meaning at this point. We could understand his words to mean that Andrew "first found his own brother" (i.e., he found him before he did anything else). Or John could mean that Andrew "found his own brother first" (i.e., before he found anyone else; he found others, but Simon was the first). A slightly different reading in some manuscripts is, "He was the first to find his brother" (i.e., the unnamed disciple found *his* brother, too, but only after Andrew had found Simon). With a bigger difference, yet other manuscripts read, "In the morning he found. . . ." It seems to me that this last understanding of the passage is unlikely (though Moffatt and others accept it), but any of the other three is possible. They all indicate the promptness with which Andrew went about his task. In my opinion the first-mentioned meaning is likely the correct one, but whichever we adopt, we get a picture of Andrew as interested in bringing his brother to Jesus, so interested that he did so very quickly indeed.

This interest continued, for every time we come across Andrew in the Fourth Gospel he is bringing someone to Jesus. The next time we meet him is at the feeding of the five thousand. The other Evangelists tell us that the disciples wanted to send the people away so that they could get food for themselves in the neighboring towns and villages. It was Jesus who suggested that they should feed them. John tells us that he first asked Philip where they should buy bread for the crowd, only to be met with the information that two hundred denarii could not buy enough bread to give them all even a little. The situation was hopeless.

It is at this point in John's narrative that we again meet Andrew. "There is a young lad here," he said, "who has five barley loaves and two little fishes." He recognized the limitations of this meager supply: "but what are these among so many?" (6:8–9).

It cannot be said that Andrew foresaw what would happen, so we are left wondering why he brought the boy to Jesus. Perhaps he felt that at least Jesus ought to have something to eat after all his hard day's work. For whatever reason, he brought the lad to Jesus. He might not have been good at understanding all that Jesus could do, but he was good at bringing people.

The final occasion on which John mentions Andrew is toward the end of Jesus' public ministry, after the triumphal entry into Jerusalem. John tells us that there were some Greeks who had come up to worship at the Passover. It is not completely clear what the term *Greek* means in this context. Since they were going up to Jerusalem to worship, the first thing we think of is that they had become converts to Judaism (proselytes). But John does not say this. It seems likely that if this were the case he would have expressed himself somewhat differently. It seems more likely that these Greeks were what are sometimes called "God-fearers" or "half-proselytes" or "devout people." These were folk who were attracted to Judaism without being fully committed to it. They liked some things about it very much indeed. For example, the Jews taught emphatically that there is only one God, and this mono-theism attracted some who had been brought up in an unsatisfying polytheism. The lofty morality of Judaism was also attractive in a world where moral values had slipped badly. Then there were the Scriptures, those tremendous words of the prophets, the riches of the Law, and the Psalms, and all the rest. They found much to attract them.

But they also found much to repel them. First-century Judaism was narrowly nationalistic with a firm belief in the superiority of all Jews to everyone else. Proselytes were accepted somewhat grudgingly and never seem to have had the same status as native-born Jews. Then again, Greeks found some of the ritual practices of Judaism repellent, for example, circumcision. Such considerations made it hard for them to become full Jews.

So they hovered on the fringe. They worshiped the one God and tried to live the life he demanded of his own people. But they refused circumcision and never became full members of Judaism. At the feasts they often came up to Jerusalem to worship, as in this case. They would, of course, not be allowed to go beyond the outer court, the Court of the Gentiles. But at least they would be in the house of the Lord at one of the feasts of the Lord.

It seems probable that John is talking about such people. They may have come from Greece, though not necessarily. Greeks lived in all sorts of places, and there were large numbers of them not too far away, in the region known as Decapolis on the other side of the Jordan. Wherever their homes were, they were not Jews by race.

They came to Philip and said, "Sir, we wish to see Jesus." Why did they come to Philip? Perhaps because he had a Greek name, but if so they were misled, because many Jews of the day had Greek names. For that matter, Andrew is a Greek name. However, whatever their reason, they came to Philip.

And they puzzled that good man. Could he bring Greeks to Jesus? *Greeks*? On the other hand, could he refuse? Did Jesus ever turn anyone away? Philip did not know what to do. So he went off and found Andrew.

Andrew had no problem. He was always bringing people to Jesus. And that was what he and Philip did now (12:20–22). There is a marvelous consistency about Andrew. Every time we meet him in the Fourth Gospel he is bringing someone to the Lord. It is a noteworthy characteristic.

William Temple is reported to have said that the church is the one organization among men that exists purely for the benefit of non-members. In this striking way he brought out the truth that mission is of the essence of the church's existence. The function of the church is not to be a cozy club for like-minded people who prefer not to go along with everything in contemporary society. It is a group of people committed to proclaiming the gospel and bringing others to Christ. Andrew understood this function of the church very well. He seems not to have tried to fasten attention on himself, but was concerned simply with getting people to come to Jesus. That, for him, was the thing that mattered.

A Lowly Man

Andrew is not usually held to have been one of the really outstanding early Christians. It is noteworthy to see him called "Simon Peter's brother" (John 1:40; 6:8), and not named for his own achievement. The first of these references is especially striking, for at that point Peter had not yet been brought into the narrative. He came in only after Andrew brought him to Jesus, but even then Andrew was in the shadow of his greater brother.

But people without great gifts are sometimes strikingly effective. I like the story of the man who for a long time had been a very poor fisherman, but who then started to bring home some fairly good catches. Thereafter he rarely failed to fill his basket. It happened that one day his wife decided to go with him when he went off to try a new spot.

When they arrived, the husband kept looking around. His wife was puzzled. "What are you looking for?" she inquired.

"An old man."

"What old man? You don't know anybody here, do you?"

"No, of course not. But I have discovered that old men know where the fish are. So I generally find one and watch where he goes. Then when he is finished, I take over his spot. It usually works."

The husband was not brilliant; he seemed to have learned practically nothing about how to go about the task for himself. But his method worked. It made him a respectable fisherman, instead of one who had to content himself with stories of the ones that got away.

Andrew was perhaps a bit like that. There is nothing to indicate that he was a great man, and much to indicate that he was rather a humble person. But he had one thing going for him—he could and did bring people to Jesus. That is what counts.

Lowly service is important. Let us never forget that it was Andrew who brought Peter to Jesus, an act which William Temple says was perhaps "as great a service to the Church as ever any man did." Andrew may not have been able to do great things, but he brought Peter to Jesus, and Peter did great things. From a human point of view, it is impossible to see how those great things would ever have been accomplished had not Andrew played his part so well.

Has not this been consistently true in the history of the Christian church? Ananias of Damascus, for one, is scarcely a celebrated name in Christian annals, but he introduced Saul of Tarsus to the Christians.

And the story has gone on. Who can tell even the name of that monk at Erfurt who taught Martin Luther the doctrine of justification by faith? He himself did little, but Luther made the teaching ring through Europe.

Or think of that Sunday-school teacher who felt led to speak to a young man about his soul. He was hesitant and not at all sure how to go about it. He spent time outside the shop where the young man worked, not quite knowing what to say. But in the end he plucked up his courage, went in, and stammered out words that told of the love of Christ for people and the love people should have for Christ. The result was the conversion of Dwight L. Moody, one of the greatest evangelists of modern times.

We could go on. Again and again we see in the shadows of great Christian leaders humble people who themselves could never do great deeds, but who knew the importance of bringing men to Christ. Without them the history of the church would have been very different and far less successful.

It is still the case that there is need for people like Andrew. Lots of them. The Lord raises up very few great leaders, but he calls many followers, people who will work humbly in lowly places and in this way set his great purpose forward. Few things are more important for the Christian than lowly service well done.

7

The First Disciples: Philip

*The next day he wished to go out into Galilee and he finds
Philip. And Jesus says to him, "Follow me." Now Philip was
from Bethsaida, from the city of Andrew and Peter. Philip
finds Nathanael, and says to him, "We have found him of
whom Moses (in the law) and the prophets wrote, Jesus the son
of Joseph, who is from Nazareth." Nathanael said to him,
"Out of Nazareth can any good thing come?" Philip says to
him, "Come and see"* (John 1:43–46).

I once heard a bishop of the church say, "Apparently
Philip was a rather stupid man." This rather took the congregation
aback, for it is not the way we expect bishops to talk about apostles.
The apostles were the great leaders of the church in its early days. The
bishops are leaders in the church in these latter days. We expect that
one lot of leaders will be respectful to another lot. So the congregation
was surprised, to say the least.

Now I am not a bishop, so I will not say such a dreadful thing. But
when you look at the record, it does seem that Philip was not very
bright. I think I understand why the bishop spoke as he did.

We depend on John for most of our information about Philip. This
apostle is mentioned in the lists of apostles in the first three Gospels,
but that is all they tell us about him. They say nothing about what
Philip said and did. For that we must go to John.

The first thing John tells us is that Jesus "finds" Philip (v. 43). This
is unusual. All the others who are said in John 1 to have come to Jesus

50

either came of their own accord or were brought by their friends. Only in the case of Philip is it said that Jesus took the initiative. This has been developed by some scholars into an argument about sources. In this chapter, they say, disciples "come" to Jesus or "are brought" to him. There is something wrong, they suggest, when we read that Jesus "finds" this man. So there is a different source behind this part of the chapter. Or perhaps there has been some editorial work. Perhaps originally Peter (who is mentioned in the previous verse), having been brought to Jesus by his brother Andrew, carried on the process by finding his fellow townsman Philip and bringing him.

But I wonder. Elsewhere John does not proceed in such a mechanical way that we can safely say, "All who come to Jesus must come in much the same way." He is not at all averse to variety. Nor does he depict Jesus as a passive personality who simply waits for things to happen. There is nothing out of character in Jesus' finding Philip, even though this is a different process from that recorded of the others.

It is also interesting that it is Philip, of all those spoken of in this chapter, whom Jesus found. Simon Peter was really a great man, the outstanding leader in the early church. Andrew was not of the same caliber, but he was a man of initiative, always bringing people to Jesus. Nathanael, of whom we read at the end of the chapter, is not a man about whom we know much, but the little we do know reveals him to have been a guileless person. As we shall see, he had at least one memorable experience under a fig tree. Since the shade of a fig tree was often used as a place for prayer and meditation, we may conclude that he was a deeply spiritual man, perhaps something of a visionary.

But it was not Andrew or Peter or Nathanael whom Jesus went out and found. It was Philip, this perfectly ordinary man, one who, as far as we know, had no outstanding quality. Jesus is not interested only in the great. He went out to enlist this humble, ordinary man personally, to number him among his apostles.

Philip of Bethsaida

The name *Philip* is a Greek name meaning "lover of horses." But we should not think that it shows that Philip was a Greek. Many Jews bore the name. For example, the tetrarch who governed the region was called Philip (some have even guessed that the apostle was named after him). Our man may well have had a Hebrew name as well as this Greek name, but if he did we have no information about it.

There seems to have been nothing wonderful about Philip. Every time we meet him he seems to be out of his depth. We do not understand what John is telling us about him if we see him as some spiritual supergiant. He is a humble, ordinary man, one with whom most of us might well feel quite at home.

On the first occasion that we meet him, he was found by Jesus. It fits in with all the rest we know about Philip that he took no initiative in this matter. It apparently did not occur to him that he should seek Jesus out. It is not quite certain when Jesus found him. John tells us that Jesus wanted to go into Galilee and he found Philip. Does this mean that he in fact went into Galilee and found Philip there? William Barclay thinks so, for he translates, "And there He found Philip." This is certainly a possible understanding of the Greek text, and it may be supported by John's reporting that Philip went on to find his friend Nathanael, who was a Galilean (21:2). It is, of course, possible that Nathanael had come into the region where John the Baptist was active, but this Gospel does not say so. So Philip may have been at home when Jesus found him. If so, it is all the more remarkable that Jesus sought him out.

But it seems to me that this is a somewhat unlikely reading of the evidence. It looks as though John 1, after the prologue, is concerned with what happened in the area where the Baptist was busy. We have his witness to Jesus, then his pointing of two of his disiciples to the Lord. This is followed by one of them bringing his brother. The most natural reading of the chapter is that Jesus went on to find Philip in that area and that Philip completed the process by finding Nathanael. This would make Philip one of the group that had gathered around John the Baptist. He may have gone along with his fellow townsmen, Simon and Andrew; that would be in character. And it would also be in line with what we read of Philip elsewhere that he followed Jesus only after having received the kind of preliminary teaching that came from the Baptist. Given Philip's nature, it is unlikely that Jesus simply found him at home and, with little advance preparation, immediately persuaded him to follow.

Philip's home was Bethsaida, a Galilean town. The exact site of the place is not known, and indeed there are some who think that there were two towns of that name, "Bethsaida of Galilee" (12:21) and "Bethsaida Julias." This latter name was given to a town rebuilt by the tetrarch Philip, who added "Julias" to "Bethsaida" in honor of the daughter of the emperor. However, our best understanding of the evidence is that there was but one Bethsaida, situated somewhere near the place where the Jordan runs into the lake of Galilee. Perhaps it had a suburb on the other side of the river, and this may have given rise to the confusion about the names. The name means "house of fishing," appropriate enough for a place on the shores of the lake where so many fishermen plied their trade.

Philip and Nathanael

Jesus said to Philip, "Follow me." John does not say that Philip did follow him, but this is the clear implication of the passage. There would be no point in recording Jesus' command if nothing had happened. It is also the case that Philip immediately went looking for his friend Nathanael. When he found him he said, "We have found him of whom Moses . . . wrote," which indicates that he was already classing himself with the disciples of Jesus. There is no real doubt that Philip followed Jesus, nor that for Philip this meant attachment to the Messiah (however he understood that term).

His first reaction was to go to his friend with the news. He said to Nathanael, "We have found him of whom Moses (in the law) and the prophets wrote, Jesus the son of Joseph, who is from Nazareth." His "We have found" may in the circumstances be a slight exaggeration, but it is understandable. The others had indeed "found" Jesus, and when Philip followed him he aligned himself with them.

He does not speak of Jesus as "the Messiah" or use a similar title. He refers to him as the one of whom Moses and the prophets wrote. The fact that these words come first in the Greek gives them emphasis. This may mean that they were important words for Nathanael and Philip, and this in turn that the two friends were of the number of the Israelites who searched the Scriptures for information about the Messiah. It seems as though they were interested in the topic and had had many discussions. They would not have lacked material; Alfred Edersheim informs us that the rabbis found as many as 456 passages in Scripture that spoke of the Messiah. We need not think that all of these would have been known to Philip and Nathanael, or even that all were thought of as messianic as early as this time. It is enough that, in the opinion of many first-century students, there were many messianic passages. These two gentlemen would not have lacked passages for study.

Philip specifies the Law as one of the places in which the prophecies were to be found. In strict usage this refers to the first five books of our Old Testament, Genesis to Deuteronomy, the books of Moses. Sometimes the expression is used loosely, with a meaning like "Scripture." But the addition about the prophets here shows that Philip has in mind the books of Moses. "The prophets" probably means more than it does with us. The Jews spoke of "the former prophets" (by which they meant what we call the historical books; e.g., Joshua, Judges, 1 and 2 Samuel) and "the latter prophets" (what we call the prophetical books; e.g., Isaiah and Jeremiah). There were some differences from our classification, for they did not include Chronicles among the former prophets, nor Daniel among the latter prophets. But the division I have given answers fairly well. What Philip is saying is that a considerable part of the Bible points forward to the Messiah. And "Moses . . . and the prophets" may be a shorthand way of referring to the whole Old Testament (cf. "the law and the prophets" [Matt. 7:12]).

Philip may be saying more by his use of but one singular verb to cover the two subjects. He may be emphasizing that it was one person of whom Moses and the prophets wrote. Their messianic passages agree. They point to the same person, and that person is Jesus.

Philip calls Jesus "the son of Joseph," but we should not read too much into this. Certainly we should not argue, as some have done, that John in reporting this is denying the virgin birth. In the first place, we cannot expect a man who has been a disciple for no more than a matter of hours to know the intimate details of the birth of Jesus. Philip could not have known more at that time than that Joseph was the legal father of Jesus.

And in the second place, it is quite in John's manner to put down a statement which his informed readers will know to be in error, and leave them to work it out for themselves. G. Salmon points out that "no one understands better the rhetorical effect of leaving an absurdity without formal refutation, when his readers can be trusted to perceive it for themselves." This kind of irony is common in John's Gospel. A good example occurs in the discourse about the Bread of Life. At one point Jesus refers to being the bread that comes down from heaven, and his opponents say, "Is not this Jesus the son of Joseph, whose father and mother we know? How does he now say, 'I have come down from heaven'?" (6:42). Had they known the truth of the matter, they would have known that this very point of Jesus' parentage, far from being a difficulty, was itself proof that Jesus had come from heaven. But John does not stop to point this out. He is content to make his point more effectively with the use of irony. So here as well.

But Nathanael is not impressed. He retorts, "Out of *Nazareth* can any good thing come?" One of the little problems that preoccupy the scholars is why Nathanael should have been so contemptuous of Nazareth. True, it was a small and insignificant place, but we have no evidence at all for thinking that there was anything evil about it, such that it would be disqualified from being the hometown of the Messiah. Nathanael's poor opinion of the place is not reflected in any other source known to us. But for some reason Nathanael was very critical. As Hoskyns puts it, "Nathanael uses intelligent human observation to set a firm limit to the power of God," a process intelligent humans have been repeating all too often ever since.

The best suggestion that has been made, it seems to me, is that there was probably a rivalry between Nazareth and Cana. They were small places not far apart, and such centers often know a local rivalry (for that matter, such rivalry is not unknown between large cities). There is not much reason behind it, and many are quite amused at it, not taking it seriously. But there always seem to be some who do, and sometimes they are not the people we would expect to indulge such whims. Some scholars hold that such a rivalry is an improbable explanation; they feel that John is not likely to have chronicled a petty local jealousy. The trouble is that the reasons they suggest for Nathanael's words are even less convincing. Until a better explanation comes along, we may as well go along with this one.

Whatever the reasoning behind it, how do you meet a question like that? Philip did not know. He made no attempt to answer the question but simply said, "Come and see." Philip thought that if Nathanael could be persuaded to see for himself, it would work out all right. He knew his friend and had come to know Jesus. Seeing no way of overcoming the difficulty Nathanael had raised, he hoped that Jesus would do it for him. We may well reflect that under the circumstances this was probably as good an answer as could be given. But nothing in what we read of Philip leads me to think that he worked through all sorts of possibilities and came up with this one as the best. I think he felt hopeless. He could not argue the point convincingly, so he could only suggest that Nathanael come and see for himself.

So Nathanael came and Jesus convinced him. The story ends well. We may profitably reflect that it is not necessary to know all the answers before we can render acceptable and fruitful service to God.

Philip and the Loaves

The next time we meet Philip in John's Gospel is at the feeding of the five thousand with the five loaves and the two fishes (6:5–7). John tells us that Jesus lifted up his eyes and saw the crowds. Then he said to Philip, "Where will we buy bread so that these people may eat?" Philip was the natural person to be asked, because he came from nearby Bethsaida (1:44). It was not that Jesus meant the purchase of bread as a serious option. Clearly the quantity needed would be enormous, and it would not be easy to get it to this deserted place even if it were purchased. John explains that the question was simply to test Philip; it was not to be taken as an indication of the way Jesus would in due course provide for the people's needs.

So Philip faced the question. It was a large crowd, and Jesus' disciples were a small band. John tells us that Philip's answer was in effect, "If we had two hundred denarii (which, of course, we have not), and if we were to spend them on bread (which, of course, we cannot do as there are no bakers' shops in this area), there would not be enough to give all of them a little taste."

That was Philip's contribution to the solution of the problem. Once again we have a man out of his depth. He could see the difficulty; that was not hard for him. But he had no idea how the problem could be solved.

Philip and the Greeks

The third time we meet Philip in this Gospel is on the occasion when some Greeks came to him at Passover time in Jerusalem (12:20–22). Jesus had entered Jerusalem in triumph, and there had been a good deal of enthusiasm among those who followed him. Knowing what Jesus had done in their territory, doubtless many of the Galileans who had now come up to the feast were full of hope that he would proclaim himself Messiah. (Did not the fulfillment of prophecy through his triumphal entry into the city point to this?) They saw him as one who could get rid of the hated Romans and begin a new era for the Jews and for Palestine. Jerusalem was always excited during the great feasts, with crowds from all over the world thronging the streets. The triumphal entry must have heightened the normal state of excitement. What would happen next?

The Greeks who came to Philip may have been proselytes or converts to the Jewish religion, but, as we saw earlier (p. 47), this is improbable. They were more likely to have been "God-fearers," people who were interested in the Jewish way and specifically in serving the God the Jews worshiped, but who were deterred from becoming full members in the Jewish community of faith because of ritual practices like circumcision. They were religious people, for John tells us specifically that they had come to Jerusalem to worship (v. 20). The fact that they were Greeks meant that they could worship only in the Court of the Gentiles. Yet the prospect of worshiping there had brought them to Jerusalem.

These Greeks heard about Jesus. We have no information, however, about precisely what it was that they heard. John brings them into his narrative without introduction or explanation. He says only that they were among those who had come up to Jerusalem to worship at the feast and that they came to Philip. It is not clear why they selected Philip, but it may have been because he had a Greek name. If so, this is only a partial explanation, for his was not the only Greek name among the apostles (Andrew, for example, is also Greek). In any case there were many Jews who had Greek names. Greek was spoken throughout the world of the time; it was the common language of communication. Many people from a variety of nationalities accordingly provided themselves with a means of identification in this common language.

We cannot, then, determine the reason for their choice. But we are told that when they came, they "asked" Philip, "Sir, we wish to see Jesus" (v. 21). The words are not strictly a question, but a question is implied. Clearly they wanted to know whether Philip would help them in their quest. They spoke of "seeing" Jesus, but they had in mind more than physical sight. It was not difficult for anyone to see Jesus as he went about Jerusalem. The Greeks wanted more than this. They wanted an interview with Jesus and looked to Philip to arrange it.

From where we sit this was no big deal. We know that Jesus was full of love for all and, indeed, that he was about to provide in his death an atonement for the sins of the world. We have so fully accepted the idea that the gospel is a message for all men that we do not often stop to think how strange that must have seemed to some early disciples. It certainly was a problem for Philip.

Could he possibly bring Greeks to Jesus? Greeks? All of Jesus' ministry had been among the Jews. Jesus was a Jew himself. All the apostles were Jews. All the disciples Philip knew were Jews. Jesus and his friends had come to Jerusalem to keep the Passover, a feast of the Jews. The feeling that Jesus' people were Jews was so strong that for many years after this quite a few Christians held that if a Gentile wished to join them, he had to be circumcised and keep the law of Moses, that is, become a Jew in the full sense (cf. Acts 15:1). In the face of all this Jewishness, how could Philip possibly bring Greeks to his Master?

But, on the other hand, how could he turn them away? After all, Jesus had occasionally taken trips outside Jewish territory, such as that to Caesarea Philippi (Mark 8:27). He had healed the daughter of the Syrophoenician woman (Mark 7:24–30). Quite apart from such specific instances, Jesus habitually welcomed those whom the Jewish establishment regarded as outcasts. How would he view it if Philip turned the Greeks away?

It was all so very perplexing. Philip did not know what he should do. There were convincing objections to either course of action. So he went to Andrew and told him all about it. But, as we have noted, Andrew had no doubts. He was always bringing people to Jesus, and now he and Philip brought the Greeks. As in the case of Nathanael, it all ended well. But Philip was certainly puzzled in the situation in which he found himself.

Philip in the Upper Room

We get just one more glimpse of Philip in John's Gospel. It is in the upper room on the night before the crucifixion. Jesus is talking to the apostles and says in a reply to Thomas, "I am the way and the truth and the life; no one comes to the Father except through me. If you had known me you would have known the Father; and from now on you know him and have seen him" (14:6–7). This may have been clear to Thomas, but it was a puzzle to Philip. What does Jesus mean? We know the Father? We have *seen* the Father? That is just too much.

So Philip blurts out, "Lord, show us the Father. That's all we want" (14:8). Thus he draws down on him Jesus' gentle rebuke, "Have I been with you for such a time and you still do not know me, Philip?" He goes on to explain, "He who has seen me has seen the Father."

Thus in all the events involving Philip, we find him out of his depth. There is a consistency about Philip, just as there is a consistency of a different sort about Andrew.

A Humble Disciple

Obviously Philip had his limitations. And I, for one, find that comforting. We generally think of our Lord's twelve apostles as something special. They represent the inner circle, the aristocracy of the Christian church. There is nobody we can set alongside the apostles. And very naturally we make giants out of them. We see them as some kind of super-Christians, people infinitely higher than the likes of us.

But were they? Philip wasn't. And maybe some others weren't either. How many of us can recall offhand the names of the Twelve? We get off to a good start because we know Peter, James, and John. After our last two studies we think readily of Philip and Andrew. Most of us remember Thomas the doubter, and Judas who betrayed his Lord. The first part of the list is not difficult, but when we get down to "Lebbaeus, whose surname was Thaddaeus," we are hesitant, and with numbers ten, eleven, and twelve most of us are struggling.

Why do we find it so hard to remember them? Perhaps because some of them were simply not memorable men. Quite unreasonably we think that Jesus must have chosen spiritual giants for his Twelve. But he seems not to have done so. Some of them certainly were great men. I think that Peter would have been a great man in any company; probably John also in a different way, and perhaps some of the others would have been, too. But it seems that some of the Twelve were perfectly ordinary men, people about whom there was nothing special. People like Philip.

God does not need great men or women and great names to get his work done. He can, and often does, use very ordinary people. It may not seem to be anything wonderful when God picks out some really outstanding people like Peter and Paul and does great things through them. But when he takes humble, unimportant people like Philip, and makes of them the very saints of God, that is really wonderful.

I find Philip very encouraging. I can find no outstanding quality about him, nothing that makes him great. But there he is among Jesus' chosen Twelve. And ordinary people like me can learn that God has a place in his service for the lowliest. He still wants and uses the service of his Philips. Let us then not be discouraged by our limitations, but let us be encouraged and go forward to do whatever small piece of service God has for us to do.

8

The First Disciples: Nathanael

Philip finds Nathanael, and says to him, "We have found him of whom Moses (in the law) and the prophets wrote, Jesus the son of Joseph, who is from Nazareth." Nathanael said to him, "Out of Nazareth can any good thing come?" Philip says to him, "Come and see." Jesus saw Nathanael coming to him and he says of him, "Look, truly an Israelite in whom there is no guile." Nathanael says to him, "Where did you get to know me?" Jesus answered him, "Before Philip called you, while you were under the fig tree, I saw you." Nathanael answered him, "Rabbi, you are the Son of God, you are the King of Israel." Jesus answered him, "Because I told you that I saw you under the fig tree do you believe? You will see greater things than these." And he says to him, "Truly, truly, I tell you, you will see heaven opened and the angels of God going up and going down on the Son of man" (John 1:45–51).

The last of those recorded in John 1 as having come to Jesus at this time was Nathanael. Very little is known of this man. In fact, we read of him only in the incident in which Philip brought him to Jesus and on the occasion of the fishing expedition in John 21. But in the fishing story we have no more than his name and the information that he came from Cana of Galilee (21:2). If Nathanael did anything on that fishing trip, it is not recorded. Accordingly, all that we really know of him is what happened when he first met Jesus.

Some hold that we do not even know this. They point out that the name *Nathanael* (like its Greek equivalent, "Theodore") means "God has given." They argue from this that we are meant to see here not an individual, but an ideal disciple, or perhaps a typical incident. This would mean that the story is a pictorial way of telling us about what "God has given," a good gift that is repeated again and again in Christian experience. But there seems little reason for taking up this position. No concrete evidence is cited. The fact that the name has a meaning is surely not enough. Many first-century names had edifying meanings, but that does not mean that they were not real names of real people. On this occasion the story of Nathanael is the last in a sequence of stories of people who came to Jesus; there is no reason for thinking that it is less factual than any of the others.

Other people attempt to enlarge our knowledge of Nathanael by identifying him with someone else. They point out that we read of this man only in John, and they argue that he may well be identical with someone known in the synoptic Gospels by another name, all the more so as the name *Nathanael* does not occur in the Synoptics. The usual candidate is Bartholomew, who is not mentioned in John. "Philip and Bartholomew" are linked in that order in the lists of the names of the Twelve in all three Synoptics (Matt. 10:3; Mark 3:18; Luke 6:14); this fits in with the fact that in John it is Philip who brings Nathanael to Jesus. In the list in Acts 1 the order is "Philip and Thomas, Bartholomew . . ." (Acts 1:13); those who advocate the identification point out that Nathanael follows Thomas in the list of fishermen in John 21:2.

Their position is supported by the fact that the name *Bartholomew* is not really a personal name at all. "Bar" is a prefix meaning "son of," so that Bartholomew means "son of Tolmai." Anyone with a title like this almost certainly had a personal name of his own as well. We find such a title in the name of the great apostle Simon Peter, who is called "Simon Barjonah" (Matt. 16:17; i.e., he was Simon, son of Jonah). So Bartholomew almost certainly had another name. It is further pointed out that all the others mentioned in John 1 became apostles; from this it is inferred that Nathanael did too. If so, he is likely to have been Bartholomew.

All this is interesting but highly speculative. We can perhaps say that if we assume that Nathanael was in fact one of the Twelve, he was probably the same man the Synoptists call Bartholomew. But why should we make that assumption? There is nothing in John 1 to indicate that he would become one of the Twelve, though that proves little, since there is not much to show that the others would become apostles either. We have that information from other sources. But I see no reason for holding that in this chapter John is writing about the Twelve as such. He seems rather to be writing about men who became followers of Jesus; whether or not they became apostles is irrelevant. Jesus had many disciples outside the Twelve, and I cannot imagine a reason why John should not write about one from this wider circle in the opening section of his book.

"Come and See"

When we were thinking of Philip, we saw that he was the one responsible for bringing Nathanael to Jesus. The narrative reads as though the two were friends. They seem also to have been interested in studying the Bible, specifically the passages in Scripture that told of the coming of the Messiah. So Philip's opening words to Nathanael were, "We have found him of whom Moses (in the law) and the prophets wrote, Jesus the son of Joseph, who is from Nazareth" (1:45). Though Philip does not say so, the impression we get is that the two friends had often discussed scriptural passages about the Messiah, which they had found in the writings of both Moses and the prophets. They had been looking for the coming of God's Great One, and Philip was now enthusiastic: "We have found him!" What a wonderful thing that the prophecies they had studied and sought out for so long should now be fulfilled. And not only fulfilled in their own day, but right where they were, and in a person whom Philip himself had met! Philip was a very happy man and he told Nathanael all about it so that he could come to share in the joy.

But Nathanael was not impressed. Presumably he had been just as interested as Philip in searching out the relevant passages in the Bible. But it was quite another matter when it came to seeing them fulfilled in someone from Nazareth. Nathanael wanted more than Nazareth. "Out of *Nazareth* can any good thing come?" he asked (v. 46). We have already seen (pp. 54–55) that there is nothing discreditable about Nazareth as far as we know, and that Nathanael's objection probably came from nothing more than the fact that it was a little village not far from Cana, Nathanael's hometown. For Nathanael, the Messiah would be an impressive figure. He would come with the aura of being the fulfillment of countless prophecies of Scripture. How, then, could he come from a little place like Nazareth? Why, it was no bigger than Nathanael's own Cana! Great people simply do not come from the Nazareths of this world.

Nathanael's scepticism must have been a surprise to Philip, who clearly had been so mightily impressed by Jesus that he went right off to tell his friend. But the friend was less than enthusiastic; he was downright cool. What was to be done, then? Philip could not argue him out of his scepticism, but he could, and did, invite him to come and see for himself. "Come and see" was a stock phrase among the rabbis. They seem to have used it when they found a somewhat difficult problem to which the solution was not at all obvious. But it was possible, and the words are an invitation to join in a search for it together. It seems also to have been an invitation to look for something new or important or both. Philip, of course, was not a rabbi. But it is not without interest that he used this expression which meant so much to the rabbis.

An Israelite Without Guile

Nathanael was sceptical, but not too sceptical to avail himself of Philip's invitation. It would do no harm to go along with his friend and meet this Nazarene.

There was a surprise for him straightaway. Jesus saw him coming and greeted him with the words, "Look, truly an Israelite in whom there is no guile" (v. 47). The word for "guile" is an interesting one. Originally it seems to have meant the bait used in catching fish. Now the art of the angler is to deceive the fish. He presents the fish with a bait that seems quite acceptable (indeed, desirable), but in fact serves the interests not of the fish but of the fisherman. It deceives the fish. The word came in time to mean any cunning device, especially one for catching something or someone. For example, it was used of the Trojan horse and of Penelope's robe. It tended then to signify not so much "bait" or the like, as "deceit" or "craftiness." It pointed to an object that would effect someone's purpose by seeming to be other than it was, and this in such a way that the simple were beguiled.

There is an interesting example of its use in the Greek translation of the Old Testament. Jacob, it will be recalled, put hairy skins on his hands and wore Esau's robe to deceive Isaac into thinking that it was his elder son and not Jacob who came to him with savory meat. This resulted in the aged patriarch's giving Jacob his blessing. In due course Esau came in from his hunting and sought Isaac's blessing for himself. When Isaac realized what had happened, he said to Esau, "Your brother came deceitfully and took your blessing" (Gen. 27:35). The word translated "deceitfully" ("with subtilty" in KJV) is translated into Greek by the same word we have here *(dolos)*. This is what Jesus says Nathanael lacks. Nathanael was not like Jacob. Not for him the cunning contrivance that deceives. He was a plain, straightforward person. William Temple brings out the resemblance to the passage in Genesis by translating at this point, "An Israelite in whom there is no Jacob!" Nathanael was an Israelite indeed. But he was not like Jacob.

It may be worth noticing that this is the only place in John's Gospel where the word *Israelite* occurs. John speaks often of "the Jews" but only here of any Israelite. He may mean us to discern that Nathanael was really all that an Israelite ought to be. Paul reminds us that a man is a true Jew if he is one inwardly (Rom. 2:29). That is what Jesus is saying about Nathanael.

This greeting astonished the man. Nathanael had never seen Jesus before and was quite sure that Jesus had never seen him. How then could he possibly know anything about him? So Nathanael explodes in an incredulous question, "Where did you get to know me?" (v. 48). Incidentally this reaction neatly proves the truth of Jesus' point about his guilelessness. A guileful person would have affected a modesty leading him to say that he really was not worthy of such a description. Not Nathanael. Since he really had no guile, he accepted the accuracy of what Jesus had said and simply asked how Jesus knew.

Under the Fig Tree

Jesus replied, "Before Philip called you, while you were under the fig tree, I saw you." This clearly meant a lot to Nathanael, but it is not at all obvious to us. We notice first that the words "before Philip called you" are put first in Jesus' reply and are thus given a certain emphasis. Jesus is not speaking of something that took place as a result of Philip's call. What he is speaking about had taken place at an earlier time.

And that is about the end of our certainty. We can engage in speculation, based on what we know of fig trees and of people and their habits. Fig trees were very much a symbol of home, especially of home in a time of peace and prosperity. Micah has an apt description of peace: "Every man will sit under his own vine and under his own fig tree, and no one will make them afraid" (Mic. 4:4). Zechariah similarly looks forward to a time of peace and prosperity: "'In that day each of you will invite his neighbor to sit under his vine and fig tree,' declares the Lord Almighty" (Zech. 3:10). Fig trees and grape vines were very common throughout Israel, and every man wanted to have them about his home. Jesus' reference, then, almost certainly points to something that took place at Nathanael's home.

We can perhaps say more. Palestine could be hot in the summer, and there were no such amenities as air conditioning. So people looked to shady trees to help them through the hot weather. The rabbinic writings give evidence that scholars often used the shade of a fig tree as a good place to study and meditate and pray. A large fig tree gives a very acceptable shade, and as the tree was common, it was a widespread practice to use its shade for pious purposes.

It seems fair to say that Nathanael had had some outstanding experience as he studied his Bible or prayed in the shade of a fig tree at his home. What it was we do not know. But Jesus knew; his words showed that.

John Calvin comments: "We should also gather from this passage a useful lesson, that when we are not even thinking of Christ we are observed by Him; and this must needs be so, that He may bring us back when we have withdrawn from Him."

The King of Israel

What is not clear to us was abundantly plain to Nathanael. He knew immediately what Jesus meant and was deeply impressed by his knowledge. He exclaimed, "Rabbi, you are the Son of God, you are the King of Israel" (v. 49). Clearly he found Jesus' words totally unexpected and totally devastating to his scepticism.

I was reading of a father who was quite out of sympathy with his long-haired modern son's interest in conservation, protest marches, and the like. But one day the father scored a neat point by remarking: "Do you realize that when you wash your hair you use four times as much shampoo as I do? And all that excess is foaming away into the ecosystem and polluting the environment!" It was a completely unexpected statement.

So with Nathanael. He had not anticipated anything like Jesus' answer, and so it had a profound effect on him. The first thing we notice is the respectful "Rabbi" which begins his response. He had not been this polite when he asked whether anything good could possibly come out of Nazareth. His opening word indicates a change of heart.

He proceeds to affirm that Jesus is the Son of God. He uses the emphatic pronoun *you*. It singles Jesus out from all others. What follows in the statement is distinctive to him.

"Son of God" has different meanings. It may be used of man, as when Paul writes, "As many as are led by the Spirit of God, these are the sons of God" (Rom. 8:14). A similar thought is implied also in the family prayer of all Christians, when we say, "Our Father." As we have been adopted into the heavenly family, we may rightly be called "sons" (and, of course, "daughters") of God.

But the expression may also be used in a more limited sense. Instead of referring to a son of God in general, we may use the term in a restricted sense to denote the unique Son of God. This marks one person as God's Son in a special way. He is Son of God in a way different from that in which all of God's people may be called sons. Nathanael is using the term in this second way. He is not saying that Jesus shares with all pious men a good relationship with God, but that Jesus' sonship is different. He is not a son of God, but the Son of God.

We noticed earlier (p. 13) that John does not use the word *son* (of God) to refer to pious people who are members of God's family; he reserves this term for Jesus. He does, of course, use "son" in the ordinary way—for human sons of human fathers; it is when speaking of the heavenly family that his terminology is distinctive. When he wants to refer to human membership in the heavenly family, he uses the word *child* (as he did in 1:12). By keeping the word *Son* for Jesus he brings out his deep conviction that Jesus is God's Son in a special way, a way different from that in which anybody else may be called a son. A good example is John's reporting of Martha's confession: "I have believed that you are the Christ, the Son of God, who comes into the world" (11:27). Obviously this was not meant as a commonplace; Martha was saying that Jesus stood in a very special relationship to God. It is the same with Nathanael. He is saying that Jesus is different, the Son of God as no one else is.

Nathanael goes on to speak of Jesus as "the King of Israel." This expression is found only three times in the whole of the rest of the New Testament. One such occurrence is in Matthew's account of the mockery as Jesus hung on the cross. The chief priests and scribes and elders called on "the King of Israel" to come down from the cross (Matt. 27:42). It is not without interest that Nathanael here uses in sincerity at the beginning of Jesus' ministry a title that others would use in mockery at the end!

Mark also records the incident reported in Matthew. But in Mark the words "the Christ" and "the King of Israel" seem to mean nearly the same thing (Mark 15:32). Jesus is no ordinary king, but the messianic King, the Christ of God, the Deliverer whom God sent.

The only other passage containing the expression is the record of the triumphal entry. John tells us that as the people came to meet Jesus, they took branches from palm trees and cried out, "Hosanna, blessed is he who comes in the Lord's name, even the King of Israel" (12:13).

It is obvious from these passages that "the King of Israel" was a title of grandeur. We might be inclined to think that to go from "Son of God" to "King of Israel" is anticlimactic. But this is not the way it would have seemed to Nathanael. For him, "King of Israel" was as high a title as could be given. It denoted the sovereign ruler over the people of God, and thus someone who had an especially close relationship to God and a special task from God. We should also bear in mind that Jesus had just greeted Nathanael as "an Israelite." Accordingly, when Nathanael calls him "King of Israel," he is expressing his own allegiance and submission. As William Barclay puts it, "Nathanael capitulated for ever to the man who read and understood and satisfied his heart."

Heaven Opened

Jesus proceeds to assure Nathanael that this is but a beginning. Nathanael had been impressed by Jesus, as we see from the fact that

Jesus' use of just one expression had caused such a reversal in the attitude of the man from Cana. But, Jesus says, he will see greater things than these: "You will see heaven opened" (1:51).

This is not a commonplace, for it is consistent biblical teaching that heaven is beyond man's grasp. The story of the Tower of Babel, back in Genesis 11, illustrates the foolishness of man in his proud assurance that a tower could be built that would bring him to heaven. It firmly makes the point that God forbids this. He puts obstacles in the way. To attain heaven by our own effort must remain forever an impossible dream. Man may want to bring it about but he never can. A little later in John's Gospel we read that "no one has gained the heights of heaven except him who came down from heaven, the Son of man" (3:13). That remains true. Man is limited; heaven may be in his aspiration, but it is beyond his grasp.

But God can open heaven if he so chooses. Three times we read in the New Testament that he has done so. It happened at the baptism of Jesus (Luke 3:21). On that occasion heaven was opened for the visible coming of the Holy Spirit in a form like a dove. This was accompanied by the voice from heaven that affirmed that Jesus is God's beloved Son. Clearly that opening of heaven was very special.

So, in different ways, were the other two. When Stephen's speech met a hostile reception, he had a vision of "the glory of God and Jesus standing at the right hand of God." He said, "I see the heavens opened and the Son of man standing at the right hand of God" (Acts 7:55–56). This was a significant occasion in the life of the church. Stephen was about to become the first man martyred for the new faith. Heaven's opening assured him that, despite what men might say, God would receive him. He might be condemned by his opponents, but he had divine approval.

The third occasion was in Peter's vision. He saw "the heaven opened" and a great sheet let down full of all sorts of creatures that Peter could not class as "clean" (Acts 10:11–16). This was God's way of bringing home to the apostle the great truth that Gentiles are as important in his sight as are Jews, a most important lesson for the early church. For that matter, it is still important. Not all Christians have come to learn that race does not matter. If God opened heaven to make this clear, why are we so slow to learn it?

Jesus is saying, then, to Nathanael that his ministry would make the realities of heaven known to men. People can never attain heaven of themselves, but God can open heaven. He has sometimes done so, and preeminently was this the case in the ministry of Jesus. He has met us where we are. He has disclosed to us what we could never know of ourselves.

Jesus also says that Nathanael will see "the angels of God going up and going down on the Son of man." Notice a small point: Jesus speaks of the angels as first "going up." We would expect him to say that they would first come down from heaven and then return. But that is not the order. And it is not the order in Jacob's vision when that patriarch saw a ladder set up from earth to heaven and angels going up and down on it (Gen. 28:12). What can this mean but that the angels are here already? God has never forsaken the people he made. His love is so strong that it is always exercised toward us. We must not think that our sin or our stupidity can ever stop God from being active among us. His angelic messengers are constantly with us.

The other significant thing is that the angels ascend and descend not on a ladder (as in Jacob's vision), but on the Son of man. Jesus is the one Mediator between heaven and earth. He brings the realities of God to us, and he lifts us up to God. It is to be his work both to teach people the way to God and to be the way to God (cf. John 14:6). He will in due course lay down his life that we may be given that life that is life indeed. This is foreshadowed in the conversation with Nathanael. Nathanael could not have understood all that was involved in the mission of Jesus. But he could understand that he was no more than at the beginning of his knowledge of Jesus. Jesus had already shown him that he knew much about him and knew something of his intercourse with God. Now Nathanael learns that Jesus has much more to show him. Jesus would be the Mediator between heaven and earth.

9

A Wedding in Cana

On the third day there was a wedding in Cana of Galilee, and the mother of Jesus was there. Jesus and his disciples had been invited to the wedding. And when the wine ran out the mother of Jesus says to him, "They have no wine." Jesus says to her, "Lady, what have I to do with you? My hour has not yet come." His mother says to the waiters, "Do whatever he tells you." Now there were set there six stone water jars for the Jewish purification rites; each held two or three measures. Jesus says to them, "Fill the water jars with water." They filled them right up to the brim. And he says to them, "Draw out now and take it to the master of ceremonies." So they took it. When the master of ceremonies had tasted the water made into wine, and did not know where it had come from (though the waiters who had drawn the water knew), the master of ceremonies calls the bridegroom and says to him, "Everyone puts out the good wine first, and when people get drunk the worse. But you have kept the good wine until now." This Jesus did as the beginning of signs in Cana of Galilee, and manifested his glory. And his disciples believed in him (John 2:1–11).

We do not know a great deal about the way a wedding was conducted in first-century Palestine. A good number of regulations survive, so that we know about things like preliminary arrangements, contracts, and so on. We know who might marry whom and who might not marry whom. In sum, we know quite a bit about weddings in general.

But what happened on the great day? Here our knowledge is limited. We have no information about who performed the marriage ceremony, for example. We do not even know whether it was a religious or a civil ceremony (if indeed there was a distinction in those days). We may reason that among a people as religious as the Jews it is unthinkable that anything as significant as a wedding would take place without a solemn religious ceremony. But the fact is that we do not know. We can reason about it. We can say, "Such and such must have happened," but we cannot point to evidence. Would there have been a rabbi there? Or a priest? A Levite perhaps? Who would conduct the ceremony? What part would the heads of families play? We do not know.

Yet there are some things we do know. The wedding was preceded by a betrothal, which was a very solemn affair and much more binding than is an engagement with us. To break an engagement in modern times is not, as a general rule, much more difficult than simply returning the ring. But in first-century Palestine it required the same procedure as divorce.

The day of the wedding was a Wednesday if the bride was a virgin and a Thursday if she was a widow. The wedding was often held in the evening, because there were processions and these were more spectacular if they were held by torchlight. First the bridegroom and his friends went in procession to the home of the bride. The bridegroom and a few of those close to him went into the bride's home, while the others waited outside (like the ten young ladies in Matt. 25:1–13). The actual ceremony, whatever its form, took place inside the bride's home. Then there was another procession, this time with all those interested going to the home of the bridegroom.

Here the marriage feast was held. This was a very important part of the proceedings. It was often a lengthy affair and might go on for a week. It was important that everything be done properly. One thing that seems strange to us is that there was a strong element of reciprocity. If one gave a feast of such and such a quality (and quantity!) when his son was married, he was entitled to an equivalent when his neighbor's son was married. If the neighbor did not provide it, he could be taken to court and sued; a wedding feast was not simply a social occasion, but involved a legal obligation. This is important for our present study. It is quite possible that the bridegroom of John 2 and his family were financially unable to provide all that was necessary for the wedding feast. It is often said that it is unlikely that Jesus would have performed a miracle like this simply to rescue people from a minor social embarrassment. Quite so. But it may well have been much more than that. It may be that Jesus rescued a young couple from a financial liability that would have crippled them economically for years.

The Wine Failed

We are told that this marriage was at Cana of Galilee. This place is rarely mentioned in early literature; in the New Testament it is referred to only here and in John 4:46 and 21:2. Each time "of Galilee" is added; apparently people needed some indication of its location. We may fairly reason that it was not an important place.

And the participants were not important people. Important people did not live in places like Cana. We are not even told the name of anyone in either of the families being linked by this wedding. Plainly the people were poor; otherwise they would have made ample provision for the wedding. They were certainly a long way from being like the customers of a New York bank of whom I read recently. For people who like to use only clean, fresh bank-notes, quite untouched by human hands, the bank provides new notes in books with tissues between the notes. This service is provided free for customers who keep a minimum balance of $25,000. Our wedding party would not have qualified. But it was for this humble, obscure, unnamed group of poor people that Jesus did his first miracle. God's priorities are not ours.

John tells us that the mother of Jesus "was there" (v. 1). Incidentally it is one of the minor mysteries about this Gospel that the author never uses Mary's name. He uses some other names freely, but he always refers to Mary as "the mother of Jesus." No satisfactory explanation of this has been given; we must simply take it that John omits the names of some people. John the son of Zebedee is himself nowhere mentioned by name (cf. John 21:2), and these two facts may be linked. John tells us that on the cross Jesus commended Mary to the keeping of the beloved disciple (19:26–27). If this man was the author of the Gospel and his practice was not to mention the name either of himself or of his brother, he may well have extended this habit to include Mary, who at the time of writing was, or had been, a member of his household.

John does not say so, but he leaves the impression that Mary was a friend of the family, and that she had been in residence with them to help with the preparations for the wedding. By contrast, Jesus and his disciples "had been invited" to the wedding (v. 2). Some, it is true, hold that they simply came by and, being there, were "invited" on the spot. They further conjecture that it was this unexpected addition to the guest list that caused the wine to run out, so that Jesus' miracle was a means of rescuing people from a difficult situation that he himself had helped to bring about. But this is to read a great deal into the passage. The plain meaning of the words before us is that Jesus and his friends had been invited in the customary way.

Evidently the family was a poor one. They had had to make the minimum preparation for the wedding, hoping that everything would work out all right. But it didn't. They miscalculated the amount of wine needed (or perhaps they could not afford more), and there was not enough.

That was a serious matter. There is a rabbinic saying, "Without wine there is no joy." We should not misinterpret this as evidence that the rabbis were given to much drinking. They were not. They were highly critical of drunkenness, and they required that when wine was drunk it should be diluted with water in the proportion of three parts of water to one of wine. The saying reflects the fact that in the first century there was not much choice of beverages. Quite unreasonably we tend to read back our rich variety; we think that if they did not have our tea, coffee, Coca-Cola, and the like, they had their equivalent. But in the first century one drank water or one drank wine. For ordinary people there was nothing else. A wedding or other feast was a special occasion. So while some people evidently had the habit of drinking water as their normal practice (cf. 1 Tim. 5:23), this was felt to be inappropriate at a feast. On such an occasion there must be wine. No one, then, could dismiss the absence of wine at a wedding feast as a matter of no importance. In that time and in that place it mattered very much.

As we saw earlier, it is likely that the family responsible was in a difficult financial position. That the wine ran out is itself evidence of the fact that they were poor. Had they not been in straitened circumstances, they would never have allowed such an occurrence. It is almost certain that some of the guests were people who had previously entertained the present hosts and were thus entitled to demand an equivalent hospitality. There may even have been the prospect of a lawsuit. We must not think of the situation as a very minor affair, with nothing much hinging on the outcome.

In this crisis Mary approached Jesus. She did not ask explicitly for a miracle, but her words seem to look for nothing less. At the least she knew Jesus to be resourceful, and she put the problem before him. But we should perhaps see more than that in her words. Mary knew the circumstances of the birth of Jesus, and she had had visits from the shepherds and the wise men. Whatever the case with other people, she knew Jesus to be God's Messiah. It may be that we should see here some natural motherly pride and perhaps a small trace of exasperation. From Luke's Gospel we know that Jesus was about thirty years old when he started on his public ministry (Luke 3:23). Mary may well have been asking herself, "When will he begin his work as Messiah?" Surely it was time. Moreover, there was the excitement arising from the events described in John 1. Disciples were gathering round Jesus. He was being hailed as the Messiah. Why then does he not do something? Mary, proud of her son, gives a gentle push. Here is a fine opportunity for him to make a beginning.

This is probably behind Jesus' words, "Lady, what have I to do with you?" (v. 4). These words are not as distant in Greek as they sound in English. For example, Jesus used the same form of address, "Lady" or "Woman," in speaking to women for whom he was doing miracles (Matt. 15:28; Luke 13:12), the woman at the well (John 4:21), the woman taken in adultery whom he rescued from being stoned (John 8:10), and Mary Magdalene at the tomb (John 20:15). And, of course, it was this form of address that he used when he spoke to Mary from the cross (John 19:26). There is no harshness in the term on any of these occasions.

Yet we should bear in mind that it was a very unusual form of address for a son to use in speaking to his mother. Apart from the examples in this Gospel, no one seems to have noticed any. Neither among the Jews nor among the Greeks is this form of address attested.

We should probably infer that Jesus, though speaking politely, is putting a distance between them. As long as he lived in the home at Nazareth he was subject to his parents as a dutiful son. But when he began his public ministry he was God's Messiah. He must now act as God leads him. His relationship to his mother is changed, and she must not presume on her position. This is also the thrust of "what have I to do with you?" It points to a changed relationship. There is no longer the tie to which Mary appealed. Jesus is now not simply her son, but God's Messiah, who must be active in doing the will and the work of God.

Jesus adds, "My hour has not yet come." This must surely mean, "It is not yet time for me to act." We would leave it at that, were it not that this is the first of a series of references to Jesus' "time" or his "hour." His time has not yet come in John 7:6, 8, 30; and 8:20. But when the cross is in immediate prospect Jesus says, "The hour has come that the Son of man should be glorified" (John 12:23; there are similar statements in 12:27; 13:1; 16:32; 17:1). In other words, this series of statements running through the Gospel up till the time of the crucifixion is a way John has of bringing out the fact that the purpose of God is worked out in the life of Jesus, a purpose that is to culminate in the cross. Until the crucifixion Jesus' hour had not arrived. At the crucifixion his hour came. This is an unobtrusive but impressive way of indicating the centrality of the cross. We are not to see the cross as a sad accident coming at the end of a life full of the promise of better things. We are to see it as the culmination, and as the intended culmination, of all that Jesus did. That for which he came into the world would be accomplished on the cross and nowhere else.

Water into Wine

Clearly Mary did not take Jesus' words to her as a sharp rebuke. She went on to instruct the servants to do whatever Jesus told them (v. 5).

Incidentally, the fact that she could give such an instruction shows that she had some standing in the household and underlines our impression from verse 1 that she was in the house at the time to help with the wedding preparations.

John now inserts a little explanation of the scene. He specifically refers to some water jars. They were made of stone and were of considerable size. He tells us that they had a capacity of "two or three measures" each. This is the only passage in the New Testament where this word for "measure" is found, but in other literature it was in frequent use (often in connection with a quantity of wine). It denoted eight to nine gallons, so that two or three measures would amount to something like twenty gallons. Six such jars would hold about 120 gallons of water. If this seems a lot, we must bear in mind the continuing need for ceremonial purification. Before eating, each guest would have a servant pour water over his hands. If the feast went on for a number of days, the process would be repeated every time the guest ate, for in the meantime he might well have contracted defilement in some way. So, with any sizable number of guests, there would be the need for a fair quantity of water.

Jesus' first instruction to the servants was to fill up these water jars. This is presumably a way of ensuring that there would be no doubt about what happened. With the jars filled right up to the brim with water, there was no chance of inserting anything else into them.

Some have seen some symbolic significance in the number six. They point out that seven was regarded as the perfect number and suggest that six should be seen as a symbol of coming short. This leads us to think of the Jewish approach as coming short, and of Christ's way as the perfect way that replaces it. I suppose that a symbolic significance of this sort is not impossible, but it is not the kind of thing we meet elsewhere in this Gospel. Against it also is the fact that there is nothing to indicate the number seven. Jesus does not produce a seventh jar, for example. Moreover, we cannot be certain that six would be recognized as an indication of falling short. The Alexandrian Jew Philo, who wrote shortly after this, thinks of six as the perfect number. He gives as his reason that it is equal to the sum of its factors ($3 \times 2 \times 1 = 6$ and $3 + 2 + 1 = 6$). We are not impressed by his logic; nonetheless, we are not in a position to say, without some indication in the context, that John is pointing to something imperfect when he uses the number six. That is not given in the number itself.

Next Jesus instructs the waiters to draw water and bring it to the master of ceremonies (v. 8). He does not say from what the water should be drawn, and some people have thought that he meant that they should draw water from the well. It is true that the verb here is often used of drawing water out of wells (though not exclusively; there are other uses). But there is nothing to show that this is the meaning here. If it is this that is in mind, why does John tell us about the water jars? And why does Jesus command that they be filled? It seems curious that they should be mentioned if they are to play no part in the story. Everything points to the water as being taken from the water jars.

John puts no particular emphasis on the miracle. In fact, he does not even say when it happened. For that matter, he does not say how much water was turned into wine, but simply assumes the miracle and says, "When the master of ceremonies had tasted the water made into wine. . . ." Some have thought that his meaning is that the whole 120 gallons became wine, others that only what was brought to the guests was so changed. If the former was the case, the change probably took place before the waiters started bringing it in; if the latter, then the transformation would have been at the time of bringing the beverage to the guests.

Some have objected to the idea that all 120 gallons were changed, on the grounds that this would be far too much for a wedding feast and would be an encouragement to drunkenness. But that is probably the wrong way to understand it. We have already seen that wine was heavily diluted on such occasions, and if we are to think of the entire amount as being changed (which I think we should), the point is that it was more than was needed for the wedding. The young couple would be able to sell the excess and start their married life with an asset instead of facing a crippling liability. While we cannot be sure which of the views is to be preferred, it seems to me that the mention of the capacity of the water jars turns the scale. If all the water was changed into wine, this tells us how much there was; it is an important piece of information. But if only what was drawn out was changed, what is the point of mentioning the size of the jars? In this view it would not matter what size they were.

One point of the miracle is that Christ makes abundant provision. There was an immediate need at the wedding, but when he supplied that need he did more: he helped the young couple get off to a good start in their married life. He gives with no niggardly hand. Paul speaks of God as supplying his people's need "according to his riches in glory" (Phil. 4:19), not simply according to their need at one particular moment.

The Result

The first result of the miracle was the comment of the master of ceremonies. He called the bridegroom and pointed out that he was not behaving as a host usually did. Evidently this man had had a wide

75

experience of festivities (as we would expect of someone appointed to preside). He remarked that the usual practice was for people to put out their best wine at the beginning. At that time the guests' palates are still sensitive, and they can remark on the quality of what they are drinking. When they have drunk a quantity (actually he says, "when people get drunk," which is a comment not on the state of the guests at this particular feast but on what happens at feasts in general), then the worse wine is brought out. When palates are no longer sensitive, people are less aware of what they are drinking.

But on this occasion the best wine had been kept back until later. It would seem that neither the master of ceremonies nor the bridegroom knew where the wine in question came from. We are told only that the waiters who brought it in knew. The master of ceremonies was not consciously commenting on a miracle; he was simply impressed by the taste. But John's readers will pick up the point that Jesus does not do things by halves. Not only is the wine that Jesus provides abundant in quantity, but it is also of excellent quality. There is nothing to equal it.

John adds a comment of his own. He tells us that Jesus did this "as the beginning of signs" (v. 11). He has his own terminology for Jesus' miracles. He never calls them "mighty works" as do the other Evangelists. He calls them "signs" or "works." The latter term points to the fact that what to us is a miracle is to Jesus no more than a work. And, as John uses the term for both miracles and the nonmiraculous, it points to the further truth that for Jesus there was no great difference between the one and the other. His life was a unity. Being who and what he was, he did some things we can class only as miracles, as well as more ordinary things. But we ought not to think of Jesus as though he on occasion transformed himself into a magician, into another person so to speak. All that he did he did as one person.

But here John uses the term *sign*. This is a way of saying that Jesus' miracles were not simply works of wonder. The essential characteristic is not that we cannot explain them, but that they are meaningful. They convey spiritual truth.

A New Creation

Accordingly, we should look for the spiritual significance of this first sign. Right at the beginning of his account of Jesus' ministry, John tells a story of transformation. He is not writing about Jesus as though he were simply a wonder-worker. He is telling us about the way Jesus transforms lives. He will go on in chapter 3 to the necessity for being reborn; there he will set forth the same truth in a different way. The divine power will transform the life of whoever comes to Christ.

We should not overlook the fact that John says specifically that the water jars in this story were set there "for the Jewish purification rites" (v. 6). It was precisely this water of Jewish purification that Jesus changed into wine. John surely means us to see that the water of Jewish ceremonial observance, water used in accordance with Jewish concentration on the law as the way of salvation, is changed by Christ into the wine of the gospel. Jesus had not come to tidy up an old system. He came to change people, to change them radically, to put a new power in them.

This may be indicated also by some unobtrusive notes with which John starts his Gospel. After his prologue, he begins his account by telling us what happened on one particular day (1:19). In verse 29, the words "the next day" move us on to Day Two. A similar expression in verse 35 advances us to Day Three. Then in verse 39 two young men come and stay with Jesus, beginning at around 4 P.M. This seems to mean that they stay the night, bringing us to Day Four. In verse 43 the words "the next day" take us to Day Five. There is no reference to Day Six, but in John 2:1 we read "on the third day," which, by the inclusive method of counting in use at the time, brings us to Day Seven. John puts no emphasis on it, but he thus begins his Gospel with an account of the happenings of one momentous week, the week that inaugurated Jesus' ministry.

We recall that the opening words of this Gospel are "In the beginning," exactly the words with which Genesis commences its description of the seven days of creation. Surely John is doing much the same thing. By his choice of opening words and by arranging his first narratives in a way that recalls the creation story, he is making the point that he is writing about a new creation. This is not a creation in the physical world, but one in the hearts of men. Jesus does not take sinners as they are and leave them like that. He transforms them. He brings a new power into life and makes them new.

John goes on to say that Jesus "manifested his glory." The sign showed something of who and what he is. He is fully man, but he is more. This "more" might be hidden from the casual observer. But John goes on to say, "His disciples believed in him." He says nothing about the effect of it all on the guests or the wedded couple or the master of ceremonies or the waiters, though these last at least knew that water had been changed into wine (v. 9). None of these saw the significance of what had happened.

But the disciples did. They were interested and committed people, and they looked into the meaning of what Jesus did. And because they looked for spiritual meaning, their faith was deepened. God always responds to the genuine seeker.

10

The Temple

And the Passover of the Jews was near, and Jesus went up to Jerusalem. And he found in the temple men selling oxen and sheep and doves, and all the moneychangers sitting. He made a whip of rushes and drove them all out of the temple, both the sheep and the oxen, and he poured out the money of the moneychangers and overturned their tables. He said to those who sold doves, "Take these things away from here; do not make my Father's house into a shop." His disciples remembered that it is written, "Zeal for your house will devour me" (John 2:13–17).

The Passover was one of the three great festivals of the Jewish year. It commemorated the great deliverance of the people from Egypt and was accordingly a time of special solemnity. It was one of the three occasions each year when all adult Jewish males were required to go up to Jerusalem (Deut. 16:16). So it is not surprising to find Jesus keeping it in the usual way and going up to the capital city.

John speaks of it as "the Passover of the Jews," from which some have drawn the conclusion that there was another Passover, the Passover of the Christians (which would in time develop into the Easter festival). But this seems highly unlikely. In the first place, it is reading too much into the words "of the Jews." John refers to Jewish customs often. In our last study we saw how naturally he referred to the water jars for the Jewish purification rites, where his expression is like that here: "the purification of the Jews" (2:6). He also uses this kind of language with respect to the Feast of Tabernacles; it is "the feast of the Jews" (7:2). Are we to think that the Christians had their own purification ceremonies and their own Feast of Tabernacles?

In the second place, this would attribute to the early Christians a greater interest in liturgical observances than the New Testament warrants. There is evidence that those among them who were Jews observed some of the Jewish liturgical requirements, such as the feasts. Some even kept the Jewish Sabbath. But there is little evidence of any specifically Christian liturgical observance. It seems reasonably clear that Sunday was kept as a day for worship (1 Cor. 16:2; Rev. 1:10), though there is not as much evidence even for this as we might have expected. And it is not easy to find any other day that the Christians kept as holy. Sometimes their language is hard to reconcile with any real concern for special days (e.g., Gal. 4:10–11).

In the third place, for the Christians the Passover could be said to have been sacrificed already (1 Cor. 5:7). This would be a very strange statement if the Christians were in the habit of keeping an annual Passover of their own.

It seems clear, then, that John simply means that the Jews held a Passover each year, and that on the occasion of which he is writing Jesus went up to Jerusalem to keep it. Not all Jews went up each year, of course, but many did. It was a great festival, and people liked to be in Jerusalem for it.

Traders in the Temple

On this occasion, when he came up to Jerusalem Jesus found a busy bazaar in the temple courts. There were people selling oxen, sheep, and doves, which would have been necessary for those who wanted to offer a sacrifice. Obviously, for people who came from a distance, perhaps from over the sea, it would be difficult and in some cases impossible to bring with them the animals needed for sacrifice. So it was important that there be those who would provide the necessary victims somewhere handy to the temple. Then the worshipers could come up to Jerusalem with their money, purchase the animals or birds on the spot, and offer their sacrifices in the normal manner.

If the sacrificial system was to be continued and if it was to be available for people who came from distant parts, it was necessary that there be provision for them to purchase what they needed for their offerings. But the point is that there was no necessity for the animals and the birds to be in the temple precincts. They needed only be somewhere handy. But the traders were evidently eager for business and set up their stalls in the temple itself. This means in the outermost court, the Court of the Gentiles. For the traders it meant good business; they were on the spot and in a position to make many sales. But for any Gentile who came up to the temple to worship it meant that prayer had to be offered in the middle of a cattle yard and money market. It is true that the service these businessmen provided was useful, but they should have provided it somewhere other than in the temple itself.

The moneychangers were needed because offerings in the temple were to be made only in approved currency. A surprising number of commentators say that this was because some coins had stamped on them the image of the emperor or some other great person or some heathen emblem. Pointing out that the Jews refused to make any representation of the human form, they hold that heathen coinage with such images was unacceptable for the temple offerings. But this overlooks the fact that it was not only permitted, but required, that offerings be made in Tyrian currency, and the heathen Tyrian coins bore representations of the human form.

The reason for stipulating Tyrian coinage is never given, but it probably concerns problems that arose when people were not strict enough with their currencies. In many states coins were of uncertain alloy. When times were hard, rulers were able to stretch their available gold and silver by making the coins a little less valuable, either by simply reducing the amount of precious metal in them or by substituting some cheaper metal for part of the gold or silver. But the Tyrians were traders and knew the value of a stable currency. So they insisted that their coins be of exactly the right weight and contain exactly the right amount of precious metal. People knew that they could trust Tyrian currency. If a Tyrian coin was supposed to contain a certain amount of silver or gold, then it would certainly contain that amount of precious metal.

The temple authorities probably insisted on this coinage for temple dues and the like because they knew what they were getting. In any case they seem to have melted down the coins and cast them into ingots, so the heathen symbols did not matter; they did not last long. Whether or not that is the reason, there is no doubt as to the practice. Anyone making an offering in the temple had to do so in Tyrian coins. So moneychangers were needed. Worshipers came from all over the world bringing their local coins, and the moneychangers exchanged their coins for Tyrian.

Driving the Traders Out

When Jesus came up to the temple, then, he found himself confronted with commercialism run riot. Instead of a quiet courtyard where people from all over the world could pray, there was this noisy trading center.

So he made a whip, probably out of rushes, though some hold that it was of cords. They find support in the fact that in the only other place where the word is used in the New Testament, it certainly means the ropes on a ship (Acts 27:32). Either way, it was not a particularly formidable weapon. But armed with this alone, Jesus proceeded to drive the traders from the temple.

Obviously one man with such a small armament could not prevail physically over a crowd of traders. There can be little doubt that he had an ally in the consciences of the traders. They knew deep down that whatever the legalities, they should not have been there. Had they combined to resist Jesus, it is not easy to see on the human level how he could have overcome them. But his selfless anger and their uneasy fears combined. They fled before his onslaught. He drove out the traders with their sheep and oxen; he poured out the money of the moneychangers and overturned their tables.

He said to the sellers of doves, "Take these things away from here; do not make my Father's house into a shop" (v. 16). The word *shop* is more literally "house of trade," and the double reference to "house" is noteworthy. They had forgotten in whose house they were and were making a house meant for the worship of God into a house for their own profit.

There is an account of a cleansing of the temple in all three synoptic Gospels. But they tell us that on that occasion (which seems to be different from the one John describes; it is at the end of Jesus' ministry, whereas John is describing what happened near the beginning of it), Jesus quoted Isaiah 56:7 and went on to complain that the traders had made the house of God into "a den of robbers" (Mark 11:17). He was complaining about the dishonesty of the traders, and there was indeed room for that. Enough examples are attested of their exorbitant charges to make it clear that they took advantage of their privileged position. But in John it is not the dishonesty of which notice is taken, but the practice itself. Whether honest or not, they should not have been there. The temple was meant as a place of worship and should not have been used as a means of amassing profits.

Notice further that Jesus speaks of "my Father's house." He does not class himself with men and speak of "our Father's house." Throughout this Gospel he never links himself with people in such a way that we can say that his relationship to the Father is the same as that of men. God is our Father, but he is Jesus' Father in a special way. We may become "sons of God"; he is "the Son of God"!

The disciples remembered the words of Psalm 69:9: "Zeal for your house will devour me." We should probably understand these words to mean that Jesus has that all-consuming zeal for God and for God's house that is characteristic of the Messiah. All that Jesus does arises from his special relationship to God and his vocation to be God's Messiah. John writes his whole Gospel to bring this out (20:31), and narrating this incident is part of the way he fulfills his plan.

Raising the Temple

The Jews answered him, "What sign do you show us, that you do these things?" Jesus replied, "Destroy this temple and in three days I will raise it up." The Jews said to him therefore, "This temple was built in forty-six years, and you will raise it up in three days?" But he was speaking about the temple of his body. When accordingly he was raised from the dead, his disciples remembered that he had said this and they believed the Scripture and the saying that Jesus had spoken (John 2:18–22).

The Jews recognized the messianic significance of what Jesus had done. Interestingly, they did not question the deed itself, but Jesus' right to do it. They expected that when the Messiah came, God would do miraculous things through him; presumably they thought that the Messiah could do more or less what he wanted to in the temple. So they asked Jesus for a sign that would accredit him. If he was going to act like the Messiah, let him produce a sign that would show him to be the Messiah. John says that they "answered" him, which means that they answered his action. What he had done spoke louder than any words. They made reply to that devastating action.

Jesus responded, "Destroy this temple and in three days I will raise it up" (v. 19). This puzzled them, but in some form or other it was remembered and distorted. When his enemies arrested him years later, they produced witnesses who said, "We heard him say, 'I will destroy this temple made with hands and in three days I will build another not made with hands'" (Mark 14:58). This is not exactly what Jesus said, and indeed in this form it is something very different. But it resembles his actual statement sufficiently for us to see that it is based on what Jesus had said. Unfortunately for their purpose, the witnesses could not agree on the exact words; this is natural if they were trying to recall a cryptic statement made some years before. Mockers also recalled the saying as Jesus hung on the cross (Mark 15:29), and Stephen's opponents seem to have had the same words in mind (Acts 6:14). In the synoptic Gospels there is no narrative relating the actual event at which Jesus spoke these words. It would seem that behind all these passages there are fragmentary and imperfect recollections of what Jesus said on this occasion.

The Jews had asked Jesus for a sign, but throughout his ministry he consistently refused to give a sign when he was asked for it in this way (cf. Mark 8:11–12). Jesus said that the only sign that would be given to the people who looked for one was the sign of Jonah, who was three days and nights in the belly of the whale, just as the Son of man would be in the heart of the earth (Matt. 12:38–40). That is to say, the resurrection would be the sign.

It is along this line of thinking that Jesus here says, "Destroy this temple and in three days I will raise it up." The language is different, but the meaning is the same. The Jews would bring about his death, and on the third day he would rise. Ironically they would themselves be the means of bringing about the sign they were demanding. Another irony is that when the sign in fact came, they did not recognize it, because they refused to recognize the resurrection.

We should notice a change of vocabulary that seems significant. In the earlier part of this account, John uses for "temple" the word *hieron* (v. 14), which is an inclusive word. It refers to the whole of the temple precincts, with the courtyards, vestries, and whatever else belonged to the temple complex. But in verse 19 Jesus uses the word *naos*, which means "the sanctuary." It was used of the central place in any temple, the shrine, the place where deity dwells. This word is sometimes used metaphorically of the believer, who is the "temple of the Holy Spirit" (1 Cor. 6:19). But its use here of Jesus probably points to the fact that God was in him in a special way.

The Jews were astonished. They thought about their temple, a magnificent structure that had been in process of construction for a long time. They spoke of forty-six years, which may mean that at the end of that period of time a certain stage in the work had been completed, so that they could speak of the temple as "built." Actually the temple was begun by Herod but not completed until A.D. 64, well after the time these words were spoken. But even forty-six years is a long time and stands for a considerable amount of work. They found it incredible that Jesus would accomplish in three days what had taken the workmen so many years.

But they had not understood Jesus. He was not talking about the stones and mortar that preoccupied them. He was talking about "the temple of his body" (v. 21). This pattern—a statement by Jesus, a misunderstanding, then a further explanation that brings out more truth—is repeated a number of times in this Gospel (and is not unknown in the others). It is an effective way of driving a point home.

John does not say that the disciples understood all this straightaway. It was only after the resurrection that they remembered the saying and

83

saw what it meant. The result was that they believed (v. 22). John's linkage of believing "the Scripture" with believing "the saying that Jesus had spoken" shows that he put the words of Jesus on the same level as those of the Bible, the Word of God. This is instructive for understanding his view of Jesus.

John sees the words as pointing to Jesus' resurrection. We should perhaps notice that there have been other interpretations. Some students think that the "body" refers to the church. They remind us that the church is explicitly said to be the body of Christ in passages like Ephesians 1:23 and 4:16. They suggest that Jesus meant that his death would result in the appearance of the church. There is, of course, truth in this, since apart from the death of Jesus, there would have been no Christian church. The atonement is the great act on which the very existence of the church depends. But it is not easy to think that it is this that John has in mind when he reports these words of Jesus. John does not call the church the body of Christ in any other passage, and we have no reason for thinking that in this Gospel a reference to the "body" without further explanation would lead his readers to think of the church. There must be a further meaning.

Others hold that Jesus was referring to the literal temple and speaking of its ultimate destruction. But he would not refer to the rebuilding of this material, physical structure, for in fact it was not rebuilt after it was destroyed in A.D. 70. So they maintain that Jesus said something about the destruction of the temple that was not fully understood. They think that the exact words have been lost in the process of transmission, so that it is now impossible to be certain of what Jesus said or what he meant. Probably, they suggest, he said something about the new way that he would bring to pass, a new way that would replace the temple and all it stood for.

The Resurrection

Such explanations are put forward sincerely, but it seems they are no improvement on what John tells us, namely, that the words refer to the physical body of Jesus, which would be destroyed, but which would be raised up in the resurrection. Let us bear in mind a number of relevant facts.

In the first place, all the other Gospels tell us that Jesus predicted his resurrection (e.g., Matt. 16:21; Mark 9:31; Luke 18:33). It is clear in all the Gospels that Jesus knew that he would be rejected by the Jews and that in the end they would succeed in having him put to death. But it is equally clear that he did not regard their triumph as permanent. He foresaw that he would rise from the dead and said so. John's explanation of his words here fits in with what we know from elsewhere.

It is also clear that Jesus said something about the temple that his enemies thought involved its destruction and used against him at his trial (as we saw earlier). They could not remember the exact words (Mark 14:58–59). This would be very natural, for the statement was made at least a couple of years before Jesus' arrest and trial; and in addition it is the kind of enigmatic saying that they would not have understood and thus might have difficulty in recalling exactly.

It is also the case that when in any Gospel Jesus speaks of "three days," he usually means the period leading up to the resurrection. He does this often and in fact does not refer to "three days" in any other way (except for one saying about people who had been with him for three days [Matt. 15:32; Mark 8:2]). It is not easy to see why anyone should attach "three days" to a saying about the literal destruction of the temple. It is much the best explanation that Jesus himself linked "three days" to a reference to the temple in a statement that foretold his rising from the dead.

A New Way

We should take the words, then, as an unusual way of referring to the resurrection after the Jews had helped bring about the death of Jesus (the "destruction" of his body). But John often has sayings that may be understood in more ways than one, and not uncommonly it seems as though he intends us to see a double meaning. This may well be the case here.

For the fact is that the death and resurrection of Jesus did mean the destruction of the temple as a viable religious system. After Jesus had offered the sacrifice that would put away the sins of the world, what place would there be for a temple in which the central act was the offering of the bodies of animals on the altar? When Jesus died, the temple died as the center of a religious system.

John is surely tying all this together. He tells us how Jesus cleansed the temple, an act that vividly rejected the Jewish system as it was practiced, with its externality and its exaltation of the profit motive. When he goes on to Jesus' words about the destruction of the temple, he seems to be saying that in due course the death and resurrection of Jesus would spell the end of the way of approach to God that his contemporaries accepted so uncritically.

R. H. Lightfoot has this to say:

There is in this story, thus set before us here, a triple depth of meaning. First, the Lord performs an act by which He condemns the methods and the manner of the existing Jewish worship. Secondly, this act, as set forth by St. John, is a sign of the destruction of the old order of worship, that of the Jewish Church, and its replacement by a new order of worship, that of the Christian Church, the sanctuary or shrine of the living God. And thirdly, intermediate between the old order and the new order is the "work"—the ministry, death, and resurrection—of the Lord, which alone makes possible the inauguration and the life of the new temple.

To see the words in this way is to see John as setting forth a grand conception. He sees the work of Jesus as the critical event in the working out of the plan of God for man's redemption. He sees what God has done as a call to us to bow in adoring worship before him who has wrought out our salvation in what his dear Son taught and did. The death and resurrection of Jesus have transformed our whole conception of the way to God. In the light of what Jesus has done, there is no place for the kind of thing that the temple symbolized. As the writer to the Hebrews put it, "no longer is there an offering for sin" (Heb. 10:18).

11

Rebirth from Above

There was a man of the Pharisees, Nicodemus by name, a ruler
of the Jews. This man came to him by night and said to him,
"Rabbi, we know that it is from God that you have come as a
teacher, for nobody can do the signs that you do unless God is
with him." Jesus replied, "Truly, truly, I tell you, unless anyone
is reborn from above he cannot see the kingdom of God."
Nicodemus says to him, "How can a man be born when he is
old? He cannot enter a second time into his mother's womb
and be born, can he?" Jesus answered, "Truly, truly, I tell you,
unless anyone is born of water and Spirit he cannot enter the
kingdom of God. That which is born of the flesh is flesh, and
that which is born of the Spirit is spirit. Don't be astonished
that I told you, 'You must be reborn from above.' The wind
blows where it wants to, and you hear the sound of it, but you
do not know where it is coming from or where it is going. So is
everyone who has been born of the Spirit" (John 3:1–8).

Jesus' conversation with Nicodemus is fascinating. In
the first place it is quite unexpected that a man of this kind would want
to talk to Jesus. John tells us that he was a Pharisee, a ruler, and "the
teacher of Israel" (vv. 1, 10). This is not the kind of person that the
Gospels tell us was usually found where Jesus was. But Nicodemus
came.

When he came he spoke with some condescension. "Rabbi," he began. Jesus was not really a rabbi, but it doesn't hurt to be polite

(especially if one's friends know nothing about it!). "Rabbi, we know that it is from God that you have come as a teacher. . . ." Is there here a note of conscious superiority? Is he implying, "Some of us are disposed to think quite well of you"? Though Nicodemus was condescending to talk to the Galilean teacher, he was still very mindful of his own position and who he thought Jesus was.

I am reminded of an incident in an American law court. A flamboyant figure strode to the witness box and was sworn in. He was instructed, "State your name," and replied, "Frank Lloyd Wright." "Occupation?" "I am the world's greatest living architect." Afterwards one of his friends said to him, "Frank, how could you say such a thing in court?" To which he replied simply, "I had to. I was on oath."

Do I detect something of this in the attitude of Nicodemus? He was not coming to Jesus (he thought) as to a superior or even an equal. He was very conscious of the relative positions of a Pharisaic ruler and a preacher from Galilee. Nicodemus might be polite, but he knew where they both stood.

But Jesus was not concerned with the kind of thing that mattered to Nicodemus. He wanted none of the polite exchanges that rested on such a foundation, but came straight to the real need of the Pharisee. His opening words are the solemn "Truly, truly," which in this Gospel introduce and emphasize important statements. "Truly, truly, I tell you, unless anyone is reborn from above he cannot see the kingdom of God" (v. 3). I am adopting here the common translation "born," but it might be noticed that the Greek verb is more naturally understood of the male parent than of the female. It is the "begotten" of old-fashioned speech. The point is that what Jesus says more naturally refers to the male parent than the female, and in this context refers to the action of God the Father. The way to the kingdom is not the way of human striving or of human excellence of any sort. We enter the kingdom because of what God does.

"The kingdom of God" is the most frequent topic of Jesus' teaching in the Synoptics, but it is rare in the Fourth Gospel. It is generally accepted that the term is to be understood dynamically; that is to say, it means "reign" rather than "realm." It points to something that happens rather than something that exists. It is the rule of God actively at work. Obviously it is important for religiously minded people that they see this kingdom, so the words were important for Nicodemus.

There is a problem for us as to the precise meaning of the expression I have translated "reborn from above." The adverb *anōthen* is held by some to mean "again." The word can mean either "again" or "from above," and the difficulty is that either translation gives a good sense in this passage. But John has the habit of using words that have more than one meaning in a way that shows he wants his readers to see multiple meanings. So it is, I think, here. The begetting of which John is writing is something new, so we should understand the adverb as "again." But it is not an earthly renewal that is in mind, a fact which is brought out with "from above." If we understand the adverb in the sense "reborn from above," we get both meanings and save ourselves the problem of trying to differentiate between them.

Clearly Nicodemus did not like the way the conversation was going. He asked, "How can a man be born when he is old? He cannot enter a second time into his mother's womb and be born, can he?" (v. 4). This is surprising. Jesus quite obviously did not mean this, and an intelligent man like Nicodemus can scarcely have thought that he did.

It is possible that it was the form of expression that bothered Nicodemus. The words are not unlike those often used of a convert to the Jewish religion. When a Gentile decided to become an adherent of the Jewish way and was admitted by way of baptism and circumcision, it was often said that he was like "a child newborn." To use terminology that fitted the latest convert to Judaism would have seemed to Nicodemus the last thing that should have been said about such a distinguished person as he, a Pharisee and a member of the governing body, the Sanhedrin. J. Alexander Findlay says it was "as though in modern times an Anglican dignitary or eminent Nonconformist divine were told to go and get converted in an evangelical mission hall!" It may be just what he needs, but he is unlikely to welcome the proposal. It may be this sort of thing that bothered Nicodemus.

But I wonder whether perhaps he was being wistful rather than just plain difficult. He may have been thinking that the past grips us with an all too firm grasp. I am what I am today because of the nature with which I was born and then what all my yesterdays have done to me. Some of them have strengthened me and made me a better man, but all too many have weakened me and dragged me down. I have learned all sorts of bad habits and made mistakes innumerable. When I try to do good, I am hindered by the fact that I am so used to doing evil.

Perhaps Nicodemus was reasoning: "How wonderful it would be to shake off the dead hand of the past! I would like to have such a 'new birth' and thereafter not be limited by all my sins and errors and mistakes. It would be tremendous to make a completely new beginning, quite unhindered by the handicaps the past has built into me. But, of course, it is impossible. The lesser miracle, the physical one of going back into one's mother's womb for birth, is impossible. How much more the greater miracle, that of breaking with the past and starting all over again! It would be wonderful. But—."

Water and the Spirit

Jesus repeats what he said before, but with slight differences. Once again he uses the emphatic "Truly, truly." What follows is important and must be listened to carefully and heeded: "Unless anyone is born of water and Spirit he cannot enter the kingdom of God" (v. 5). We should probably not read much difference between "seeing" the kingdom (v. 3) and "entering" it (here). It is John's habit to introduce slight variations of expression with no great difference of meaning. In both places the meaning is that the way into God's kingdom is not a way worked out by man. The natural man always likes to think that he can merit acceptance by God by the kind of life he lives, the great deeds he does, or some other aspect of human striving. But twice over Jesus says that nothing of the sort is the way. The way is by regeneration, by being reborn by the power of God.

A further difference is that whereas before Jesus had spoken of being "reborn from above," here the process is described as being a birth "of water and Spirit." This is not an easy expression, and commentators have tried to explain it with a fascinating diversity of results. But the many explanations tend to fall into one or another of three groups.

One interpretation sees "water" as referring to cleansing of some sort. It may be the kind of cleansing that John the Baptist preached. He called on people to repent and accept his baptism as a sign of their repentance, with a view to the forgiveness of their sins. Some scholars place no stress on the connection with John the Baptist, but simply see "water" as a natural symbol for being made clean. According to this view Jesus is saying that to enter the kingdom one must first be cleansed from one's sins and then be given the positive endowment of the Holy Spirit of God, who enables people to live uprightly. There is a negative aspect to salvation (cleansing by water) and a positive aspect (the work of the Spirit). This view is attractive and must remain a possibility.

A second view sees "water" as connected with natural birth. This view may take more than one form. Thus "water" may refer to the fluid that surrounds the unborn child and from which it emerges during the process of birth. If this is the way to understand it, the expression is simply a reference to the natural process of being born.

Another way of understanding "water" is quite foreign to us, but seems to have been quite congenial to first-century Jews and, for that matter, to quite a number of other people at that time. Words referring to something wet were often used as euphemisms for the male semen: "water," "dew," "drop," "rain," and other words were all used in this way. We could take this meaning here and understand the expression in much the same way as that which we have already noted. It would then simply mean natural birth. In both cases the meaning would be that the way into the kingdom means (1) natural birth ("water") and (2) birth from the Spirit.

But there is another way of understanding "water" as a reference to the male semen. In the Greek text, "water" and "Spirit" go closely together in this passage (there is one "of" that covers them both). Some have thought accordingly that the birth in question is one of water-and-Spirit, that is, a birth of "spiritual seed"; one must be born with the birth the Holy Spirit provides. It is a support to this view that a little later Jesus speaks of being born "of the Spirit" (v. 8); and as we noted earlier, it is John's habit to use expressions that differ from one another slightly but have essentially the same meaning.

A third way of understanding the expression is to see a reference to Christian baptism. Then the meaning would be that the Holy Spirit is at work when one is duly baptized, and it is this that brings entrance to the kingdom. The strongest reason that can be urged in favor of this view is that at the time when this Gospel was written this meaning might well have occurred to many readers. The weakness is in seeing how Nicodemus could possibly have understood Jesus if that was what he meant. Christian baptism had not yet begun, and it is not easy to see why Jesus should puzzle an inquirer with a reference to a nonexistent sacrament. So, while this view is popular in many circles today, it seems best not to accept it. The words must have made sense to Nicodemus.

It seems to me that the second way of taking the expression is the best way, and that in the sense of being "born of spiritual seed." This way of understanding the words would be natural for a learned Pharisee like Nicodemus, and it makes excellent sense. Jesus would then be saying that the way into the kingdom is the way of divine action. We enter a completely new existence by virtue of what the Holy Spirit does in us. So thoroughly are we remade that the process can be described as a being born all over again, a spiritual rebirth. It is quite distinct from the natural process of birth or, for that matter, from any natural process. Jesus is referring to the power of God to remake people.

Flesh and Spirit

Jesus proceeds to develop the thought. "That which is born of the flesh is flesh," he says, "and that which is born of the Spirit is spirit" (v. 6). Sir Edmund Hoskyns brings out the meaning of these words neatly when he says, "There is no evolution from flesh to Spirit."

The word *flesh* is used in more ways than one in the New Testament. In Christian teaching it is often associated with "the world" and "the devil" (as in "the temptations of the world, the flesh, and the devil"). We find this meaning sometimes in Paul, for example, when he tells us that "the mind of the flesh is death" (Rom. 8:6; in the next verse it is "enmity against God"). But we do not find it in John. He prefers to use the term to point us to the physical weakness that is an inevitable part of this mortal life. It may refer to limitations on the way people carry out actions like judgment (8:15). But it may also refer to Jesus' becoming human for us (1:14), or to "the flesh" that he would give "for the life of the world" (6:51).

If John does not use the term for what is sinful, he certainly does use it for what is limited. That is his meaning here. We like to dwell on those things that we can accomplish. Human achievement means much to us. But Jesus is saying that it is limited to this earth. When it comes to entrance to the kingdom of God, the best human efforts are of no use. For that we need divine energy.

Jesus goes on to say, "Don't be astonished that I told you, 'You must be reborn from above'" (v. 7). In view of the principle just set forth, there is nothing really surprising in the statement that it is necessary for a rebirth to take place if anyone is to enter God's kingdom. Jesus makes it clear that what he is saying applies not only to Nicodemus. In Greek there is a distinction between the singular and the plural of "you," just as in old-fashioned English we had "thou" as well as "you." Here Jesus uses the singular when he says, "I told you" (i.e., "I told thee"), but the plural in the words, "You must be reborn from above." This is not a private principle that applies only to Nicodemus, a kind of solution to his own personal problems. It did have its personal application to Nicodemus, but it applies universally as well. It is true of us all that rebirth from above is the one way into the kingdom.

Notice also the strong word *must*. Jesus is not saying that rebirth is on the whole a good idea. He is not just recommending it for people in some special situation, perhaps with difficult problems of their own. He is making it of universal application. This is true of everybody. There is no exception.

It is said that George Whitefield, who was associated with the Wesleys in the Methodist Revival, preached on this text again and again. When one of his friends asked him, "Why do you preach so often on the text, 'You must be born again'?" he replied, "Because you *must* be born again." It was a good answer, and one that brought out this great evangelist's firm grasp on this central spiritual truth.

The Spirit and the Natural Man

There is a little uncertainty about the way to understand Jesus' next words. The difficulty is that the word we have translated "spirit" up till now, has also in Greek the meaning "wind" or "breath." It would seem that from the earliest days people noticed that when anyone ceased to breathe he died. Now breath seemed nonmaterial; it was not like, say, a piece of wood or metal, which could be seen and handled. Equally the spirit of man could not be seen or handled. So the same word came to be used in a number of languages for "spirit" and "breath." Since wind is no more than a lot of breath going somewhere in a hurry, the word was used to mean "wind" as well. It is only the context that enables us to say which meaning should be understood in a given passage.

Jesus' words in verse 8 may accordingly be understood as "the wind blows where it wants to" or as "the Spirit breathes where he wills." A point in favor of the second translation is the fact that the same word has been understood earlier in this chapter in the sense "spirit." We would thus expect it to have this meaning here also. The meaning of the verse would then be that the Spirit moves as he wills. People cannot predict what he will do. Nor do they know what motivates anyone who has been reborn by the agency of the Spirit. Just as the Spirit of God is unpredictable to the natural man, so the person re-made by the Spirit is quite incomprehensible to him. He does not know the Spirit, so he does not know the Spirit-led man.

This understanding of the words is consistent and gives a good sense. It would unhesitatingly be accepted were it not for the fact that Jesus goes on after the difficult words to say, "and you hear the sound of it." Now the unbeliever can scarcely be said to hear the "sound" or the "voice" of the Spirit. How can he possibly do that? Because of this difficulty it seems necessary to look at the other way of taking the words. They will then mean, "The wind blows where it wants to, and you hear the sound of it, but you do not know where it is coming from or where it is going." This gives an excellent sense also, and is free from the disadvantage attending the first interpretation. We should surely take Jesus' words in this way.

He is saying to Nicodemus, then, that the familiar wind is myste-rious. Was there a gust of wind at this point in the conversation? It would underline the point that it is possible to hear the wind without knowing either its origin or its destination. It is like that for the un-spiritual person. He may indeed come into contact with one who is indwelt by the Spirit of God, but he cannot understand him. It makes no sense to him when the Spirit-filled man or woman forsakes a life of ease and comfort for difficult and demanding and lowly service. For the true Christian it is a commonplace that the site of one's service may be in slums, among the down and outs (or, for that matter, in the penthouses, among the up and outs!). Or it may be among some primi-tive tribe in a distant land. It may mean forsaking comforts and pros-pects and friends. For the worldly-minded the question always arises, "What do you get out of it?" Such people cannot understand those who prefer to ask, "What can I put into it? How can I best serve?"

The Radical Novelty of Christianity

The mystery of rebirth points us to the great distinctive that separates the Christian way from other ways. In antiquity, as in modern times, there were many religions that emphasized the importance of good works. But Jesus says that no one can so live that eternal life is owed to him. It is neither a reward for good conduct nor the result of diligent search. It comes from being reborn.

We noticed earlier that the figure of rebirth was sometimes used of the proselyte, the convert to Judaism from among the Gentiles. But though the figure of rebirth might be used of him, he did not enter into eternal life in the way Jesus was teaching. The proselyte thought that when he became a Jew it was necessary that he merit his salvation by the life he lived. He was still bound by the idea of good works. He thought that he earned his salvation by his own efforts.

So it was with other religious systems. There were, for example, a group of religions that today we call "the mystery religions." Not as much as we would like is known about them, but it is known that the novice went through some horrifying experience by way of initiation and then was brought into a condition of peace. In a way this was a gift. But in a way it was also his reward. He had of his own free will submitted to the rites of initiation. He had done the right thing; he had performed all that was prescribed for him and thus earned his salvation.

This continues in the modern world. There are "religions" like communism and humanism that hold out before people a very limited idea of salvation. But common to them, and to every purely human system, is the thought that in the end salvation depends on what we do. We must, for example, cease to rely on superstition. Instead we must educate people; we must work to establish communism or humanism. This is the supposed way of "salvation." In both cases the end result is proportional to the effort we make.

The fact is that it comes naturally to the human animal to rest his ultimate salvation, however he may understand it, in his own strong right arm. In the end, he thinks, everything depends on what he does. But in the end, Jesus says, that will never do. At best, what we finish up with is "flesh," some human system with all the typical faults of a human system. He is saying that reform is not enough. It is a noble ideal, but it operates only on fallible human flesh. Over against that he insists that "you must be reborn from above." It is in being remade by the Spirit of God, not in dusting off a few of our worst habits, that the way of salvation lies.

It is as true of our generation as it is of all others: "You must be reborn from above"!

94

12

The Death of Christ and the Life of Men

"No one has ascended into heaven except him who came down from heaven, the Son of man. And just as Moses lifted up the snake in the wilderness, even so must the Son of man be lifted up, so that everyone who believes may have eternal life in him. For God so loved the world that he gave his only Son, in order that everyone who believes in him should not perish, but have life eternal. For God did not send his Son into the world to condemn the world, but so that the world should be saved through him" (John 3:13–17).

Jesus is still talking to Nicodemus. He has made it clear that the way to life is the way of being reborn from above. Nicodemus's puzzlement upon hearing this (v. 9) leads Jesus to refer to the Pharisee's position as "the teacher of Israel" and to the contrast between heavenly and earthly things (vv. 10–12). If Nicodemus could not understand earthly things, how could he comprehend the heavenly?

Then Jesus proceeds to the truth that rising to heaven is not a human achievement (v. 13). In a way this is the thrust of the previous section. The point about being reborn is that man in his natural state cannot attain the highest. Jesus now puts the same basic truth in another way. He says that no man has ever gained the heights of heaven. That belongs only to "the Son of man." This is the way Jesus normally refers to himself. It is a puzzling expression, but we need not go into all the problems it presents and for which the scholars have no agreed solutions.

What is clear is that Jesus uses it of himself in his official capacity, so to speak. Where people today often speak of Jesus as the Messiah, he preferred to refer to himself as the Son of man. This term has an obvious reference to his humanity, but it is also a way of bringing out his heavenly origin, for the expression seems to have been taken from Daniel 7:13–14, where we read that "one like a son of man [came] with the clouds of heaven," and "approached the Ancient of Days." To this Son of man were given "authority, glory and sovereign power; all peoples, nations and men of every language worshiped him. His dominion is an everlasting dominion that will not pass away, and his kingdom is one that will never be destroyed." Clearly the Son of man is a divine person with great dignity.

But since this term seems not to have been in common use in Jesus' day, most people would not have seen him as claiming any particular place for himself when he used it. It was a way of both concealing and revealing his messiahship at the same time. It concealed it from those who did not look too hard, yet revealed it to those who saw a link with the passage in Daniel. Nobody else seems to have referred to Jesus in this way, with the exception of the dying Stephen (Acts 7:56). It was Jesus' own way of referring to himself, and he used the term frequently.

In this passage, then, he is saying that it is his work to come from heaven to save people. People cannot attain heaven, but he can come down from heaven and raise them up. In Isaiah 14:12–13 we read that the "morning star, son of the dawn," said in his heart, "I will ascend to heaven; I will raise my throne above the stars of God." But he could not bring this desire to pass. No created being can rise to heaven by his own efforts. But the Son of man is on a different level. He could and did come down to raise men to heaven.

The Snake in the Wilderness

Jesus goes on to explain something of what this means (v. 14). He reminds Nicodemus of the story in Numbers 21, where some fiery snakes were biting the Israelites with fatal results. Moses prayed for the people, and God told him to make a fiery snake in bronze and put it up on a pole. Whoever looked at it would live (Num. 21:6–9). The lifting up of the bronze snake in this way was clearly connected with life and salvation.

So now Jesus likens this to what would happen on the cross. He speaks of the Son of man as being "lifted up." Though he does not explicitly mention the cross at this point, it is clearly in mind in the following verses, and we need not doubt that this is so here as well. In a later part of his Gospel, John appears to give an explanation of what he understands by this term. Telling us that Jesus said, "I, if I be lifted up from the earth, will draw all men to me," John proceeds to add his own explanation of what this meant, "This he spoke, signifying by what death he would die" (12:32–33). This is an intelligible way of referring to the cross, though an unusual one.

It is unexpected for another reason. The verb John uses is rarely employed in this way. It is much more usual to find it employed in a sense that we would translate by "exalt" or the like. We find it, for example, in Peter's sermon on the day of Pentecost, when that apostle said of Jesus, "Having therefore been exalted at the right hand of God . . ." (Acts 2:33). And it occurs in a compound form when Paul writes, "Therefore also God has highly exalted him" (Phil. 2:9).

In an earlier study (pp. 21–26) we saw that John has a highly individual use of the term *glory*, applying it freely not to majesty and splendor, but to lowly service. It is like that here. The supreme exaltation is that on the cross, for there the Son of God laid down his perfect life for others.

Notice further the little word *must*. Jesus is not saying that there are various possibilities before him and that from them all he chooses this one (though he might have chosen one of the others). That is not the way of it at all. He says that he "must" be lifted up in this way. We do not know in what the necessity lay, but we find the word *must* used a number of times in connection with what Jesus would do in carrying out his mission. So here. It points to a compelling divine necessity. It was the way people would be saved, and so, though it meant pain and grief and difficulty, Jesus chose to endure it. Being who and what he was, there was no alternative. He would save people, even though it meant dying for them on a cross.

Faith and Life

Jesus goes on to speak of the purpose of his death. It was "so that everyone who believes may have eternal life in him" (v. 15). Faith—or more exactly, believing—is a very important concept in John. The verb *to believe* is found ninety-eight times in this Gospel (though interestingly, the corresponding noun *faith* does not occur at all). It is clear that the idea of trusting Christ or God (John puts little difference between these two activities) is supremely important. Its importance arises from what we have seen in our earlier studies, that men cannot attain salvation by their own efforts. This is something that must be brought about by God if it is to happen. To receive salvation, people need simply trust God. If we do not trust him, we place ourselves

97

outside the salvation he offers. If we trust him, we enter into all that this salvation means.

Sometimes John speaks of "believing in" Christ (v. 16), sometimes of believing that what Christ or God says is true (e.g., 5:24). Sometimes he sees faith as having content, and refers to "believing that . . ." (e.g., 8:24), and sometimes he uses the term absolutely, speaking of people as simply believing (9:38). So fundamental is faith that it is not necessary to say in whom we believe. When we take God's way we become believers.

It seems likely that this is the meaning here. I know that some translators and commentators take the words in the sense "everyone who believes in him. . . ." But the construction found here is unusual; it is certainly not John's normal way of saying "believes in him." It is probable that "in him" should be connected with "eternal life" rather than with "believes." John then means us to understand the words in the sense "everyone who believes may have eternal life in him." In any case this is a small point, because elsewhere it is said that people are to believe, that they are to believe in Jesus, and that life is in him. All these points are taught in this Gospel; it is only a question of which of them is found here.

John often refers to "eternal life." To see what he means we must refer to the Jewish concept of time. For the Jews all time could be divided into three ages: the age before the creation, the present age, and the age to come. The age to come is the age that would be ushered in by the coming of the Messiah. There is an adjective that literally means "pertaining to an age" and that might theoretically be used of any of these ages. But in practice it is always used of the age to come. It is this adjective that John uses here. It gives the meaning "life appropriate to the age to come."

The traditional translation "eternal" draws attention to one aspect of that age: it never ends. But that is only one aspect. Much more important is the quality of life that people will then have. As B. F. Westcott put it, "It is not an endless duration of being in time, but being of which time is not a measure." It is this life of quality of which Jesus is speaking. Elsewhere in this Gospel he brings out the point by saying, "I came that they may have life and have it abundantly" (10:10). The point, then, is that to believe in Christ "lifted up" for us is to enter a wonderful life, a life whose quality nothing earthly can produce or match.

The Love of God

This leads on to John 3:16, the best-known text in the whole of Scripture: "God so loved the world. . . ." The love of God is the great basic reality on which the whole Christian edifice is built. Without that great love there would be no Christianity. That love is not aroused by some great merit in the beloved. It is emphasized throughout the Bible, in the Old Testament as well as the New, that God loves sinful people. We are not required to overcome evil before God will begin to love us. Twice we read, "God is love" (1 John 4:8, 16), which assures us that love is God's essential nature. God loves, if we may put it that way, because he can do no other. It is his nature to love. Fundamentally he loves because he is love.

This truth is of priceless value to all of us, full of shortcomings as we are. We can know with certainty that God's love does not depend on our being good. If that were the way of it, we might well despair. But because his love depends not on what we are but on what he is, we may have confidence. God loves because he is a loving God. That being so, he will never cease to love us.

John assures us here that God loves "the world." This was a new thought. Though it is often said in earlier writings that God loves his own people, there appears to be no Jewish writing from those early days that says that God's love reaches out to all mankind. It is a new idea, and a wonderful one, that God loves everybody in this sorry old world. Elsewhere we read that God sends his sunshine and his rain upon the wicked and the good, upon the just and the unjust (Matt. 5:45). It is like that here. God's good gifts are bestowed because it is his nature to love: they are not bestowed on account of human merit.

The Gift of God

Not only did God love the world, but he gave the world a gift. He gave his Son. There is an interesting construction in the Greek which means not simply that God loved the world enough to give his Son, but rather that he loved the world so much that he actually gave his Son. The fact of the gift receives emphasis.

We may say that God gave this gift in part when he sent the Son into the world. This is a truth that John insists on over and over again. More than any of the other Gospel writers he brings out the truth that God sent the Son. Quite often he reports Jesus as referring to "the Father who sent me"; in fact Jesus characterizes the Father as "the having-sent-me-Father" (an expression he repeats several times). The mission of the Son is of great importance in this Gospel. The coming of the Son into the world means, of course, that illumination has come to men. John often uses the figure of light to bring out what Jesus has done: he has revealed to us what God is like (1:18).

But there is more than revelation. The gift of God was brought to its climax and consummation on the cross. It was there that our redemption was wrought out, the central act that made salvation possible.

It is noteworthy that the cross is here said to show the love of the Father. It is possible to see it also in terms of the love of the Son (as in Gal. 2:20). This is a very true and very meaningful part of our understanding of the cross, but we should not overlook the fact that the love of the Father is there as well as that of the Son. Christians have not always given due attention to this. They have sometimes pictured the Father as somewhat stern, laying it down that sin must be punished and holding out before unrepentant sinners nothing but doom. When Christians think of the Father in this way, they tend to stress the fact that it was the Son who came to die for them.

But it is important to see that the love of the Father is involved as well as that of the Son. God is love. It was he who sent the Son to be the Savior of the world. The great act of atonement was not in defiance of the will of the Father but rather the outworking of that will. Paul gives expression to this tremendous truth: "God was in Christ, reconciling the world unto himself" (2 Cor. 5:19). It is because the Father loves us that we are saved.

William Temple points out that the passage we are discussing "is the heart of the Gospel. Not 'God is Love'—a precious truth, but affirming no divine act for our redemption. *God so loved that He gave.*" This is the essential point. Love is not to be thought of as some beautiful but helpless thing wringing its hands, so to speak, in the face of evil, but unable to do anything about it. The love of God is active, and we see it in the cross (Rom. 5:8; 1 John 4:10). God so loved that he gave.

Sir Harry Lauder told a story that brings this out well. He spoke of a man who, during the difficult days of World War I, was taking his small boy for a walk. The lad noticed that there were stars in the windows of some of the houses they passed.

"Daddy, why are there stars in some of the windows?" he asked.

His father replied, "That comes from this terrible war, laddie. It shows that these people have given a son."

The little fellow went on silently digesting this information. Then he looked up and there was the evening star, shining brightly in the sky. He said, "Daddy, God must have given a Son, too."

That is it. In the terrible war against evil, God gave his Son. That is the way evil was defeated. God paid the price.

Life Eternal

This, John tells us, was "in order that everyone who believes in him should not perish, but have life eternal." Again we have a reference to believing, this time with the addition "in him." This is a frequent construction in John, one that brings out the importance of a personal faith in a personal Savior. To believe in someone in John's terminology means to give one's full trust. It means to rely wholeheartedly on the object of the trust.

The means whereby sin was dealt with is the gift of God, the death of his Son. The means whereby this becomes effective in the life of any one person is believing in him. The "him" may refer to God himself or to the Son, but in John there is no great difference. Throughout his Gospel he depicts the Father and the Son as so close that to honor one is to honor the other, to despise the one is to despise the other, to believe on one is to believe on the other. The point being stressed is that salvation comes through the gift of God, not through the effort of man. All that is required from the human end is that we trust. This is not a meritorious action so that we are rewarded, so to speak, for being trusting people. Rather our trust is the means whereby we receive God's good gift.

John goes on to speak of not perishing but having life eternal. We saw earlier that "life eternal" is life appropriate to the age to come, life of a different order from anything we see here on earth. Here it is set over against "perishing." John does not explain what he means by this, but obviously it is a most unwelcome fate. It is a reminder that it is a very serious thing to refuse the gift of God.

Throughout the New Testament there is emphasis on this truth, though not always with the same terminology. Jesus spoke of hell (Luke 12:5), and of "the hell of fire" (Matt. 5:22). He spoke of cutting off hand or foot or casting out an eye rather than going to hell (Mark 9:43–47). On the last occasion he added, "where their worm does not die and the fire is not quenched." He spoke of evildoers being "cast into the outer darkness; there there will be wailing and gnashing of teeth" (Matt. 8:12). Elsewhere we read of sinners for whom "the blackness of darkness" is reserved (Jude 13). Or they may be "lost" (2 Cor. 4:3), or lose their souls (Mark 8:36). Again, the fate of the wicked is death (Rom. 6:23).

It is not easy to see what that state can be that is capable of being described in so many ways. Fortunately we are not called upon to understand it, but to escape it. John is saying that when we trust God in Christ, we are delivered from the ultimate horror. We pass from death to life (5:24).

God's Purpose

John has set before us the alternatives of "perishing" and "eternal life." He has shown us that God gave his Son to deliver those who trust him. He goes on to the thought that while the condemnation of the finally impenitent is a reality, that is not the purpose of God. "For God did not send his Son into the world to condemn the world, but so that the world should be saved through him." There is a little problem in that elsewhere John tells us that Jesus said, "For judgment I came into this world" (9:39). On the surface these two statements do not agree, but only on the surface.

John's basic idea is that God sent his Son and gave him on the cross in order that people might be saved. That purpose of salvation runs through John's Gospel, as through the rest of the New Testament. But it is also the case that the offer of salvation divides people. Some gladly trust God and accept his offer. Some turn away from it. The latter enter into judgment (or condemnation), just as surely as the former escape it.

Someone has said that it is not the purpose of the shining of the sun to cast shadows. But if the sun shines on opaque objects, shadows are inevitable. The shadows are, so to speak, the other side of the sunshine. So it is with condemnation and the coming of the Son of God. He did not come in order that people be condemned. But there are great moral issues involved, and those who refuse salvation thus condemn themselves. The condemnation is as real as the salvation.

The last words of this verse are "through him." We may well close this study by reflecting that God's purpose is salvation. This stems from the love of God and is brought to us "through" the Son. Both are involved, for both love sinners.

13

Judgment: A Present Reality

"He who believes in him is not condemned; but he who does not believe has been condemned already, because he has not believed in the name of the only Son of God. Now this is the condemnation, that the light has come into the world, and men loved the darkness rather than the light, because their deeds were evil" (John 3:18–19).

H e who believes in him is not condemned." John has just been speaking about the love of God for the world. God's love gave Jesus so that people might be delivered from perishing and brought into eternal life. John has said that the reason that God sent his Son into the world was not condemnation, "but so that the world should be saved through him" (v. 17).

Now he goes on from that point. First, he makes it clear that, from the human side, salvation is a matter of faith only. Nothing more is required. John brings this out by a couple of his favorite stylistic devices. One is repetition. Every now and then he emphasizes a point by the simplest of all devices: he simply repeats it. So here. "He who *believes* in him is not condemned; but he who does not *believe* has been condemned already, because he has not *believed*. . . ." The verb occurs three times. The thought is hammered in. Believe, believe, believe. That is the important thing. It is *believing* and not some other thing that matters.

The other device John uses here is the placing together of a positive statement and a negative one. This brings out the truth by putting it

103

two ways. First, "He who believes in him is not condemned." Then the other side of that particular coin, "he who does not believe has been condemned already."

John's verb is in the present tense; he is speaking of a reality here and now. But this carries with it, of course, the thought that the present reality continues. The believer need not fear, not now and not in eternity. There is for him no condemnation. His deep need has been met.

In a story among the legends of India of a time long ago, two kings were about to go to war. They appeared before the god Krishna prior to the battle. He said, "To one of you I will give ten armies of soldiers, to the other myself unarmed." One king was very happy to have chosen the ten armies of soldiers and went off congratulating himself. The other seemed just as happy to have the god alongside him. Krishna asked him, "Why did you choose me?" To which the king replied, "Because I need a Great Companion."

A profound truth is enshrined in this legend, a truth that comes home to all of us from time to time. Life is not easy. There are problems, perplexities, difficulties. It is not unusual to feel alone, unsupported, vulnerable. If I am without anyone to stand by me in a hostile and difficult world, I am in an impossible situation. I need a Great Companion. It is not simply that it is advisable, that it would be a help. For to live life in the conviction that I am on my own, that there is no one to stand with me, is disaster.

John is saying that this disaster never happens to the believer. To put one's trust in Christ means to have that constant companionship that suffices for all of life, life now and life in the hereafter.

"He who believes in him is not condemned." The believer has quietness and calm and peace. He knows that no condemnation lies before him. He is not condemned now, and he will not be condemned in the life to come. Anyone who has Christ as his companion can walk through life serenely. Nothing in life can disturb him deep down.

This does not mean that the believer will not have troubles. Of course he will. Christians have all the troubles that other people have. Becoming a believer does not mean taking out a kind of insurance policy so that God now shields from every unpleasantness. That is not the way the Christian life works out. The Christian is in the same world as the non-Christian. Probably every saint at one time or another has wanted to be taken out of the world, but it is right here in the world that he belongs. The believer is sent to live a life of service, service to God and to his fellow creatures, and he is sent to live it amid the same kind of difficulties everyone else has. Indeed, he has a few more, because it is characteristic of the world to mock believers and sometimes to persecute them.

But all this is external. It belongs to the outward circumstances. It does not get to that place where trouble really counts, deep down inside one. When there is inner turmoil, a feeling that we cannot cope, then we are in real trouble. I am not saying that the believer never knows this sort of thing. Believers are fallible and sometimes they take their eyes away from their Lord (as Peter did [Matt. 14:30]). But this is out of character. It is not the Christian way. Believers characteristically trust Christ and in trusting find serenity. There is no condemnation and no sense of condemnation.

Unbelief

John goes on to the point that the condemnation that the believer never knows is not a phantom. It is a grim reality for the unbeliever: "He who does not believe has been condemned already." John is not saying that the unbeliever will be condemned on judgment day. That is a truth he expresses elsewhere (5:28–29), but it is not what he is saying here. Rather he is saying that the unbeliever is condemned here and now. Because of his unbelief he has entered the state of condemnation, of life without Christ. He does not have the Great Companion. He lives a life of an altogether different quality from that of the person who has come to believe. John places a great emphasis on the here and now. Without ever overlooking the fact that eternal realities are more significant than anything that happens to us in this present life, he yet brings out the truth that spiritual attitudes are important for life here on earth. He does not postpone either bliss or loss to a distant world beyond the grave. Life right now is what it is because of our spiritual attitudes.

Why is the person condemned? "Because he has not believed in the name of the only Son of God." Perhaps we should notice a little point about the Greek construction John employs. The two verbs translated "has been condemned" and "has not believed" are both in the perfect tense. In Greek that points to something permanent, a lasting state. John is not talking about a passing moment of doubt or unbelief. He is talking about the person who has entered a continuing state of unbelief. That person no longer keeps open the possibility that Jesus might be the Son of God and the Savior of the world. Unbelief is the atmosphere in which he lives. He knows of Christianity as a way of life some people choose, but for him it is irrelevant. He knows that Christians talk about faith, but for him it is just a word. He is not really interested, and he certainly does not know what it is to trust in the sense in which Christians trust Christ. That for him is totally unknown territory. He lives in unbelief, continuing unbelief. He wants nothing else and accordingly he gets nothing else.

John says the unbeliever has not believed "in the name" of the Son of God. Among the people of antiquity, names meant far more than they do with us. With us a name is simply a label, a distinguishing mark whereby we separate one person from another (we have a problem when we meet two people with the same name). A number would serve as well, and in fact many institutions today identify us by number rather than by our name.

But not all people use names merely as distinguishing labels. In my younger days I read stories about American Indians who had wonderful names like Hawkeye or Deerfoot or Sitting Bull. I did not know then, though I have since been informed, that the Indians thought that the name and the quality somehow went together. When an Indian brave gave his little boy the name Hawkeye, he thought that the little fellow would see just a bit better because of the name, while the little chap called Deerfoot would run a bit faster. The name and the quality somehow went together. (To this day I have never been quite sure exactly what the father had in mind when he called his son Sitting Bull, but I have no doubt that it was something great and meaningful.)

I am not saying that the men of antiquity regarded names in the same way as the American Indians did. They did not. Their concept of names was quite different. I am simply drawing attention to the fact that our way of regarding names is not the only possible one. There have been others.

In antiquity there was a widespread view that the name and the person were somehow bound up together. There was an interesting application in the realm of magic. Among the papyri that have come down to us from the ancient world are some that record the spells used by magicians. Sometimes these scrolls contain a long string of names, which may be followed by a string of nonsense syllables, apparently on the theory that a spirit might well have a name very different from any that the magician might know. The reasoning behind all this was that the name and the spirit went together. If, somewhere in his list, the magician had managed to hit on the name of a powerful spirit, then that spirit would do his will. To have the name meant to have power over the spirit. The name and the spirit went together.

If the name and the person are bound up together, then to believe "in the name" means to believe in all that the name stands for, to trust the whole person. "The name of the only Son of God" points us to him who for our salvation came down from heaven. It points him out as the one whose love was so great that he left all that heaven means and lived a life of service and rejection, a life that would end in a death that atoned for sinners. For us. John has written of the cross, which is a vivid illustration of God's love and the means of bringing salvation to us. To

106

believe in the name means to put one's trust in a God who loves like that.

The Condemnation

To choose not to believe in the name is to condemn oneself. "Now this is the condemnation," writes John, "that the light has come into the world, and men loved the darkness rather than the light, because their deeds were evil" (v. 19). An interesting point arises from his choice of word for "condemnation"; he uses the Greek word *krisis* and passes over *krima*. The two words are often used without much difference of meaning and, as John shows a marked preference for *krisis*, there may not be much significance in his choice here. But nouns ending in -*ma*, like *krima*, strictly denote the concrete embodiment of the verbal action; *krima* thus denotes the sentence of judgment. Nouns ending in -*sis*, like *krisis*, point to the activity in process—in this case the process of judging.

John is not saying, "God has passed judgment, and this is his sentence." Rather he is saying, "This is what judging means. This is the way judgment works out." The condemnation goes like this: light has come into the world, and men loved darkness. He could have said, "One day men will be judged for what they have done. One day God will come down on sinners like a ton of bricks, and he will punish them because they loved darkness and rejected light." But he does not say this. Rather he says that to love darkness is itself condemnation.

John is writing about the sentence of judgment that people impose upon themselves. Elsewhere he speaks of judgment day and, for example, refers to the resurrection to life and the resurrection to judgment (5:28–29). But here his concern is with the present, with what people do to themselves. They choose darkness and not light, and in doing so they sentence themselves.

I do not know how to bring this out better than by drawing attention to a little rhyme I came across in C. J. Wright's book on John's Gospel. It has to do with Judas Iscariot and his betrayal of Jesus:

> Still, as of old,
> Man by himself is priced.
> For thirty pieces Judas sold
> Himself, not Christ.

Consider Judas at the moment when his betrayal of Jesus was completed. As he stood there with the thirty pieces of silver in his hands and Jesus in the grip of the enemy, he had succeeded perfectly in what he set out to do. He had received his price; he had the money. He had sold his Master; Jesus was in the hands of the enemy. All had gone as Judas planned it.

But that is a superficial view. There is a very real sense in which Judas did not do anything to Jesus. Centuries before Jesus was born, the prophet wrote of him: "He was despised and rejected by men, a man of sorrows, and familiar with suffering. Like one from whom men hide their faces he was despised, and we esteemed him not" (Isa. 53:3). Then he went on with a surprising revelation:

> Surely he took up our infirmities and carried our sorrows, yet we considered him stricken by God, smitten by him, and afflicted. But he was pierced for our transgressions, he was crushed for our iniquities; the punishment that brought us peace was upon him, and by his wounds we are healed. We all, like sheep, have gone astray, each of us has turned to his own way; and the Lord has laid on him the iniquity of us all (Isa. 53:4–6).

Right from the beginning of his life, the cross lay before Jesus. God had always intended that his Son should come and die to put away men's sin. That is the way sin would be dealt with and overcome. Had Judas remained faithful and loyal and true, that would not have meant that Jesus would not have been crucified. Some other way would have been found to get him to the cross. That is what he came for. Salvation at the cost of his life was the purpose of God for his Son.

In a very important sense, then, Judas did not do anything to Jesus. But if he did not sell Jesus, how irrevocably he sold himself! And the price Judas put on his immortal soul? Thirty pieces of silver.

"Still, as of old,/Man by himself is priced." To this day it is all too often the case that our attainment of our aim is itself our ultimate condemnation. We set out to do something, as Judas did. And we succeed in what we aim at, not realizing that it is simply our form of loving darkness rather than light. We write our own sentence of condemnation.

Years ago I was a curate working in a parish that had a new housing area. I recall that one day, when I was walking through the area, I came to a house just as the new people were moving in. The moving van was at the curb and the furniture was being carried in. It was not the right time for a lengthy speech, but I greeted the man and his wife, welcomed them to our area, assured them that the church was a going concern and that we would be glad to see them any Sunday.

The new arrival smiled a funny little smile as he said, "We might send the kids to Sunday school, but I don't think you'll see us."

"Oh," I said. "Why on earth not?"

He looked at me astonished. "Look," he said, "we're just moving in! The house is new; I've got to paint it. There's no garden; I've got to plant one. There's no shed; I've got to build one. And the only day I have to do things like this is Sunday."

I pointed out to him that the only day he didn't have to do those things was Sunday: "Six days shalt thou labor and do all that thou hast to do. . . ." But I rather felt that I was on the losing end of that one.

And so it proved. I passed by the house from time to time, and it was very obvious that the householder was at work. He planted his garden, and a very attractive garden it was. He built his shed, and from the outside it looked a neat and competent piece of work. I never did get inside the house, so I don't know from personal observation what the painting was like, but I have no doubt that it was well done. And from what I could see, most of this work was done on Sundays. It took the man years, and by the time he was through, any lingering affection he may once have had for the house of God and the things of God had long since vanished.

Now it would be quite wrong to think of God as a grim tyrant looking down from heaven at this man and saying, "You make your house nice and I won't have you in my heaven!" That's not it at all. God is love. God sent his Son to die for us. He is not bent on shutting people out of heaven.

No. "Still, as of old,/Man by himself is priced." The man of whom I am writing chose to pursue his own aims and not the service of God. He put his house before his God. And the price he put on his immortal soul? A garden, a shed, and some buckets of paint.

"Still, as of old,/Man by himself is priced." We see this sometimes in the business world. Here is a man who decides that he will get to the top of his particular tree. He applies himself with great diligence and builds up his business. He finds it easier (and financially more profitable) if he cuts a few corners; his determination to be rich is greater than his concern for uprightness. His commercial success and his moral failures are alike great. He succeeds in what he set out to do, but his very success is his failure. He has priced himself out of the kingdom of heaven. He has set his love on darkness rather than light. He has condemned himself.

John's imagery is that of a man in a dark room. All the walls are black. The ceiling is black. The floor is black. There are no windows, and the door is shut. It is absolutely dark, and the man is shut in there with no light at all. He has an impoverished, limited, narrow existence with only what the darkness can give him.

But he need not stay there. The door is not locked. All he has to do is give it a push and walk out into God's good sunshine. But he does not do it. He "loves the darkness rather than the light." To love darkness rather than light is itself the condemnation. It is to shut oneself up in a cramped, mean, narrow existence in place of the liberty and the love and the light that God freely offers us.

That says something to every one of us. "Still, as of old,/Man by himself is priced." We are all quite capable of writing our own sentence of condemnation, and far too many of us do just that. The thing in which we succeed is so often the thing that condemns us. We have our goals. We may want to make a million dollars or be popular or powerful. We may aim at sporting or social success, at community achievement, at any one of a hundred goals each of which we may dress up to look acceptable. And in the process we may sell our souls. We set a price on ourselves by that for which we sell our lives. When we put anything before our Lord, that is our equivalent of the thirty pieces of silver.

At a time when our Lord is calling us to be his servants and to stand up for him in the middle of a generation that is all too often materialistic, secular, racist, insensitive, unloving, sensual, and just plain selfish, all too often we simply go our own way. We choose our particular piece of darkness and love it so much that we refuse to come out into the light of the gospel of Christ. By that refusal we write our own binding sentence of condemnation, for "Still, as of old,/Man by himself is priced."

14

He Must Increase

A dispute about ceremonial cleansing arose between John's disciples and a Jew. They came to John and said to him, "Rabbi, he who was with you on the other side of the Jordan, to whom you bore your witness, look, this man is baptizing, and everyone is coming to him." John replied, "A man can receive nothing except what is given him from heaven. You yourselves bear me witness that I said, 'I am not the Messiah,' but rather, 'I have been sent before him.' It is the bridegroom who has the bride. The bridegroom's friend, who stands and listens for him, is full of joy at the bridegroom's voice. This is my joy and it is full. He must increase, but I must decrease" (John 3:25–30).

The Dead Sea Scrolls have shown us that there was a very great deal of interest in ceremonial purification at the time the Christian movement began. The Qumran covenanters evidently went in for ceremonial washings in a big way, and there were others who showed an interest in this sort of thing. The movement associated with John the Baptist came under this heading because John called on people to repent and to be baptized. His very title, "the Baptist," shows the emphasis he put on the rite. Since different people had different ideas about what was effective in the way of ceremonial purity, it is not surprising that disputes should arise from time to time about what was the right thing to do. So we read that one day some of John's followers had a dispute with a Jew on this subject. It may be significant that it was John's disciples and not John himself who were caught up in the discussion. Followers are often inclined to be more pernickety about minor matters than are their leaders.

I am reminded of the tourist who, having spent some time in a rather sleepy little village with very few inhabitants, remarked to one of the local people, "I see you don't have much of a population problem here." To which the local replied, "That's where you're wrong. Almost all of the problems round here are caused by the population!" It would seem that on this occasion John's problem was caused by the population.

There is no indication of the precise question at issue. We know no more than that there was a difference of opinion. Perhaps the man argued that all the talk about baptism was most confusing. Here was John making disciples and calling on people to be baptized, while Jesus, whom John had baptized, was now busy making disciples of his own and perhaps even having them baptized (4:1–2). Maybe the man was asking why he should get baptized by John when Jesus was doing so much better. Perhaps he was saying that with different leaders operating at the same time it was not easy to see who was right. All that we can be sure of is that in some way Jesus' success was drawn into the discussion.

So some of John's people came to John and complained. Evidently they had not been able to refute the Jew with whom they had been arguing, so they came to John to try to get things set right. Clearly they were very loyal to their leader. They were glad to be his followers and wanted to see his cause advanced. They knew that he had borne witness to Jesus, but apparently they had taken little notice of what he had said. John had told them plainly that he was not the Messiah and that they should follow Jesus. Many, including Andrew and his friend, had done just that—they had left John and followed Jesus (1:35–37).

Not these people, however. They had attached themselves to John so firmly that they refused to be detached. This appears to have been a problem among the followers of the Baptist, for at a much later time some men who had been baptized with John's baptism apparently still counted themselves as his followers. They had not gone on to link themselves with the followers of Jesus (Acts 19:1–7).

It is easy to be so happy with whatever good we have that we cut ourselves off from anything further. We have a proverb: "The good is the enemy of the best." It would seem that these followers of John are an apt illustration of what is meant. They had heard John's preaching, they had realized their sinfulness, they had repented and been baptized. They had also heard John's teaching (see Luke 3:7–17). All this must have been a wonderful spiritual experience for them.

The Baptist had spoken of the near approach of the kingdom of God and had said that he himself was no more than the herald of the kingdom. It was the Mighty One who would follow who would bring in the kingdom, not John. As plainly as a man can do it, the Baptist had pointed people to the Messiah who would come. But these people were well content with where they were. It was wonderful that they had come to grips with the need for repentance and had experienced all that John's baptism meant. They were thrilled to hear their leader continue with his exhortations to people to turn from their sin. But there they stayed.

They might have gone on to all that fellowship with Jesus meant. They might have entered into the kingdom of God. They might have known continued spiritual growth under Jesus. Instead they chose to remain at the early stage of repentance. Let nothing be said to diminish the importance of repentance. It is the necessary preliminary to all that forgiveness means; as long as people commit sin, there is the necessity for them to turn from it in repentance. But repentance is no more than the preliminary. It opens up the way to many blessings, and if we do not go on, we cut ourselves off from them all.

That is what these disciples of John were doing, and that, alas, is what many of us still do in different ways. It is well to reflect that we are called to spiritual growth. If we are still at the stage at which we entered the Christian life when we were converted, if we have not gone on to maturity, we are repeating the mistake of those well-intentioned followers of John.

They come to John with their complaint. They do not speak Jesus' name, but complain about him "who was with you on the other side of the Jordan" (v. 26). They are clear that their John had done his part; for they say, ". . . to whom *you* bore your witness" (their "you" is emphatic). It is as though they are saying, "It's not fair! You did your part. You bore your witness and did it well. Why can't he help you instead of building up a large following of his own?" They are indignant. The tense of their verb *bear witness* is perfect, which conveys the meaning that there was something permanent about the witness John bore. He had left it on record, so to speak. Even these people who are so upset about the success of Jesus are clear that John had spoken well of him. And indeed John did speak well of Jesus. Much later, when Jesus came into the area where John had baptized, people were able to remember that while John had done no miracles, "all things that John said about this man were true" (10:41). And John's testimony at that late time brought people to believe in Jesus.

What Is Given from Heaven

John's followers might be upset and angrily determined to uphold the place of their master, but John himself was not of that opinion. He had come to bear his witness to Jesus, and single-mindedly this is what he did. It would not have been surprising if he had delivered a sharp rebuke to those who had so misunderstood the central point in his teaching. But, after all, they are his followers, and he speaks to them kindly. He simply points out to them that God is in control of every-thing. "A man can receive nothing except what is given him from heaven" (v. 27). This last expression means "from God." The Jews out of reverence often avoided using the name of God, and "heaven" was a regular substitute. John is saying that one has only what God gives to him.

This might be understood in either of two ways. It might refer to the Baptist himself. There is no point in his followers' getting upset be-cause he does not have the supreme place. God did not give him that supreme place. He has what God gave him, the place of the forerunner. That is a very significant place. Indeed Jesus said that there is nobody among those born of women who is greater than John (Matt. 11:11). His following statement that the least in the kingdom of heaven is greater than John is to be taken as a mark of the wonderful thing that membership in the kingdom is, not as a criticism of John in the slightest degree. But John's point here is that, great or small, the place he has is the place that God has assigned him. It is true of all of us that God has given us such and such gifts, those and no more.

It is important that we make the best use of our gifts. We will cer-tainly do more in the service of God and find life more rewarding if we do use them to the full than if we spend our time complaining that we do not have such and such a gift. The Baptist's calm acceptance of the place God has assigned him is an object lesson to all of us.

It is possible, however, that John was speaking more of Jesus than he was of himself. It was true of Jesus, as it was true of John, that in his incarnate life he had what God had given him. There was no point in anyone's complaining about Jesus' success, for that is what God had given him. John had always taught that God would send the Great One who would bring in the kingdom. And when he saw the Holy Spirit descend on Jesus at his baptism, he had hailed him as that Great One. Let his followers recognize that, and then they would not be so upset about what was happening. What was happening was what God was doing in the world. It was not some man's interfering with God's plan and striving after kudos that he did not deserve. There is never a reason for being unhappy about the success God gives, especially about the success that he gives to his beloved Son.

John goes on to remind his followers of what they already knew. He had borne his witness to Jesus as they had said (v. 26). In their turn they could bear witness to John. They had heard him say that he was not the Messiah. They could testify to it. Why then should they be upset when the Messiah made his appearance and was acclaimed by some of the people? John's "you yourselves" points out that they had the answer in the facts of which they had knowledge if only they would give attention to them. John had made it very clear that he was not the Christ, the Messiah (1:20). When he was asked to tell the delegation from Jerusalem who he was, he had replied that he was "a voice," that and nothing more. And that voice moreover was a voice bearing witness to the coming of the Christ. John never claimed more, and it was sheer misunderstanding on the part of his followers if they thought anything else. They just weren't listening.

Listening

Failure to listen is a fault to which we all are prone. It is much easier to hear what we want to hear than what someone is really saying, especially if what is being said is something we do not greatly like. John's followers had attached themselves to him because they thought he was a very great person and was giving very important teaching. Having done the right thing (so they thought) and attached themselves to this superb teacher, it was unsettling to be told that they should leave him. Why should they leave him? He was a great man, and they had left whatever it was they had been doing before simply in order that they might be near him. They listened with eagerness to John's preaching. Wasn't it wonderful to hear him call the religious leaders "sons of snakes"? And how he thundered out his warnings about an angry God who would soon be showing people what he did when he was angry! And those calls for repentance! The priests and the Pharisees certainly did not want to hear any of that. There was never a dull moment when John was telling people off.

So these followers of John were very happy with his preaching and did not want to go anywhere else. It was so wonderful to stay where they were. If he spoke of some coming Great One, this was probably no more than politeness. For them it was John who was the Great One. If he said something about leaving him and following someone else, they were probably hearing it the wrong way. It would be better to stick around with John till they got it clearer. Being John's loyal men, they were not going after someone else.

So when the man from Nazareth started preaching and teaching and people began to follow him, John's disciples thought this could not be anything other than a rival movement. This Jesus had even been baptized by John. They had seen it happen. Did it not follow that he was a disciple of John? Now a disciple has no business branching out on his own. His job is to follow his leader. In their opinion, Jesus should certainly have remained loyal to John. That was surely what they were going to do.

John had said that he was "sent before" the Great One, meaning that he was no more than the forerunner, the man who was to prepare the way for the Greater One who would follow. But in antiquity there was often the thought that the greatest person was the one who came first. People held to the idea of "the good old days." They thought that in the infancy of the race there had been a golden age when things were wonderful and men were incredibly wise. History was all downhill from then on. Each generation was apparently a bit worse than its predecessor. So it was with teachers. The great teachers were those of earlier ages who had established the body of teaching that was handed on from generation to generation.

Probably reasoning in this way, John's disciples made out a case for his being a greater and wiser teacher than Jesus. Did he not come first? Had he not baptized Jesus? Did this not mean that Jesus had publicly declared himself to be a follower of John? Since John must be the greater of the two, it would be folly to leave John for Jesus. So they misunderstood John's teaching about being the forerunner.

Now the Baptist repeats it. And he repeats it in a way that must make them think again. Over against the Christ he is no more than the one who has "been sent" before him (v. 28). The idea of being sent certainly contains the idea of subordination. John is in no doubt that he is a lowly person, not the great man that his followers have made him out to be.

The Bridegroom

John proceeds to an illustration that should make the point clear. "It is the bridegroom who has the bride," he says, and goes on to speak of the best man, with his important, but subordinate, place (v. 29). The New Testament writers do not often speak of Jesus as the Bridegroom, but we read a number of times of the church as the bride of Christ, which, of course, means the same thing. There are several picture words used to bring out the relationship between Christ and his people: the church is the body of Christ, the church is a building, and so on. Each tells us something important about the way we should see the church and the way the church relates to its Lord.

The imagery of the bride and bridegroom emphasizes the place of love and commitment. A tender love binds bride and groom in any rightful marriage, and this is of the essence of the relationship of the church to Christ. The thought of the church as a body or a building does not bring out this aspect as well. But we are all familiar with the importance of love in a true marriage. Indeed, without love we have no real marriage at all but a travesty. Love is of the essence of marriage. The church is the object of the love of Christ, a love so great that Christ died for the church. It is important that church members respond to this love with love. There is nothing more important in the living of the Christian life than love.

Commitment is likewise important. In marriage the bride gives herself wholeheartedly to the bridegroom. She pledges herself to him and to him alone. So with the church. Christians do not think of Christ as merely one of a number of interesting religious teachers. They are not religionists but *Christ*-ians. They have attached themselves to Christ, not to religion. They see Christ as their Savior. It is central to the Christian way that Christ died on the cross to put away our sins. He is our teacher certainly, but he is more. He is our Savior. We may have many teachers, but there is only one Savior. To see the church as the bride of Christ is to see her as pledged entirely to the Bridegroom, the Bridegroom who saved her at the cost of his own blood.

This imagery springs from the closest tie between human beings. No two people are bound so closely together as are husband and wife. We are thus reminded that the church is closely bound to Christ. Sometimes the thought is that the bride should prepare herself (Rev. 19:7). A young lady will certainly put everything into her preparation for her wedding. On that day everything must be done in the best possible way. So Christians are called on to prepare themselves for Christ and the glorious consummation that awaits us at the end of the age. One great scholar reminds us: "A Marriage is the union of two which grows into perfect unity through love." That tells us something very important about the church and its relationship to Christ. And John's use of the term *bridegroom* tells us something very important about the place he gave Christ. At a wedding no man is as important as the bridegroom. For John, Jesus is the central figure, the one round whom everything else revolves.

The Friend of the Bridegroom

And that helps John bring out his own place. He is the "bridegroom's friend," the equivalent of the best man at our weddings. But the best man in antiquity did some things that today's best man does not. He was often responsible for arranging the wedding in the first place and subsequently had other duties, the most important being that of bringing the bride to the bridegroom. He was a well-known and highly respected figure.

John's point here is that he was not the bridegroom. For all his importance, he was necessarily number two. No one can compete with the bridegroom for center stage. A wedding is about a bridegroom and a bride. It is not about a best man. The best man is no more than someone who helps to bring the marriage about. John is emphatically making the point that he is a subordinate. He is not minimizing his own place, for, after all, at a wedding the best man is a very important person. But it is the bridegroom who matters. John does not want his followers to be in any doubt about that.

He adds a very important point. The friend of the bridegroom is a very happy man at a wedding. He is neither torn by jealousy because he does not have the bride, nor concerned because people are more interested in the bridegroom than they are in him. He sees the wedding as a very happy occasion, one on which he rejoices with his friend. It is precisely because he is the friend of the bridegroom that he is happy. His friend has the bride, and the best man is delighted. His rejoicing is brought out with an emphatic expression that means literally "he rejoices with joy." It is not that the best man merely puts up with what is going on with as good a grace as he can muster. No. He is genuinely happy, filled with joy because of his friend's joy. He is there for that reason—to promote the joy of the bridegroom—and when that is realized, his own joy is complete.

And that is what the Baptist says about himself. He is not jealous of the success that his followers tell him Jesus has had. That is what John has come for. He is there to set forward the coming of the Messiah. Now that he has come, John can say, "This is my joy and it is full." He is not simply mildly pleased that Jesus has come and is having success. He is deliriously happy. He is full of joy. That is what the mission of John is all about. His followers may be distressed and displeased, but not John. What they tell him about Jesus is just what he wants to hear.

"He Must Increase"

John goes on to some of the greatest words ever to fall from the lips of mortal man: "He must increase, but I must decrease" (v. 30). John had not come in order to be a leading figure. His message had always been that one greater than he was coming. He never wavered in his conviction that he was no more than the forerunner of the Christ.

We should not view this as though it were the most natural thing in the world. It is not natural. What is natural to all of us is to want the best place for ourselves. We may have very different ideas as to what that place is, but there is no wavering in our desire to have it.

Somewhere I read a story of a new nation that in its endeavor to keep up with the developed world set up a national television service. There was but one channel, and through it the government told the people the things it thought they should know. In time it became apparent that the people were not completely happy with this arrangement, and their discontent became so strong that the powers-that-be in their wisdom decided to arrange for a second channel on which more popular programs might be viewed. But one night the president had a specially important message for the nation, and everyone was commanded to watch Channel One. One citizen loyally watched his president for an hour, but then felt that he had had all he could stand. So he switched to Channel Two, only to find that on that channel he was confronted with a soldier pointing a gun at him and saying, "Switch back to Channel One!" The story is apocryphal, but it certainly illustrates our natural penchant for wanting to have things our own way. Be we presidents or ordinary citizens, we want to be number one in our own circle, and we tend to take what action we can to see that this is brought about.

But John was wiser. And humbler. He was not consumed by a passion for popularity and success as the world counts success. He saw clearly that he was to be the Messiah's forerunner, that and nothing more. And he rejoiced in that role, which meant that as time went on people would increasingly put Jesus at the center ("He must increase") and John at the periphery ("I must decrease"). So be it. John would then be doing what God had for him to do, and God's purpose would be set forward.

It is good when God's servants today are content to serve well in whatever place he has assigned to them and do not set their hearts on some higher place that is not theirs. Humility and the conviction that what matters is that God's purpose be set forward, not that I should be seen to be wonderful, are still essential in the work of God.

15

Samaritans and Jews

He had to pass through Samaria. He comes then to a city of Samaria called Sychar, near the piece of land which Jacob gave to Joseph his son. Now Jacob's well was there. Jesus then, being wearied from the journey, was sitting thus at the well. It was about noon. A woman from Samaria comes to draw water. Jesus says to her, "Give me a drink." (For his disciples had gone off into the city to buy food.) The Samaritan woman says to him, "How is it that you, being a Jew, ask a drink from me, being a Samaritan woman?" (For Jews do not use [drinking vessels] with Samaritans) (John 4:4–9).

He had to pass through Samaria." This reads strangely in a writing about Jews, for the Jews of the time normally had as little as possible to do with the Samaritans. Most Jews seem to have hated Samaritans on principle and avoided all contact with them. Strict Jews, for example, when traveling from Galilee to Jerusalem, would cross the river Jordan, travel south on the eastern side of that river, and then cross it again for the ascent to Jerusalem. Though this meant going extra miles, it also meant that they avoided the territory of the Samaritans. If the need was pressing, they might go through Samaria, but not otherwise. The Jewish historian Josephus uses language much like that of John here when he says, "For rapid travel it was necessary to take that route [i.e., through Samaria]." But only dire necessity would cause strict Jews to do this.

The quarrel between the two nations went back a long way. It is not unlikely that at the time when the Hebrews were divided into two kingdoms, those in Judah had a feeling of superiority towards those in Israel because the one temple for the worship of God was in their territory, in Jerusalem. There were shrines in northern Israel and the golden calves that King Jeroboam had made, but the one place where the true God was to be worshiped was in their great city. Those in the north had to come there or else go astray in their worship.

Then came the dreadful time when the mighty Assyrians came down with all their awesome military power and destroyed forever the northern kingdom, Israel. The Assyrians (and some other conquerors in antiquity) had a habit of moving large numbers of conquered peoples. The theory appears to have been that if they broke up the subject nations into small groups, there would not be the cohesion for them to launch revolts. So they took large numbers of the people in the ten tribes in the northern kingdom and set them down in other parts of the vast Assyrian Empire. They could not leave the land of Israel depopulated, of course, so they moved other peoples in there, people from Babylon, Cuthah, Avva, Hamath, and Sepharvaim (see 2 Kings 17:24).

These new settlers ran into trouble. Lions killed some of them, and this made the survivors feel that they needed instruction about how to worship the God of the land. Evidently they felt that each god had a territory of his own. They had been quite happy with their own gods back in the lands from which they had come. And indeed they thought that those gods still had some power where they were, for they continued to worship them. They made idols in their usual fashion and followed their old customs, like the dreadful one of burning their children in the fire as sacrifices to their gods (2 Kings 17:30–31). But since worship of their own gods did not prevent them from being killed by lions, they sought information about the God the Israelites had worshiped.

The Assyrians sent back an exiled Israelite priest, and this induced the new population to add the worship of the true God to their other religious practices. "They worshiped the LORD, but they also served their own gods" (2 Kings 17:33). But as the years passed the worship of these other gods seems gradually to have dropped out, and the people in Samaria and the surrounding regions worshiped only the God of the Jews. It might have been expected that this would create some form of bond between them. After all, it was only the Jews and the Samaritans in all the world who worshiped this one God. But it did not work out that way. While the Jews were glad that the Samaritans worshiped the true God, they were not happy with the way they went about it. Take, for example, the Bible. The Samaritans had as their Scripture the five books of Moses—the books from Genesis to Deuteronomy—these five and no more. They knew nothing of the teachings of such wonderful books as the Psalms and all the books of the prophets. The Jews saw the Samaritans' worship as impoverished.

Bitterness grew. There came a time when the people of Judah, like the northerners earlier, were defeated in war and taken to the land of the conqueror as captives. This time the conquerors were not the Assyrians but the Babylonians. But in due course Persians defeated the Babylonians and allowed the Jews to return to their own land. They found it a shambles. Their cities had been overthrown and apparently not rebuilt. There was destruction everywhere.

One thing that particularly worried them was that their beautiful temple had been destroyed. So they set about rebuilding it. When the Samaritans heard of this, they offered to help. Did they not worship the same God? Was it not proper that they should assist in the construction of the new temple? But the Jews wanted no help from Samaritans. Were they not astray in many of their ideas? Would God be pleased with a temple built with the help of heretics? So the Jews refused to let the Samaritans help them, and the Samaritans in turn refused to worship in Jerusalem. The Samaritans in due course built a temple of their own on Mount Gerizim. But when the Jews became strong again, they were able to control Samaria and burned down the Samaritan temple. For them it was basic that there could be only one temple to God, and that temple was at Jerusalem.

Not surprisingly all this created an atmosphere of bitterness. There were some notable exceptions, but for the most part the two nations detested each other. In one of the apocryphal books, written between the Old and the New Testaments, we read: "With two nations my soul is vexed, and the third is no nation: those who live on Mount Seir, and the Philistines, and the foolish people that dwell in Shechem" (Sirach 50:25–26). Shechem was an important Samaritan city, and "the foolish people" are the Samaritans.

All this means that at the time of Jesus there was a strong mutual antagonism between the two peoples. It was not an antagonism that Christians shared. There is not much about the Samaritans in the first two Gospels. Luke, however, has the parable of the good Samaritan and also the information that one of the ten lepers Jesus healed was a Samaritan (the one who came back to thank him). Luke also tells of a time when the people in a Samaritan village refused to receive Jesus and his disciples because they were clearly going up to Jerusalem, an attitude that distinctly annoyed James and John. Not sharing their annoyance, Jesus rebuked them (Luke 9:52–56). John's Gospel adds to our information. In addition to this story of the Samaritan woman at the well, he tells us of an occasion when the Jews called Jesus a Samaritan (8:48). Clearly they discerned a friendliness in Jesus' attitude toward these people, a friendliness of which they did not approve.

It should not surprise us that there is little about the Samaritans in the Gospels, since Jesus' whole life was spent among the Jews. But enough is said for us to see that he strongly opposed the Jewish attitude. And when the early Christians began their work of preaching the gospel, it was not long before they were evangelizing the Samaritans (Acts 8:5–25).

But the antagonism so common in Jesus' day makes it noteworthy that John says that Jesus "had to" go through Samaria. We are surely to understand this as pertaining to his mission, not to the necessities of his journey. Jesus could scarcely have been in such a hurry that he had to take a shortcut. If he was, John tells us nothing about it. No, the necessity lay in who Jesus was and what he was doing. For the Son of God the bitterness that divided the two nations was not something to be complied with but something to be overcome. God loves Samaritans as well as Jews, and it was necessary accordingly that the Son of God should go through Samaria and meet the needs of Samaritans.

Jacob's Well

So Jesus came near a village called Sychar, the exact location of which is not known for sure. But near it was a well that people thought was dug by Jacob centuries before. Jesus rested by this well while his disciples went into the village to get some food. Whether Jacob really was responsible for the well is, of course, not known. He did buy some land in the general area (Gen. 33:19) and later he did give some land to Joseph (Gen. 48:22), though we have no way of knowing whether it was the same land. There is no record of his having dug a well there, but there is nothing improbable in the suggestion. And the fact that this well is a very deep one (over a hundred feet) has been drawn into an argument that it was in fact Jacob who dug it. Since there is normally plenty of water in the area, it is suggested that only a stranger in the land would have gone to all the trouble to dig so deep a well! Be that as it may, there was a well there, and Jesus rested by it.

That he was weary is an interesting detail. It shows that he had been working hard and traveling much or both. It also brings out the true humanity of our Lord. John consistently shows us that Jesus is the divine Son of God; it is impossible to read his Gospel without seeing this. But John is equally sure of Jesus' genuine manhood. The Son of God came right where we are. If we are wearied with what this world does to us, let us reflect that Jesus knows all about that. He was weary too.

Water at Noon

John quite often tells us the time of day when things happened, and he does so here. It was about "the sixth hour," that is, noon. A woman from the village came to draw water. It was not unusual that a woman should do this; after all, the drawing of water was a common chore for the women, as it still is. What was unusual was the time. Mostly the women came at around sunset, when the heat of the day was over. It could be very hot in the middle of the day, and few women would venture forth for the heavy work of carrying water at such a time. Yet we should bear in mind that there is at least one other record of water being drawn at this hour. In Exodus 2:15–17 we read of Moses helping some young women with watering their flock from a well; the Jewish historian Josephus says this happened at noon. We have no way of knowing whether this is accurate, but the fact that he says so shows that in his day drawing water at noon was not thought of as impossible. But it was certainly unusual.

Indeed this may be the reason why the woman chose to come at noon. She could be sure that there would not be many others drawing water at that time, and it may be that that suited her fine. As we see from later stages in the narrative, she was not a woman of good reputation and may have been more comfortable in getting her supply of water when there were few other women around—or better, none at all. At least she would not hear what they were saying about her!

And that may be the very reason she chose to use this particular well. There would have been other wells closer to her home than this one (people do not usually carry water farther than they have to). It has been suggested that the quality of the water in this well may have been better than that in other wells closer to her home. This may have been the case, but if so we have no way of knowing it. John says nothing about it. Some believe that the woman may have been attracted by the association of the well with the name of the great patriarch and thought that a well bearing his name would be better than other wells. Again this is a possibility, but since the woman did not say why she came, in the end we are left to guess.

What we do know is that Jesus asked her for a drink (v. 7). It was usually women who drew water, so from one point of view it is not surprising that Jesus should ask her. From another it is, as the woman's reply in verse 9 shows. She recognized that Jesus was a Jew, though John does not tell us how. Was it the way he dressed? Or the way he spoke? At any rate she knew. And she knew that Jewish men did not normally ask her, or for that matter any other Samaritan, for something to drink. The reason is usually translated, "For Jews have no dealings with the Samaritans," or words to that effect.

But we have been told that the disciples had gone off to the village to buy food (v. 8). If that is not having dealings with the Samaritans, I do not know what is. The expression will bear closer examination. The verb is an unusual one and is found only here in all the Greek New Testament. It is a compound that means literally "use with," so that the expression means "Jews do not use with Samaritans." People have reasoned that "use with" must mean something like "associate with," "meet up with," and thus in general "have dealings with."

But it might have been better had they asked, "What is it that Jews do not use with Samaritans?" In this situation the answer must be drinking vessels. Jesus did not have anything with which to get water from the well (v. 11), and presumably this means that he had nothing like a cup either. If the woman were to give him a drink, he would have to use a drinking vessel that she supplied. And she knew that Jews did not do this.

Ceremonial Defilement

In our culture we do not have the concept of ceremonial uncleanness, so the point of this is not as obvious as it would have been to a Jew or a Samaritan of the first century. For them it was accepted as obvious that contact with anything ceremonially unclean brought defilement to the person who made contact. A well-known example is contact with a dead body. Anyone who had contact with a corpse was unclean for seven days according to a Jewish law (Num. 19:11). It was not even necessary to make physical contact. If anyone even entered a tent where there was a dead body, he became unclean (Num. 19:14). The same passage tells us that everything in the tent became unclean and, of course, contact with an unclean object conveyed defilement. Moreover, when a person became unclean he would make unclean any clean person he touched. And the unclean could not engage in religious activities like worship. All in all, ceremonial uncleanness was to be avoided. It made life intolerably complicated and cut one off from all sorts of useful and interesting activities.

Unfortunately nobody in antiquity seems to have set down exactly how relationships between Jews and Samaritans were organized. At that time everybody knew, so why write about it? The result is that we do not know today. We are left to gather our information from statements about other things. Sometimes there was a comparatively friendly attitude between the two groups. There was a Jewish regulation that if three people ate a meal together, they must say grace together. That is to say, none of them must say grace for himself, but a common grace would be said by one of them to cover them all. And one rule says that a Samaritan might be included in the number. That would mean that sometimes Jews and Samaritans shared a common meal and prayed together. Indeed a Samaritan might be the one who said grace for them all, for it is laid down that in that case Jews must not say "Amen" until they have heard the whole prayer (who can tell what heresy a Samaritan might introduce before he finished?).

But some Jews were more strict. Rabbi Eliezer used to say, "He that eats the bread of the Samaritans is like to one that eats the flesh of swine." Clearly this godly man was taking no risks! And from the general tone of references in the writings of the rabbis it seems that the hard line was not uncommon. We must not build too much on the "friendly" references. It seems that many had as little to do with Samaritans as they could. Certainly the woman at the well had no high expectations of a Jew. She expected that a Jewish man would not want to use her drinking vessels and was surprised that Jesus evidently did not take this attitude.

Don't Talk with Women

Actually Jesus' request was the beginning of a lengthy conversation, and this too must have surprised her. We today scarcely realize the extent to which women were excluded from important aspects of religion. To start with, there was a strong feeling among the Jews that women should not be allowed to study the Law, which meant that they were cut off from education, for it was the Law that was studied in the rabbinic schools. Rabbi Eliezer said, "If any man gives his daughter a knowledge of the Law it is as though he taught her lechery." It was not only that women were in fact not educated; many rabbis thought it was a sin to educate a woman.

This extended beyond formal education to ordinary conversation. Rabbi Jose ben Johanan of Jerusalem pointed out that "the Sages have said: He that talks much with womankind brings evil on himself and neglects the study of the Law and at the last will inherit Gehenna." I like the little story about a pious woman who had learned this lesson well. Rabbi Jose the Galilean was once uncertain of his route and happened to meet this woman. He asked her, "By what road do we go to Lydda?" She rebuked him by retorting, "Foolish Galilean, did not the Sages say this: Engage not in much talk with women? You should have asked: By which to Lydda?" If he had put his question this way, he would have saved a few words and thus have talked less with a woman!

The rabbis had a firm view that women were inferior to men in every way. There is an ancient prayer, "Blessed art thou, O Lord . . . who hast not made me a woman," which takes this view into worship and gives expression to a lordly sense of male superiority. There is a corresponding prayer for a woman, "Blessed art thou, O Lord, who hast fashioned me according to thy will." Presumably this prayer was composed by some male and was meant to convey the thought that it is good for a woman to reflect that, though she does not have the great privilege of being a man, she still has some place in God's scheme of things. If we look closely at the two prayers, we may well feel that the woman had the better of it. It is certainly much more a matter for thanksgiving that one is made according to the will of God than that one is not a member of the opposite sex. But that is a modern and Christian attitude, not an ancient Jewish one.

All One in Christ

Jesus was not bound by the prejudices of his time. From a number of incidents in the Gospels, it is plain that he did not share the common view regarding the Samaritans. Did he not have a Samaritan as the central figure in one of the greatest of the parables? And when he healed ten men who were lepers and one came back to thank him, did he not speak appreciatively of this man, Samaritan though he was? Racial prejudice might have been common in Jesus' day (as, alas, it has been common in most periods of human history), but he had none.

This is a lesson that the early church learned. Paul writes, "There is neither Jew nor Greek, there is neither slave nor free, there is neither male nor female, for you are all one in Christ Jesus" (Gal. 3:28). He does not, of course, mean that there is no difference between Jew and Greek, between slave and free, between male and female. Of course there are differences. What he is saying is that these differences give us no ground for taking up an attitude of lofty superiority. He is saying that there is a unity in Christ that transcends all kinds of human barriers.

To be a Christian is to know that you are a sinner, but that your sin has been put away at terrible cost, the cost of the death of the sinless Son of God. Really to take that in and to put your trust in Christ means to enter into a new way of living. Among other things, it means that you see racial prejudice as sinful. Racial prejudice erects barriers that are meaningless in a context where the whole human race needs salvation, where the really significant problem is sin, not race. If we understand what the death of Christ means, we understand that racial prejudice has no place in our lives.

And we understand that sexual prejudice likewise has no place. As that ancient Jewish prayer reminds us, women are fashioned according to the will of God. The most ardent male chauvinist cannot claim more. The sexes are not in some form of competition but are created in fulfillment of the divine purpose. In this world they belong together, and each is impoverished without the other.

127

Paul could write, "Receive one another, as Christ received you, to the glory of God" (Rom. 15:7). In this he showed that he had learned an important lesson from his Master. Because of what Christ has done for us, we are to act toward other people in the way he acted. That means an end to stupid practices like racial prejudice and sexual harassment. Unity in Christ is an important Christian concept.

16

Living Water

Jesus answered her: "If you knew the free gift of God and who it is that says to you, 'Give me a drink,' you would have asked him, and he would have given you living water." The woman says to him, "Sir, you have no bucket and the well is deep; from where then do you have the living water? Are you greater than our father Jacob, who gave us the well and drank from it, he and his sons and his cattle?" Jesus replied, "Everyone who drinks of this water will thirst again; but whoever drinks of the water that I will give him will never thirst again, but the water that I will give him will be in him a fountain of water leaping up into life eternal" (John 4:10–14).

Jesus asked the woman of Samaria for a drink. This led to her expression of astonishment that a Jew would make such a request of a Samaritan woman. We have looked into the mutual antagonism of the two races and seen something of the tolerant attitude that Jesus brought into a tense and difficult situation. But the woman's statement was there, and we now resume our study of the incident by going on to the further conversation.

Jesus points to some things that the woman did not know. The first is "the free gift of God" (v. 10). Jesus here uses a word *(dōrea)* that is somewhat unusual among the Evangelists (this is the only place in any of the four Gospels where it is used to denote a gift, though it is used adverbially with the meaning "freely, in the manner of a gift"). He does not explain what the free gift is, but in view of the context it seems likely that he means the living water of which he goes on to speak. The woman in her remote Samaritan village and with her inadequate knowledge of the ways of God knew nothing of the living water that God could give her. She was in danger of rejecting a good gift that she was not yet in a position to evaluate.

The second thing of which she was ignorant was the identity of him with whom she was speaking. The whole conversation gives the impression that she did not take Jesus seriously. She was evidently not in a hurry and found it pleasant to spend some time gossiping by the well. The stranger was unusual for a Jew, but until later in the conversation she thought no more of him than that. She had at this time not the slightest idea of the great privilege that was hers.

This is a mistake that many of us make. Of course, if we were to see our Lord in all his splendor, we would bow down to him. If he appeared in his heavenly majesty, we would do anything he asked and do it gladly. But do we not often fail to recognize him when he comes to us in a way that we do not expect? And are we not at times guilty of failing to do for him the things we should? Jesus said that on judgment day there will be some very surprised people. On that day some will be rewarded for feeding the Lord when he was hungry, for giving him something to drink when he was thirsty, for welcoming him when he was a stranger, for clothing him when he was naked, for visiting him when he was sick, and coming to him when he was in prison. This will puzzle them, for they will have no recollection of doing any of those things. Then they will be told, "Inasmuch as you did it to one of the least of these my brothers, to me it was you did it." And others will be equally surprised at being condemned for failing to do these things for the Lord, only to be told that when they did not do these things for the least of his brothers, they did not do them for him (Matt. 25:31–46).

It is not given to most of us to walk in high places, to be constantly in the presence of the great. Mostly we live and move and have our being among very ordinary people. Indeed they are sometimes far too ordinary for our tastes! We perhaps create fantasies of the wonderful service we would render if our lot were cast in different places. What the Samaritan woman did not realize was that she stood in the presence of the Lord of all. It is important that we realize that when we have the opportunity of meeting human need, even the need of very lowly people, we too are in the presence of the Lord of all.

Flowing Water

Had the woman known the realities of the situation, she would have asked for the gift of "living water." This is not an expression that we use very often (unless we are talking about this part of the Bible or a similar passage). But the expression was not uncommon among people who lived in first-century Palestine.

It was used of water that flowed, water in a river, or water poured out, that is, water in motion as opposed to stagnant water, water in a pool or a cistern or a basin. "Living water" was vital in the many ceremonies of purification that mattered so much to the people of that day. When a person contracted ceremonial defilement and had to be cleansed, it was "living water" that was needed. For example, scrupulous people commonly washed their hands before a meal. For they might have accidentally picked up some defilement as their hands touched many things, and if they conveyed that pollution to the food they ate, they would be entirely defiled.

But washing did not mean, as with us, washing in a basin of water. The water had to be poured over the hands. Elisha could be described as the one who "used to pour water on the hands of Elijah" (2 Kings 3:11); that is to say, he helped him in the process of washing. It had to be "living water," water that moved, if it was to remove defilement.

The rabbis do not seem to have used the expression "living water" in metaphorical senses. For them it was always water that flowed. They often used the word *water* metaphorically, mostly to refer to the Law, the first five books of our Old Testament. They found this revelation of God so necessary and so refreshing that "water" was a natural way of referring to it. But "living water" was different. That was always flowing water, water that moved.

We rarely find this expression in the Old Testament, but there are some passages that come close. Thus we read, "The words of a man's mouth are deep waters, but the fountain of wisdom is a bubbling brook" (Prov. 18:4). Again, "The teaching of the wise is a fountain of life" (Prov. 13:14). Water is a natural symbol of what is invigorating and refreshing.

There are some other Old Testament passages that associate "living water" closely with God. Twice Jeremiah speaks of him as "the spring of living water" (Jer. 2:13; 17:13), and the psalmist prays, "With you is the fountain of life" (Ps. 36:9). In Ezekiel's vision there was the mighty stream that flowed from the temple, and though we do not have a specific statement that this was living water coming from the Lord, we are not far from such a statement. We should also notice that the bride is "a garden fountain" and "a well of flowing [literally, living] water" (Song of Sol. 4:15). Such passages link "living water" with God, and we should not overlook this scriptural teaching when we find Jesus claiming to give the living water. The claim he makes here is one that puts him very close to God the Father. It is a striking claim indeed.

But Jesus seems to be putting more meaning into the words "living water" than do the Old Testament passages. He does not explain here

131

what "living water" stands for, but he uses the concept again later in this Gospel, when he says of the believer, "Rivers of living water will flow from his innermost being." John goes on to explain, "He said this about the Spirit which those who believed on him would receive" (7:38–39). This later passage is very important and will repay close study. But here we simply notice that it explains for us the meaning of "living water." Jesus is talking about the gift of the Holy Spirit.

"Our Father Jacob"

But the woman is not thinking in terms of deep spiritual realities. She is polite as she addresses him, "Sir." (This word could be used in the sense "Lord." Indeed it is often used in that way in the New Testament, but there is no reason for thinking that the woman as yet saw Jesus in that light. She is simply being polite.) The word has perhaps a note of formality about it when used in this manner. She is putting a distance between them.

Her sternly practical mind goes to the fact that Jesus has no bucket. (Her word in verse 11 means anything that could be used for drawing water; most travelers would probably have a skin bucket to meet such needs as they journeyed.) "The well is deep," she adds. The water did not lie near the surface, and a person without equipment would not be able to get at it. She is taking Jesus' reference to water quite literally; she sees it as the kind of water that she would draw from the well. As Jesus had no way of getting at the water in the well, she dismisses his words. No bucket, no water. That's all there is to it!

But Jesus had spoken of "living" water, and now she asks where he will get this "living" water. She has made it clear that she is thinking of ordinary water and has pointed out to her own satisfaction that the water Jesus is talking about is not going to come from the well. Where, then, could it come from? She sees no other source of water in that place.

She raises a further objection that seems to her to make Jesus' position quite impossible: "Are *you* greater than our father Jacob?" (v. 12). Her "you" is emphatic. It is ridiculous to think that such a person as Jesus appeared to be could possibly be greater than Jacob. But he would have to be much greater if he was going to get water in this place without so much as a bucket. She reminds him that Jacob had not come up with a tiny quantity of water. He had produced enough to provide not only for his own drinking needs, but also for those of his sons and his cattle. That was a lot of water. It would require someone much greater than she thought Jesus to be to do that.

This is a good example of the irony that John introduces from time to time. To the woman it was impossible that Jesus was greater than

Jacob, but the truth was that he was indeed greater by far than that patriarch. John often leaves statements like this one unrefuted if his informed readers would immediately recognize the truth. The woman did not realize it, but her words pointed to an important truth.

It is perhaps curious that the woman speaks of Jacob as "our father." As we saw in an earlier study, the Samaritans were a mixed race and had no real claim to descent from Jacob. But the claim was certainly made, and the historian Josephus, for example, tells us that the Samaritans considered that they were descended from Joseph through his sons Ephraim and Manasseh. Evidently the woman was repeating a claim that Samaritans were fond of making, though, as far as we can see, without historical justification.

J. C. Ryle has a sharp comment that brings out another aspect of the situation: "Dead teachers have always more authority than living ones." It is a common failing of the human race to think that those of an earlier time were greater and wiser than those more recent. The woman clung to the thought that the well from which she drew was sanctified in some way because Jacob dug it. Jacob was the ultimate source of her supply, and she was not going to let anything interfere with that comforting thought. She would not look past Jacob, even though this meant cutting herself off from the most wonderful thing there is, the gift of life from the Son of God himself.

I like the story of the comedian who gave one of his children a birthday gift of a bulldog. A friend asked why he had chosen such an unusual and downright ugly gift. "He will see that ugly face," replied the father, "and in time he will discover all the love behind it. He'll never take anything at face value again." Whether it worked with that child I do not know. But I do know that it is important not to put our trust in surface impressions, as the woman was doing at this point. She was in danger of missing out on the best there is because of her casual impressions of Jesus and her firm commitment to a great one of the past.

Never to Thirst Again

The woman is determined to keep to the kind of water that is in Jacob's well. So Jesus continues to talk about it. He makes the single devastating point that whoever drinks of that water will certainly thirst again (v. 13). That is the nature of that water. There is nothing about it that even raises the possibility of a permanent quenching of thirst. That the woman was there to draw water was a witness to the fact. The water she had drawn previously was exhausted. She had drunk it and now was thirsty again. There is no permanent satisfaction that way.

133

Perhaps it is not inappropriate to point out that this is characteristic of the world. It is not only the water supply that must be renewed every day and the food supplies that must be obtained again. The way of worldliness is the way of permanent dissatisfaction.

There was a commanding officer in a certain army unit who had been a heavyweight boxer in his pre-army days and was held in a good deal of respect accordingly. On one occasion he was dealing with a group of soldiers who were guilty of various military offenses. Having received his sentence, one of them told a friend who was waiting to be dealt with, "He offered me the choice between seven days of confinement to barracks and three rounds in the boxing ring with him. I chose the seven days of confinement, and he roared at me, 'Coward, take fourteen days of confinement to barracks.'"

When his turn came, the friend was glad of a little inside information. "Will you take seven days of confinement to barracks or will you go three rounds in the ring with me?" the officer asked.

Thankful that he had some idea of what was involved, the soldier promptly replied, "I'd prefer the three rounds with you, sir." But to his consternation the officer shouted, "You'd take advantage of an old man, would you? Fourteen days in barracks for you!"

The way of worldliness is a bit like that. There is no means of ultimately pleasing it and meeting its demands. No matter which way we try, we cannot attain final and lasting satisfaction. The modern world is a study in dissatisfaction; with all its sophisticated pleasures it is a classic example of boredom and discontent. Surely never in the history of the race have there been so many ways of attaining pleasure, so much in the way of technical devices to make life easy and enjoyable (think of all the gadgets with which our homes are adorned). And never have so many been bored and unhappy, seeing life as a frustrating business, an exercise in futility. I do not want to give the impression that I can state the world's problems in one sentence and give the solution in another. Life is too complex for that. But there can surely be no doubt that part of the difficulty arises from the fact that "everyone who drinks of this water will thirst again." There is nothing lasting about this world's satisfactions.

Jesus contrasts with this the drinking of the water that he will give. We might notice an interesting change of tense in the Greek. When he says, "Everyone who drinks of this water . . ." (v. 13), the verb *drinks* is in the present tense, a tense that can depict continuous action. This kind of drinking goes on and on. It has to, because of the kind of water that is involved.

But when Jesus says, "Whoever drinks of the water that I will give him . . ." (v. 14), the verb *drinks* is in the aorist subjunctive, with a meaning like "whoever has drunk once for all." He is talking about a decisive happening. When anyone comes face to face with Christ and, abandoning an old way of life, turns to him for salvation, for the "living water" that he alone can give, then something permanent has happened. That person has entered into an experience from which he will never want to go back. He has drunk of the water that is permanently satisfying.

This does not mean that the Christian life is a kind of flat, bovine contentment, such that the believer has nothing to reach out for, no attainment in the service of Christ that is yet before him. Jesus pronounced a blessing on "those who hunger and thirst for righteousness" (Matt. 5:6). The believer is always aware that he has not yet attained the standard which he ought to attain. He is never ignorant of the fact that there are greater experiences yet before him. With Paul he cries out, "Forgetting the things that are behind and stretching out towards what is before, I press on toward the mark for the prize of the high calling of God in Christ Jesus" (Phil. 3:13–14).

The Water That Leaps

The water that Jesus gives "will be in him [who drinks of it] a fountain of water leaping up into life eternal." The Spirit-filled life is dynamic. Jesus brings out something of what this means by the use of an unusual word for the action of water. His verb for "leap" is not normally used for the action of inanimate things, but rather for living beings, people or animals, that jump in the air. There does not appear to be another example of its use for the action of water. It is true that a fountain is water in motion in a way that might aptly be described as "leaping," and we do sometimes speak of a fountain in this way. But that was not the way the ancients described it. They used other verbs. Jesus is not referring to an ordinary process, a natural force, but to something that is very unusual. When the Holy Spirit enters the life, there is vital force that finds vigorous expression.

This may perhaps be indicated by another piece of John's language in this chapter. He has used the word *pēgē*, "spring," of the source of the woman's water supply (v. 6). It is uncertain why this word would be used of a well. Theoretically there might have been a spring at the bottom of the well, and if so the well would have had a magnificent source to replenish its supplies. There is no spring there now, so if the word is being used strictly, the spring has since dried up. But it seems more likely that the word simply means "well." It is apparently used without regard to the way the water got into the well. But the more usual word for a hole in the ground is *phrear*, and this is used in verses 11 and 12. There is something static about this word. It simply refers to a ditch, a hole in the ground.

But when Jesus refers to the living water he uses *pēgē* again, and there is a point in his choice of word. This is a real fountain; it contains vital force as it leaps up. And that corresponds to the life of the believer. When the Holy Spirit comes into anyone's life, there is a new power as well as a new sense of direction. Jesus is not calling people to a worldly life with one or two of its worst habits eradicated. He is calling them to something radically new.

He speaks of this radically new existence in terms of eternal life. As we saw in an earlier study (p. 98), this refers to life that is proper to the age to come, but it is life that Jesus has made available here and now. The wonderful thing about the gift of the Holy Spirit is that those who have it do not live out their lives solely in the possibilities of this present world and its resources. Something of the power and the vision of the age to come is theirs now.

It is this wonderful prospect that is held out to the woman of Samaria. There is nothing extraordinary about her. As we read the chapter we do not see her as a woman with outstanding achievement or potential. We have already seen that Jesus does not always choose outstanding people. Many of his miracles of grace are worked in what the world would count as very unpromising people. That is one of the things this chapter is saying to us. The gift of the living water is not a reward for meritorious service. It is a gift that brings to anyone who receives it, no matter how insignificant and limited he or she may be, a totally new experience, a new power, a new life—the life that is life eternal.

17

Worship in Spirit and Truth

He says to her, "Go call your husband and come here." The woman answered him, "I have no husband." Jesus says to her, "Well did you say, 'I have no husband,' because you have had five husbands and he whom you now have is not your husband; this you said truly." The woman says to him, "Sir, I see that you are a prophet. Our fathers worshiped in this mountain, and you say that in Jerusalem is the place where we must worship." Jesus says to her, "Believe me, woman, an hour is coming when neither in this mountain nor in Jerusalem will you worship the Father. You worship you know not what; we worship what we know, for salvation is from the Jews. But an hour is coming and is now present when the true worshipers will worship the Father in spirit and truth, for the Father seeks such as his worshipers. God is spirit, and those who worship him must worship in spirit and truth" (John 4:16–24).

When Jesus spoke of living water that would give permanent satisfaction, the woman asked for it so that she would not have to come to the well to draw water (v. 15). Clearly she was not serious. The water Jesus was offering was not the kind of water that would relieve those who drank it from having to make visits to wells. She did not think that Jesus had anything in particular to give; rather, she was simply humoring an unusual acquaintance.

But Jesus saw that the time had come to bring things home to the woman and he asked her to bring her husband (v. 16). It has well been

137

pointed out that the gift Jesus would give is not a gift to be enjoyed alone, but it is to be shared with other people. And with whom could the woman share better than with her husband? This may have been part of the reason for Jesus' request. But it seems more likely that he wanted to bring home to the woman the fact of her sin and the importance of doing something about it.

She said, "I have no husband," to which Jesus replied, "Well did you say, 'I have no husband,' because you have had five husbands and he whom you now have is not your husband; this you said truly" (vv. 17–18). Clearly the woman was an expert at divorce! We, by contrast, know little about divorce among the Samaritans of the time, though it seems a fair assumption that their customs did not differ greatly from those of the Jews.

According to the law of Moses, a man could divorce his wife, but a woman's rights were more limited: she could not divorce her husband. That, however, was not the whole story. She was sometimes allowed to petition the court, and if the judges thought it right, they could direct the husband to divorce her. Some wealthy women were known to have paid their husbands to divorce them. So there were ways that women could get around their nominal inability to get rid of unwanted husbands.

Theoretically there was no limit to the number of valid marriages anyone could contract, but the rabbis thought that a nice girl would not have more than two husbands, or three at the most. Jesus may mean that the woman had had more than the allowable number of marriages, so that her present union was not legal. Or, in accordance with the way he looked at marriage (Matt. 19:3–9), he may be saying that she was not really married at all. Or again, it may be that the woman had become so used to getting in and out of marriage that in the last case she had dispensed with the formality of marriage altogether.

Wonderful Mount Gerizim

Whatever the precise circumstances, the woman's home life clearly did not bear close examination. She wanted to get off the topic, so she tried to pick an argument on a religious theme. A good argument is often a useful way of avoiding an unpleasant subject. She paid Jesus a compliment, "Sir, I see that you are a prophet," and went on, "Our fathers worshiped in this mountain, and you say that in Jerusalem is the place where we must worship" (vv. 19–20). That should end the unpleasant topic of husband or no husband!

There was continual dispute between the Jews and the Samaritans over the right place for worship. The Jews held that the only place in the whole world where a temple could rightfully be built for the worship of God was Jerusalem. They did not mind synagogues in all sorts of places, but the temple must be in Jerusalem. The Samaritans, by contrast, held that Mount Gerizim was the right place. They found in their Scripture that Abraham and Jacob had made altars in the general vicinity (Gen. 12:7; 33:20). They found also that Mount Gerizim was the place where the people were to be blessed (Deut. 11:29; 27:12), and that God had commanded that an altar be made on this mountain (Deut. 27:4–5). In our Bibles the mountain where the altar was to be made is Mount Ebal, but in the Samaritan Scripture the mountain is Gerizim. They thus felt that they had good grounds for seeing Gerizim as important. They added to their argument by understanding Gerizim to be in view whenever an expression like "the goodly mountain" occurred.

With this way of reading the Bible, Mount Gerizim became a most significant and historical spot. The Samaritans thought that almost every important happening in the days of the great patriarchs took place on or near Mount Gerizim. They accordingly had strong feelings about their beloved holy mountain. This is illustrated in a story that was told about a Samaritan who got into conversation with a traveler, evidently a Jew. The traveler said that he was going up to Jerusalem to pray. The Samaritan replied, "Would it not be better for you to pray in this blessed mountain rather than in that dunghill?" With emotions like this so easily aroused, we can see that the woman might well feel that if she could get a good argument going over the rival merits of Jerusalem and Gerizim, her family circumstances would be forgotten.

"You Worship You Know Not What"

But Jesus was not going to be drawn into the kind of discussion the woman wanted. He had something more important to do than engage in futile argument. He pointed out that the place of worship is not important and further that times were changing. They lived in a troubled era, and soon people would worship neither in Gerizim nor Jerusalem. So they should not put too much emphasis on the place.

Then he drew attention to a defect in the whole Samaritan approach. "You worship you know not what," he said (v. 22), drawing attention to the poverty in spiritual things that necessarily followed from the Samaritan refusal to use any part of Scripture other than the first five books of our Old Testament. That meant that they did not have the historical books, Joshua and Judges, the books of Samuel, Kings, and Chronicles, and those of Ezra and Nehemiah. They did not know of the way God had watched over his people through the centuries, working out his purposes in both blessing and judgment. They did not know of the people whom God had raised up to do his will, nor did they know of the way God's demand for righteousness had worked out in history.

And they did not have the Psalms. To cite but one, the Shepherd Psalm (Ps. 23) is surely one of the great devotional treasures of Scripture, and to be without it is to be impoverished. So with other psalms that give an insight into the heart and mind of the true worshiper of God. To lack the psalms is to be robbed of truths of inestimable value. And think of Proverbs, that storehouse of practical wisdom, with its insights into the way God would have his people live.

The books of the prophets are part of the treasures of the whole human race. All sorts of people, whether or not they are worshipers of the God of the Bible, find these writings unique in their insight into the ways of God and man and the relationship between the two. The prophets have much to tell of the way God regards our sins and spiritual ineffectiveness, and of what is necessary in the path of service to God.

The Samaritans did worship the true God. But they had turned their backs on much of the revelation that God had given, and thus they incurred the condemnation, "You worship you know not what." Since Jesus says "what" and not "whom," it may be that he is pointing to the whole system of worship as well as to the God being worshiped. It was good that they were worshiping the true God, yet tragic that they did not know what they were doing. They had rejected too much of the revelation to know what they were about.

Perhaps we should ask ourselves how all this applies to us. It may well be that of many modern worshipers it can also be said, "You worship you know not what." Certainly God has made a rich and full revelation for us in Scripture, but when we go to church on Sunday, all too often it seems that our approach to God ignores much of it. It is easy to have our minds firmly made up as to what God is like and then not listen to what God says about himself in Scripture. How many of us, for example, take seriously such words as "our God is a consuming fire" (Heb. 12:29)? But they are part of the Bible, and when we worship we should bear in mind God's vigorous hostility to everything that is evil. So with the rest of the revelation. When we come before God, it is not good enough to be hazy and uncertain about what has been revealed. Worship is too serious a matter for that.

But we seem often to be in a state of ignorance. If we were truthful about our knowledge of God, many of us would have to confess that we are somewhat like a certain weatherman who was called as a witness in a trial. He was to give expert testimony as to the amount of the snowfall at the time of the crime. He gave his evidence competently and answered crisply all the questions asked of him. Then as he was about to leave the witness box the judge inquired, "What's the weather going to be like for the rest of the day?" "I'd rather not say," replied the weatherman. "I'm under oath."

An uncertainty like that tends to creep into much of our worship. It is all too easy to drift into a customary pattern without giving it any real thought. But God has revealed a great deal in the Bible, and it is plain that he expects us to take that revelation seriously. If we are to worship acceptably, it will be because we have come to know God as fully as we can and because our worship flows from that knowledge. It is a terrible thing if it can be said of us that we do not know what we are doing when we engage in worship.

"We Know"

Over against the uncertainty of the Samaritans, Jesus sets the certainty the Jews had. He is not saying that every Jew worshiped more acceptably than every Samaritan, but rather that the Jewish system took account of all of Scripture and thus, in principle at least, the Jews had a better knowledge of him whom they worshiped than did the Samaritans. Of course an individual Samaritan might be more sincere and might worship more acceptably than an individual Jew. But that is not what Jesus is talking about. He is talking about the approaches of the two groups taken as a whole.

There is a calm confidence in Jesus' words, "We worship what *we know*." The Jews' worship of God was not based on their desires, their hopes, the opinions of their liturgical experts, or anything like that. Jesus is saying that their worship was based not on speculation but on knowledge. This is an indispensable part of true worship. Thus David could say, "The Lord is my Shepherd" (Ps. 23:1), and Paul could say, "I know whom I have believed" (2 Tim. 1:12). There is a quiet certainty about the approach of the worshiper who takes seriously what God has revealed in his Word. It is there for our information. Since God means what he says, we may have confidence when we approach him in accordance with his revelation.

Assurance is an important part of the Christian faith. God has made certain promises and he will keep them. We may rely on that. We are not meant to be left uncertain, wondering whether in the end we will or will not be saved. There is a whole book of our New Testament written to bring us this assurance. As John comes toward the end of his First Epistle he says, "These things I have written to you who believe on the name of the Son of God in order that you may know that you have life eternal" (1 John 5:13). He is not writing to the general public, nor is he penning an evangelistic tract. He is writing to believers. And he wants believers to be in no doubt. They are to *know* that they have

141

eternal life. God has promised it to those who believe (John 3:16; Acts 16:31). Well, then. Let them act on the certainty that God will do what he says he will do. The assurance of salvation is one of God's good gifts.

Salvation Is from the Jews

When Jesus goes on to say, "Salvation is from the Jews," he is not engaging in some narrow nationalism. His word *salvation* is actually preceded by the definite article: he says *"the* salvation." He is not speaking of any kind of salvation that people might think of, but THE salvation, the salvation prophesied in the Old Testament, the messianic salvation. When the Samaritans refused to accept most of the Old Testament writings as sacred Scripture, they cut themselves off from an understanding of the salvation that God would provide in due course.

Jesus' words are not to be understood as ascribing some great superiority to the Jewish nation as such. He is pointing to the prophecies of Scripture about the Messiah and saying that those prophecies meant that when the Messiah came he would come from among the Jews. There is no way of reading the Old Testament and concluding that the Messiah would be a Samaritan. In his great purpose God chose the Jewish nation as the one to which he would make his supreme revelation and among whom in due course he would send his Messiah. The other nations have their gifts and their callings in the life of the world. But it is only to this nation that God would send the Messiah. People may argue as they will about the merits of Gerizim and other holy places. Nothing can alter the fact that God has determined that his Messiah and the salvation that the Messiah would bring would come to this one nation, the Jews.

And that salvation is desperately needed. There is in every modern nation, just as there was in the Jews and Samaritans, that which shrieks aloud of our inability to make this world the kind of place in which we would like to live. I have a certain sympathy with the ninety-four-year-old man who was told that he needed a hearing aid. He declined with decision, saying, "No, I've heard enough!" Unfortunately we cannot keep out the world's evil by simply refusing to listen. The evil is real. And our need of salvation is real.

True Worshipers

Jesus moves on to what real worship means. Disputes between Jews and Samaritans might stir people like the woman to whom he was talking, but they had no real substance. Things were changing, he said.

"But an hour is coming and is now present" (v. 23) points to the entrance of something new into human life. And that new thing is, of course, the coming of Jesus. Before his time people could dispute about Gerizim and Jerusalem as rival places of worship, but his coming means the end of the old ways. He would in due course die on a cross to put away people's sins and thus make obsolete the ways in which people worshiped in the rival shrines. The coming of Jesus means the end of ways of worship like those in Jerusalem and on Mount Gerizim.

The woman could not have been expected to work out all that the presence of Jesus in this world means. She had just met him and had no way of understanding the nature of his messianic vocation. She could not know that in due course he would lay down his life on a cross, but she could understand more than she had so far evidenced. Her talk of worship had centered on place. She was interested in whether Gerizim or Jerusalem was the better *place* to approach God. Jesus now turns her thoughts to the better *way* to approach him.

He speaks of "the true worshipers." It is possible, of course, to approach God mechanically and formally, but such worship is not true worship. If the woman wants no more than formality, let her keep on with discussions about the better place for a temple. But if she is really concerned with approach to God, if she wants to be a true worshiper, then she will have to take a different tack. It is easy enough to be a false worshiper, to be concerned simply with being in the right place at the right time. Which of us has not felt the temptation to be preoccupied with the outward? It is so easy to concentrate on being in our customary place of worship, on taking up our habitual position, on standing and sitting and singing and speaking (and, of course, taking part in the offertory) at the usual times.

But all of that is not worship. True worship is done "in spirit and truth." Some have thought that "spirit" here refers to the Holy Spirit, but this seems unlikely. It is true that the Holy Spirit is involved in our worship. Paul writes of the way the Spirit helps us in our weakness in prayer; we do not know what to pray but the Spirit himself makes intercession (Rom. 8:26). So, too, we are to pray "in the Spirit" (Eph. 6:18). But it is not this sort of thing of which Jesus is speaking. He is surely referring to the human spirit and saying that true worship can never be accomplished in what is merely outward. True worship means right inward dispositions; it means being involved at the deepest level of our natures.

When we come to worship, other people may see whether we are in our usual place, whether we have a reverent demeanor, whether we are joining in the hymns and responses. But only God knows whether our spirit is involved and thus whether we are really worshiping or merely going through the motions. In our worship we must always keep in mind the truth that we cannot deceive God. We can deceive our neighbors and we can deceive ourselves. But God always knows whether our worship is "in spirit and truth" or whether it is a sham.

Jesus says that right worship is done "in spirit and truth" (not only "in spirit"). In John's Gospel truth has a large place. It is linked in some way with Jesus himself, for he said, "I am . . . the truth" (14:6). We should bear this in mind when we think of worship, for it is only because of what Jesus has done that we Christians can approach God in the way we do. We close many of our prayers with "through Jesus Christ our Lord," and rightly. It is because of what Jesus has done that we can come to God. And it is in the measure that we see the truth in Jesus that we will worship as we should.

We generally think of truth as a quality attaching to words; people speak the truth or they tell lies. This, of course, is quite biblical, but there is also the idea that truth can be a quality of action; people may "do the truth" (3:21). It is perhaps something like this that is meant here. If we are to worship rightly, we must "do the truth" as we worship. We must be completely sincere.

We should notice another small point. Some translations, as, for example, the King James Version, read "in spirit and in truth." This reads well in English, but in Greek there is only one "in." The preposition is not repeated before "truth." In other words Jesus is not saying two things: we must worship in spirit *and* we must worship in truth. He is expressing one complex idea: we must worship in spirit and truth. The two go together. They make up one acceptable attitude.

God Is Spirit

We should understand Jesus' words about God in verse 24 in the sense "God is spirit" rather than "God is a spirit." In Greek there is no indefinite article like our "a." When we translate we put the article in or leave it out according to the general sense of the passage. Here Jesus is not saying that God is one spirit among many, which would be the meaning of "God is a spirit." Rather he is saying that God's essential nature is spirit. Jesus' statement is like "God is light" (not "a" light) or "God is love." The word order puts emphasis on "spirit." It is important that we understand this truth about God.

It is important because our worship must be the kind of worship that accords with the nature of God as he is. Since God is spirit, our worship must be in spirit; it must be of a spiritual kind. Of course, the outward does have its place. Jesus is not saying that it does not matter. But he is saying quite firmly that its place is a minor one. What matters in the most important sense is that we realize something of God's nature as spirit and that our worship accordingly must proceed from our inmost being. It must be worship in spirit.

Notice the word *must* in this verse. Jesus is not saying merely that it would be a good idea for people to worship this way. He is saying that it is absolutely necessary. In our free and easy democratic ways we often feel that worship is an individual matter. Each of us may worship when and how he or she chooses. It is all up to the individual.

But Jesus is denying this. He is saying that our worship must accord with the kind of being God is. He has just rebuked the Samaritans with the words, "You worship you know not what." It is something like that which is in mind here. It is important to know what God has revealed of himself if we are to worship acceptably. I am not saying that we must have a full and perfect understanding of God before we can worship acceptably. If that were the case, nobody could ever worship, for our knowledge is always partial (1 Cor. 13:9, 12). But we are not in control of worship. It is not the worshiper who determines what shall be done and how it shall be done. Worship must always be such as to agree with the kind of God being worshiped. Since God has revealed to us something of his essential being, our worship must be such as accords with that revelation.

Worship is a great privilege that God has given us. Let us then use it rightly.

18

The Great Harvest

Jesus said, "I have food to eat which you do not know about."
The disciples therefore said to one another, "Surely no one has
brought him anything to eat?" Jesus says to them, "My food is
to do the will of him who sent me and to accomplish his work.
Don't you say, 'Four months yet and the harvest comes'? Look,
I tell you, lift up your eyes and look at the fields, because they
are white, ready to harvest. Already the reaper is receiving his
wage and gathering fruit to life eternal, so that he who sows
may rejoice with him who reaps. For in this is the saying true:
'One man sows and another man reaps.' I sent you to reap that
for which you did not labor. Others have labored and you have
entered into their labor" (John 4:32–38).

The disciples had come back from the village with the
food they had bought. They were surprised that Jesus was talking with
a woman (v. 27). As we have seen, men in general did not talk much
with women, and this was especially true of religious teachers. But the
disciples had been with Jesus long enough to know that he did not
always do what people expected. In any case he was their leader. They
could scarcely say to him, "Why are you talking with her? Don't you
know that a teacher like you does not talk to women?" Nor could they
very well rebuke the woman for talking to a great religious figure
(though they probably felt like doing so). Since Jesus accepted her,
they could scarcely drive her away. So they said nothing. But the problem was solved for them when the woman decided to go back to the

village and tell people of her great discovery. So she left her water pot (the reason for her journey in the first place!) and went off (v. 28).

The disciples reasoned that Jesus must be hungry (they had probably been clean out of food when they went off to do their shopping), so they tried to get him to eat something. They were met with the surprising statement: "I have food to eat which you do not know about" (v. 32). Not unnaturally, they interpreted this to mean that somehow Jesus had obtained some food while they were absent. But how? Who could have given him anything? There were no people about. No one could have done it! Perhaps we should notice in passing that in John's Gospel we often read of people who took literally words that Jesus used of spiritual realities. The Jews did this when Jesus spoke of destroying and raising the temple (2:20), Nicodemus did it with the new birth (3:4), and the woman did it with the living water (4:15). Now the disciples do it with the food that Jesus eats. This kind of misunderstanding persisted to the end (14:8; 16:17–18). The revelation that Jesus brought is not obvious and open to everybody. There is mystery about it, and we do not recognize its meaning unless Jesus explains it.

This episode shows us an important truth about the way that Jesus used his miraculous powers. Since he had already done a number of miracles (2:23), the disciples would not have been unaware of his abilities. But it never occurred to them that he might work a miracle to meet his own needs, even legitimate ones. The miracles were always worked for other people; they were never used for selfish purposes, whatever the personal needs of Jesus might have been. And the disciples knew this. They knew that Jesus would not have worked a miracle for himself. If he had had food, someone must have brought it to him.

Doing the Will of God

But how could it have happened? Jesus explained: "My food is to do the will of him who sent me and to accomplish his work" (v. 34). We should notice that Jesus is speaking specifically about himself. His "I" is emphatic when he says, "I have food to eat," and the word *my* is emphatic when he says "my food." However it might be with other people, this is the way it is with him.

His food was to do the will of God. It was meat and drink to him to set forward the divine purpose. That was why he had come to this earth, and fulfilling the divine purpose was more important to Jesus than the food the disciples had gone off to buy. He does not say "God," but "him who sent me." This is characteristic of the Fourth Gospel. Again and again in this Gospel we read of the Father as having sent the Son. John has two Greek verbs for "to send," one of which he uses twenty-eight times and the other thirty-two times. In many of these instances he refers to the Father as sending the Son. Clearly the thought of mission is important to this Evangelist ("mission" is derived from a Latin verb which means "to send"). It is possible to speak of the Son as "coming" into the world, and John does this. It matters to him that for our salvation Jesus came. But it matters also that in this Jesus was at one with the Father. The Father is involved in this work of salvation. He *sent* the Son.

Jesus speaks of "accomplishing" the Father's work. The verb shows something of his persistence. He is not speaking of an occasional good impulse, but of carrying through right to the end the good work that he does. It is easy to grow weary in well-doing and to decide that we have done enough. Not so is the work of the Father accomplished. That demands persistence. It may also be implied that this is work that the Father began and that Jesus now carries on. If that is in mind, it would fit in very well with the saying "one man sows, another man reaps," which comes a little later. And it would also see the whole life of Jesus as one great "work." Sometimes in this Gospel we read of the "works" that Jesus did. That takes his deeds one by one and looks at them as individual acts. But this way of speaking sees his whole life as a unity, as one great act of God. Both ways of looking at what Jesus did are important.

Four Months to Harvest

It looks as though Jesus proceeds to quote a proverb in verse 35. His "you" is emphatic: "Don't *you* say . . . ?" This is not his saying, but theirs. Some reject the view that this is a proverbial saying on two grounds: such a saying is not found anywhere in the extant literature, and in any case it takes longer than four months to get a crop to the stage of harvest in Palestine (six months is more likely). The first objection is not a strong one. When I worked in a remote parish in the Australian bush, I found that the farmers had a lot of sayings that I have never read in any book. This is surely true of people everywhere. Not only farmers but city-dwellers tend to evolve short, pithy sayings that arise out of their way of life.

The second objection is a bit stronger, but not much. It does take longer than four months to grow a crop in Palestine. But it seems that the men on the land in ancient Israel tended to divide the year into six two-month periods: sowing time, winter, spring, harvest, summer, and extreme heat. And in what is probably the oldest Hebrew inscription in existence, commonly called the Gezer Calendar, we read that there were two months of sowing, two months of late sowing, one of pulling flax, another of barley harvest, then the general harvest. From both the general practice and the Gezer Calendar, we see that from the end of sowing to the beginning of harvest there are four months. While the saying does not mean that crops grow in four months, it does mean that a period of at least four months intervenes between the end of sowing and the commencement of harvest. "Rome was not built in a day," we say—some things just can't be hurried. A proverb like this makes good sense.

The alternatives do not look attractive. Some suggest that we have here a remark made by the disciples as they looked at the crops. But a chance remark like that is not the kind of thing that is recorded in the Gospels. A further objection is that if in fact it was four months before the harvest, the crops would be in the early stages of growth, and that is not a time of scarcity of water. A weary traveler would find water on the surface; he would not depend on a woman coming to the well to draw water if he wanted a drink.

On all counts it seems better to think of the words as a proverbial saying which conveyed the thought that some things cannot be hurried. There is plenty of time. The farmer must just wait for the months to pass. He cannot get his harvest until the right amount of time has elapsed. Now this has a certain force in the processes of agriculture. There is a limit to what can be done to get the crop in early. We may use fertilizers and irrigation and chemicals, but in the end we must still wait for the plants to grow. Patience is a necessary virtue for the farmer, as James points out (James 5:7).

The Harvest of Souls

But the spiritual harvest does not run on the same lines as a crop of wheat. It is all too easy to think it does and to use that as an excuse for doing nothing. I like the comment of Campbell Morgan on this verse: "If those disciples had been appointed a commission of enquiry as to the possibilities of Christian enterprise in Samaria I know exactly the resolution they would have passed. The resolution would have been: Samaria unquestionably needs our Master's message, but it is not ready for it. There must first be ploughing, then sowing, and then waiting. It is needy, but it is not ready." Can't you hear many of our ecclesiastical assemblies passing such a motion? We are always ready to recognize needy areas, but just as ready to find perfectly good reasons why we should do nothing for the present.

And it is that kind of attitude that Jesus is opposing. "Look," Jesus says, "lift up your eyes and look at the fields, because they are white, ready to harvest." The imagery is plain enough, but there is a problem as to the detail, namely the use of "white" as indicating readiness for harvest. What crop is white at harvest time? Certainly not wheat, and even the city-dweller knows of "the golden grain." Some of my farmer

149

friends point out that if wheat is not reaped when it is ripe, it turns a whitish color (they call it "rotten ripe"!). If this is in mind, Jesus is saying that the harvest is overdue. But I am not aware of any writer in antiquity who sees wheat as white, nor is the color associated with any other crop.

I think that H. V. Morton may give us the clue. He speaks of being in this very vicinity: "As I sat by Jacob's Well a crowd of Arabs came along the road from the direction in which Jesus was looking, and I saw their white garments shining in the sun. Surely Jesus was speaking not of the earthly but of the heavenly harvest, and as He spoke I think it likely that He pointed along the road where the Samaritans in their white robes were assembling to hear His words."

The harvest of which Jesus is speaking is surely to be understood in terms of people. He is not directing the apostles to agriculture, but to the harvest of souls in which they should be interested. In that harvest there is no reason for waiting. The harvest is there to be reaped, and there is an urgency about it. They must give themselves to the work of harvest and not comfort themselves with the reflection that there is no hurry because a harvest takes time to ripen. This harvest must be reaped now.

Urgency

There is an "already" at the end of verse 35, which many translations take with the preceding words: "the fields are already white. . . ." But this does not accord with the way John normally uses the word (he puts it early in the sentence, not at the end). And the sense of urgency in the passage seems better conveyed by taking it with what follows. It seems much more likely then that "already" goes with verse 36: "Already the reaper is receiving his wage." Since the normal procedure was for the laborer to be paid for his work at the end of each day, this indicates that the disciples are far behind. The day has gone, the energetic reaper is already being paid, and what have they done? We should probably not try to identify those who are already being paid. They form part of the imagery Jesus is using, and the point is simply that time is going on—there must be no delay.

There is a fine sense of urgency in a saying of Rabbi Tarfon (c. A.D. 130): "The day is short and the task is great and the laborers are idle and the wage is abundant and the master of the house is urgent." That is the way it always is in the service of our Master. In Christian work there never seems to be enough time, and there is always more to be done than we can easily accomplish. And is it not true that all too often the laborers are idle? We can so easily find good reasons for not doing the work that God sets before us. But the wage is abundant; our Lord never begrudges his people anything (cf. Luke 10:7). And the Master is urgent. We may be slack in our obedience, but the command to preach the gospel is plain enough, and the obligation to live the Christian life is abundantly clear.

Jesus brings out the overwhelming importance of the task by saying that the reaper gathers fruit "to life eternal." The task is not some insignificant one, where it does not matter much whether or not it is done. Jesus is talking about work in a field where the eternal welfare of people is at stake. Christians are called to work for the eternal well-being of those to whom they bring the gospel.

We are never to take the attitude that it does not matter much whether people respond. There are many invitations given in any normal society where it does not matter whether people accept them. When I am invited to a party, I may choose to go or not go. That is up to me. If I do not go, I miss the party. But that is all. I may have something better to do with my time. There may be other parties I can attend later. And if worse comes to worst and I simply stay at home and am miserable when I could have been rejoicing with my friends, that is soon over. In the long run it does not matter greatly whether or not I attend a particular party.

So it is with a multitude of organizations. There are innumerable clubs and societies which we receive invitations to join. If we accept, there are certain consequences, many of them beneficial. But we are not permanently handicapped if we do not. We may be impoverished by our refusal and may cut ourselves off from the possibility of doing useful service for our community. But whether we accept or decline, the results do not last forever.

It is otherwise with our work as Christians. The issues at stake here are eternal. If we are able to bring someone to trust Jesus, then we have accomplished something lasting. As James puts it, "He who converts a sinner from the error of his way will save his soul from death" (James 5:20). *From death!* That is a tremendous result. And of course, if a sinner refuses to turn from his evil way, that too is of lasting significance. When we evangelize we should be clear that we are doing something of great and permanent significance. Our concern is with eternal issues.

The Sower and the Reaper

The sower and the reaper rejoice together. They must never forget that they are working together for the same end result. The work of one would not be worth much without that of the other. If someone sows and no one comes along to reap in due course, the sower has wasted his labor. And if someone comes to reap where no one has sown, there is nothing he can do. The sower and the reaper are partners. Each depends on the other.

Sometimes Christians forget that. They did at Corinth. There they had developed cliques in the church, grouping themselves around the names of their favorite preachers. There were those who said they went along with Peter, those who aligned themselves with Paul, those who said that Apollos was the man, and even those who, apparently disgusted with the other factions, said they belonged to Christ (but don't all Christians?).

Paul would have nothing to do with such nonsense. He did not even congratulate those who put him in first place. He asked, "Has Christ been divided up? Was Paul crucified for you? Were you baptized in the name of Paul?" (1 Cor. 1:13). It is ridiculous to think of any but Christ as having brought salvation and accordingly as having first place. People like Peter and Apollos and Paul are nothing more than "servants through whom you believed." Paul goes on to explain a little more fully: "I planted, Apollos watered, but it was God who gave the increase" (1 Cor. 3:5–6).

That is the way it must always be in Christian service. There is no place for rivalry or jealousy. We are engaged together in a great work, the work of God. One may plant and another water, one may sow and another reap. But it is God and only God who can give the increase. We are all partners in doing God's work, channels through whom he accomplishes his purpose. If we understand what we are doing—and, more importantly, what God is doing in his world—we understand that the harvest is the important thing, not the part that this worker or that plays in bringing it about. As long as the harvest comes, sower and reaper can rejoice together.

So Jesus goes on to quote another proverb: "One man sows and another man reaps" (v. 37). It often happens on a small farm that the one who sows is also the one who does the reaping. But sometimes this is not the case; it matters little as long as the crop is got in. In the metaphorical application of the proverb it often happens that the one who sows is not the one who reaps. And again we may say that it matters little as long as the crop is got in. The task is the important thing, not the part of it that any particular worker accomplishes.

Entering the Labor of Others

It is often the case in life that people enjoy the fruits of the labor of others. Perhaps someone does a lot of hard work and then dies, and it is his heirs who enjoy the fruit of his labor. Or it may happen in other ways. When I retired I was able to buy a house with a very lovely garden. It had obviously been prepared with loving care by someone who knew much more than I do about the wonders and beauty of plant life. Every day I rejoice in the beautiful surroundings in which I live. And the beauty is not of my creating. It has been brought about by someone who is no longer here. He labored, and my wife and I have entered into his labors.

In the Christian task, one person often does a good deal of "spade work" and is then transferred, leaving it to others to reap the benefits of the hard work that they themselves did not do. Though the principle is clear, it is not easy to see in detail what Jesus meant here.

Some suggest that we must apply the words rigorously to the scene John is describing. It was Jesus and the woman who labored. Jesus taught the woman about the living water, and the woman passed on the good news to the people of the village and brought them to Jesus. All that the disciples did was go into the village and buy food. But now a crowd of believers was being formed and would enter into fellowship with them. The disciples had done nothing but would enjoy much. We must accept this as part of Jesus' meaning.

But others think that we must look back beyond the current happenings. Since John the Baptist had worked in this area, it is suggested that Jesus and his disciples were building on the work of John. This too is true. The Baptist had called on his hearers to repent because the kingdom of God was drawing near. He had told them of the coming of the Great One who would follow him and baptize with the Spirit. Where people accepted this teaching they were ready to respond to what Jesus and his followers said. Here it is true that John the Baptist labored and those who came later reaped.

For some this is not going back far enough. They see a reference to the prophets of the Old Testament, who had spoken in the name of God and prophesied of the Messiah whom God would send in due course and of the salvation he would bring. Those who read the ancient Scriptures with spiritual perception were prepared for the coming of God's own Son and responded to him when they met him.

Still others suggest that we must look to the future rather than to the past. Jesus would send the apostles ("apostles" means "sent ones") in due course, and they would reap what he had sown. This view reminds us of a truth we should never forget, that Christianity depends on the cross. There is but one way of salvation, and that way depends on the fact that Jesus died to put away our sins. Later Jesus said that a grain of wheat that does not fall into the ground and die produces nothing, "but if it dies, it bears much fruit" (12:24). It is the death of Jesus that results in Christian "fruit." Without that death there is nothing.

Many notice that in later happenings in that very area we have an excellent illustration of the principle involved. Philip went to Samaria and preached, with the result that many Samaritans believed. Only

153

after that did the apostles Peter and John come down and enter into Philip's labors (Acts 8).

It is not difficult, then, to see many applications of this principle in the work of the servants of God. But for us the primary thing must always be the work that Jesus has done. Paul speaks of him as the one foundation (1 Cor. 3:11). His atoning death is the necessary basis of the Christian life. Without his taking away of our sins we would still be in the ways of death. In a very real sense Jesus is the basis of our every Christian activity. In everything we do we enter into the work Jesus did. We could go further. When we try to win people for Christ or to build up those who know him, we always find that Christ has been there before us. "I sent you to reap that for which you did not labor," he said to the apostles (v. 38). The same is true for us today. We go, not because it seems a good idea to us necessarily, but because he sends us. And when we go we find that all our reaping is done in a field that he himself has prepared.

19

The Healing of the Officer's Son

So he came again to Cana of Galilee, where he made the water wine. And there was a royal officer whose son was sick in Capernaum. When this man heard that Jesus had come out of Judea into Galilee, he went to him and asked him to come down and heal his son, for he was at the point of death. Jesus then said to him, "Unless you people see signs and wonders you will not believe." The royal officer says to him, "Sir, come down before my little lad dies." Jesus says to him, "Go, your son lives." The man believed what Jesus said to him and went off. As he was now going down his slaves met him and said that his child was alive (and well). He inquired of them therefore the hour at which he recovered. So they said to him, "Yesterday at the seventh hour the fever left him." So the father knew that it was at that very hour at which Jesus said to him, "Your son lives." And he believed, he and all his household. This is now the second sign that Jesus did when he had come out of Judea into Galilee (John 4:46–54).

His work in Samaria finished, Jesus completed his journey to Galilee and went to the village of Cana once more. Up till this point John has recounted only one miracle, which he now recalls by reminding his readers that Cana was the place where Jesus had turned the water into wine. That had been an outstanding event, and John expects it to linger in the memory of his readers.

155

He now introduces a gentleman whom he calls a *basilikos*. This word is connected with the idea of royalty (*basileus* means "king"), and some feel that here it means someone of royal blood, a member of the royal family. As far as the language is concerned this is possible, but there is nothing in the narrative that points to anyone so exalted. It seems much more likely that it means someone in the royal service, so I have translated it "royal officer."

Exactly what position the man held is not clear. Elsewhere we read of people in Herod's service, such as Chuzas (Luke 8:3), but the word used of that man is not the same as that here. We also read of Manaen, "the foster-brother of Herod the tetrarch" (Acts 13:1). Of this title F. F. Bruce says, "The title 'foster-brother' was given to boys of the same age as royal princes, who were brought up with them at court." It does not seem as though that is meant in the present passage. Some suggest that the officer was the manager of Herod's estates, others that he held some political office the exact nature of which has not come down to us. We do not know. All that we can say for certain is that he was a trusted official.

Some have felt that Chuzas or Manaen was the person meant here. This is, of course, possible, and it is pointed out that if Chuzas was the father of the boy who was healed, that might explain why his wife was later found among the group of women who followed Jesus and supported him out of their means. But since John says nothing that will enable us to link this man with anybody else in the New Testament, all such identifications must remain pure speculation. For John what mattered was what Jesus did and how the man and his household came to believe, not the satisfying of our curiosity about just who the man was.

A little bit of human nature comes out in the use of the word *basilikos* ("royal"). In this context it must refer to someone in the service of Herod, even though Herod was not really a king at all. He was a "tetrarch," which means "ruler of a fourth part." This title seems to have been used originally in Macedonia, where it denoted the rulers of the four regions of Thessaly, but the Romans used it more generally for the ruler of almost any part of a province. When King Herod ("Herod the Great") died, his territory was divided among his sons. Archelaus received Judea, Samaria, and Idumea; Herod Antipas got Galilee and Peraea; while Philip's lot was Trachonitis, Ituraea, Batanaea, and Auranitis. It could be said that Archelaus got about half, and the other two about a quarter each, which would make the title *tetrarch* very appropriate. But, as I have said, the Romans did not use this title with exactness. Whatever he ruled, the Herod of this story was not a king at all but a tetrarch. Human nature being what it is, Herod remembered that his father had been a king, and he fancied the title for himself. And so he was sometimes called King Herod (see Mark 6:14 for an example).

The father in our story, then, was in all probability one of the officers of Herod the tetrarch. He lived in Capernaum, about twenty miles away from Cana. His son had a fever (v. 52), though this is not a very precise description of his illness, as the term was used for a variety of ailments. Still we can see the general character of his illness. Clearly the boy was in a bad way. His father feared that he would die. Hearing that Jesus was in Cana and evidently knowing that at an earlier time Jesus had worked a miracle there, the father now sought Jesus out with a view to having him cure his son.

He asked Jesus to "come down," which is a little mark of accuracy, for Cana is in the hills, while Capernaum is by the lake. He asked Jesus to heal his son and brought out the urgency of this request by saying that the boy was at the point of death. It was this that had caused the father to undertake the twenty-mile ride on horseback in an endeavor to get the boy cured.

Signs and Wonders

Jesus' response is unexpected: "Unless you people see signs and wonders you will not believe" (v. 48). His plural (which I have tried to bring out by the translation "you people") shows that he is not speaking particularly about the man who made the request. It is not even clear whether Jesus is including him. He may be making a general remark about the reaction of the people to his ministry. In every age, not least our own, people have loved the spectacular, and it would seem that this was true of first-century Galilee. Jesus looked for people to trust him and follow him in faith. But many were more interested in spectacular miracles than in their spiritual need and the importance of following Jesus, whether or not that was popular.

We have already come across John's use of the word *sign* (p. 76). It is one of his important words for Jesus' miracles, a word which points to the fact that there is spiritual truth demonstrated in the miracles. In the literal sense of the word, miracles are "*sign*ificant." They have meaning. The careless and superficial rejoice in the wonderful happening and do not get down to the spiritual truth to which it points; it is this to which Jesus is objecting. "Wonders" is a term that directs attention to the marvel in the miracle. It is something that people see but cannot explain. They can only stand before it in awe and amazement. The word occurs sixteen times in the New Testament. It is noteworthy that it is never used alone, but is always joined with "signs," as it is here. The point is that although the miracles are surely wonderful and we certainly cannot explain them, that is not the most important thing.

157

That is subordinate. The important thing is what God is doing through them.

When people came to Jesus simply on the basis of the wonderful miracles they saw him do, they lacked the genuine trustfulness that is the mark of the true disciple. It is still the case that people who look for the spectacular and the sensational have not understood what the Christian way means. Perhaps that is the reason why so many in these days do not walk in the way of Christ. Loving the spectacular, they find uncongenial the humble, quiet, steady service that is the lot of the servant of God. I do not want to dismiss the spectacular altogether. Certainly the hand of God is in the extraordinary. But that is not the usual way in which God does his work in the world. And for most of his servants it is in what the hymnwriter calls "the trivial round, the common task," that the path of true service lies.

Faith

Jesus looked for faith, a truth that John makes clear over and over and is seen here in his "you will not believe." It was faith that was important, not an attitude that looked for signs and wonders. In the Gospels as a whole we see that Jesus normally did his miracles in response to the faith of those who came to him. "Do you believe that I am able to do this?" he asked the two blind men who sought sight (Matt. 9:28). "All things are possible to him who believes," he said to the father of the boy who had fits (Mark 9:23), which drew from the man the classic reply, "I believe; help my unbelief" (v. 24). "Don't be afraid, only believe and she will be saved," he said to Jairus when that man had been informed that his daughter was dead (Luke 8:50). It was trust in him that mattered, and Jesus demanded it constantly.

But Jesus' power could also operate when there was no faith. We shall see an example of this when we come to the next chapter, where Jesus heals a man who has been lame for thirty-eight years. The interesting thing about this miracle is that the man did not even know the name of the One who healed him, let alone trust in him. Sometimes faith followed the miracles, and we can trust that this happened in the case of that lame man. Certainly Jesus speaks of people who sought him out after the miraculous feeding because they had eaten the food and not because of the signs (6:26). Clearly Jesus thinks it would have been better if it had been the signs that had moved them. And in the upper room Jesus said, "Believe me that I am in the Father and the Father in me, but if not, believe on account of the works themselves" (14:11). While Jesus looked for the faith that simply trusted him without any support other than a knowledge of him, it is better to believe on the basis of the miracles than not to believe at all.

We should not despise such lowly faith. I am reminded of a wise college president who was addressing a gathering of fellow presidents. "Always be kind to your A students and your B students," he said. "One day one of them will come back and make a good professor for you." He went on, "And always be kind to your C students. One day one of them will come back and build you a two-million-dollar science block!"

We need not have quite this outlook to see that there is value in the lowly. All faith, even that which brings people to Christ for imperfect reasons, is precious before God. But this Gospel makes it clear that, though he welcomes all who come, it is better to come in simple trust in Christ for what he is than for the wonders he can perform.

Yet Jesus was prepared to welcome all who came to him, no matter if their coming was with inadequate motives. And who of us ever does come with the completely right motive? We are simply too imperfect. Yet he always welcomes us. He takes us with what little faith we have and makes us into the very saints of God.

The Gift of Healing

But the father in the story was desperate. He had come because his boy was dangerously ill. He needed help urgently. So he did not proceed with a discussion of how much or how little faith he had, nor did he try to defend himself against a possible accusation that he had come with a view to seeing Jesus do "signs and wonders." "Sir," he said, "come down before my little lad dies" (v. 49). Earlier John had used the term *son* of the sufferer, as did the father when he first spoke to Jesus (vv. 46–47). But his affection comes through when this time he speaks of "my little lad." The diminutive may be used to express smallness of size but is also used affectionately, and we need not doubt that this is the case here.

Jesus' reply must have been totally unexpected: "Go, your son lives" (v. 50). It is plain that the father was anxious that Jesus should return with him to Capernaum and was hoping that he would be able to get him there in time. It apparently had not occurred to him that Jesus could heal without being there. The centurion of whom we read in Matthew 8:5–13 was different. He was used to giving commands and knew that when he told a soldier to do something, that something would be done. He did not have to be there supervising. So he did not ask Jesus to come to his home. He wanted no more than that he speak the word. But this kind of faith was unusual. "I have found such faith in no one in Israel," Jesus said (Matt. 8:10). The royal officer here in John's Gospel certainly did not have it. He wanted Jesus to "come down."

So Jesus' words represented a hard test for the father. He had nothing to go on except Jesus' assurance. Jesus did not give him a sign of any sort. He simply said that the boy lived and told the man to go. The man passed the test. Without anything other than Jesus' word he went on his way: "The man believed what Jesus said to him and went off." He had his values right and acted on his faith in Jesus.

I have read that the singer Marian Anderson was once told by Toscanini that she had the voice of the century. On one occasion she gave a concert at the While House for the king and queen of England and the Roosevelts. On one Easter Day she sang beneath the Lincoln statue in Washington to a crowd of more than seventy-five thousand, including many of this world's great ones. So, when a reporter asked her what was the greatest moment of her life, she had plenty to choose from. But her answer was, "The day I went home and told my mother that she needn't take in washing any more." For all her greatness, Marian Anderson had her sense of values right.

So with our royal officer. He knew enough about Jesus to trust him. And he was prepared to act in accordance with that trust.

We should not misunderstand Jesus' words. Modern translations often have something like "your son will live" (Revised Standard, New English Bible, Good News Bible) or "your son is going to live" (Goodspeed). Such translations can be defended, but they miss the point that Jesus is not just giving an optimistic forecast of how the fever will turn out. He is speaking a word of power. The fever did not gradually clear up but left the boy at the moment Jesus spoke. John is not giving an account of an interesting prognosis Jesus made, which was vindicated by later events. He is telling us of a "sign" that Jesus accomplished.

The Hour of Recovery

As the man was going home, some of his slaves met him with the news that the boy was better. The boy is described in three ways. At the beginning he is the man's "son" (vv. 46–47). Later the man uses the affectionate "little lad" (v. 49). In verse 51 the slaves call him the "child." Godet comments that the slaves "in their report, use neither the term of affection *(paidion)*, which would be too familiar, nor that of dignity *(huios)*, which would not be familiar enough, but that of family life: *pais, the child.*" John has preserved these lifelike touches.

The father immediately asked when the boy got better and received the answer, "Yesterday at the seventh hour the fever left him" (v. 52). This raises the question of the way time is measured in this Gospel. First-century Jews measured time from sunrise or sunset and spoke of "the first hour of the day" or "the first hour of the night" and so on. On this reckoning the seventh hour would be about 1 P.M. If that was the hour at which Jesus told the man to go, he would have had plenty of time to get back to Capernaum that day. And he would no doubt have been anxious to see for himself that what Jesus said had indeed happened. Why would he stay in Cana overnight?

So some have suggested that John is using a different method of computing time. They suggest that he is using the Roman method, which counted hours from midnight and from noon. On this reckoning the seventh hour would be our 7 P.M. At such an hour the man might well decide to stay the night rather than return home immediately. This would make good sense, except for the fact that the so-called Roman method does not seem to have been used in ordinary life. It was a legal method of computing time, used, for example, in determining when a lease expired. But though fairly common in such circumstances, it does not seem to have been used in daily life. Roman sundials, for example, have VI and not XII for the middle of the day.

So it would seem that we must see the miracle as taking place at around 1 P.M. We can only guess at the reasons why the man did not immediately return home. His anxiety had been relieved, for he believed what Jesus had said to him. There may also have been the practical problem of his horse. No doubt he had ridden the animal hard in order to get to Jesus before the boy died, and the animal might not have been in a fit state to begin the long journey home. For whatever reason, the man stayed there overnight and went home the next day.

It was on the way home that his slaves met him with the great news that the boy was well again. Evidently the household had been so thrilled at the sudden recovery that they could not wait for the master to return but sent slaves to let him know. And when they told him the time of the sudden recovery, he recognized that it had occurred at the very hour when Jesus had spoken his word of healing. Jesus spoke in Cana, and the healing took place in Capernaum. Distance is no barrier to the power of God. Jesus could do works of healing without being physically present.

Notice that the words "your son lives" in verse 53 are exactly repeated from verse 50, and almost exactly the same expression is found in verse 51. John has a habit of repeating words and phrases for emphasis (usually with some small variation). So it is plain that he regards these words as important; they are the key to our understanding of the miracle. They are words of power, not simply a prophecy that the boy would get well in due time.

A Household of Faith

The result was that the man "believed, he and all his household." The fact that the man went on such a journey to get Jesus to come and heal his boy shows that he had some kind of faith. Then, when Jesus spoke his words of power, we are told that "the man believed what

161

Jesus said to him" (v. 50). That involves some kind of trust, but the expression itself means no more than that he took the words Jesus spoke at face value. He accepted Jesus' saying and believed that what he said had happened.

But when John now says, "He believed," this means that he had a genuine trust in Jesus. He had come to faith in the full sense. He no longer simply looked for a miraculous cure; he had faith in the person. John's whole Gospel is written in order that people may come to put their trust in Jesus (20:31), and here we see an example of what is meant. The man believed. And not only the man; his whole household believed as well. We have no way of knowing how much they knew of Jesus and how much they trusted him before the miracle. But the healing made a tremendous difference to them. They recognized that what had happened showed the power of God, and that made full believers out of them too. The whole household came to a place of faith.

The Second Sign

John rounds off this story by telling us that this is "the second sign that Jesus did when he had come out of Judea into Galilee" (v. 54). But he has already told us that Jesus had done "signs" in Jerusalem, so that many believed (2:23). How, then, is this the second sign? Some scholars think that John is making use of a book someone had written about Jesus' miracles, a "Book of Signs." This is not impossible, for the miracles are always attractive to Christian people; to this day we love to hear of how Jesus made people well. Some early Christians may have decided to write a book telling of the miracles. But this does not seem likely. The fact is that all the books we have from the early Christians include teaching as well as miracles, and it is not easy to think that anyone would want to write about Jesus as simply a miracle worker. He was that, but he was much more.

It seems more likely that we should understand John as Rieu does when he translates, "Thus once again Jesus wrought a miracle after leaving Judaea for Galilee." It was not Jesus' second miracle, but it was the second time he had worked a "sign" after he had gone from Judea into Galilee. It may indeed have been the second one he did in Galilee. We must bear in mind that there is a great deal that Jesus did that we know nothing about. The Gospels record only a few of the many things he did. But as far as our information goes, this was Jesus' second Galilean miracle, and both were done after he had been to Judea and returned.

The earlier miracle was the changing of water into wine (chapter 2). Perhaps John wants us to notice something of an advance. That was a miracle done on the spot; this one was done at a distance. That was a change in an inanimate substance (water was changed into wine), but this one concerned a living being. That one marked a continuance of social life. This one took a boy as good as dead and gave him life.

20

A Lame Man Healed

After these things there was a feast of the Jews and Jesus went up to Jerusalem. Now there is in Jerusalem by the Sheep Pool a pool that has five colonnades, called in Hebrew "Bethesda." In them there lay a crowd of sick people, blind, lame, paralyzed. Now there was a man there who had been thirty-eight years in his illness. When Jesus saw this man lying there and came to know that he had been like this for a long time he says to him, "Do you want to be made well?" The sick man answered him, "Sir, when the water is stirred up I have no one to help me into the pool; while I am coming someone else gets down before me." Jesus says to him, "Get up, pick up your pallet and walk." Immediately the man became well and he picked up his pallet and walked (John 5:1–9).

The miracle of healing we have been considering in the previous study took place in Galilee. John now moves to Jerusalem. His "after these things" is a time note he uses now and then to convey the thought of an indefinite interval. He is not telling us everything that happened nor does he let us know how long an interval elapsed before the next incident took place. He is interested in the things Jesus said and did, not in the precise sequence.

It happened at "a feast." This time John does not tell us which feast it was, as he often does. He is very interested in the Jewish feasts; in fact, there is more information about them in this Gospel than in any of the others. John uses the word *feast* a total of seventeen times. Matthew

164

and Mark each have it twice and Luke three times, so John's use is distinctly exceptional. Not only does he use the general term *feast* often, he names particular feasts. We read of three Passovers in this Gospel (2:13; 6:4; 11:55; the third Passover is mentioned several times). We read also of the Feast of the Dedication (10:22) and the Feast of Tabernacles (7:2). Each of the feasts, of course, had deep religious significance and pointed to important spiritual truths. Apparently one of John's minor aims is to show his readers that Jesus perfectly fulfilled all that the feasts typified. What they symbolized he brought into existence.

All Jewish adult males were required to go up to Jerusalem for the three most important feasts of the year, the Passover (or Feast of Unleavened Bread), the Feast of Weeks, and the Feast of Tabernacles (Deut. 16:16). They often tried to go up also on other occasions, for there was clearly something special about observing a feast in the capital city, the one place where there could be a temple. As John does not tell us which feast this one was, we do not know whether or not it was one of the great feasts. We have nothing to go on, so the suggestions that are made are mere guesses. Since John does not mention the disciples in this incident, it is possible that Jesus went up without them. Though they often accompanied Jesus, we should not suppose that he never went anywhere without taking them with him.

The Pool

"Now there is in Jerusalem . . . ," says John, and his use of the present tense ("is") may be significant. It has been drawn into discussions of the date of the writing of this Gospel. The city of Jerusalem was destroyed by the Romans in A.D. 70, and if the present tense is used in its normal sense, this would mean that this Gospel was written before that date. In my opinion it was written before A.D. 70, but we cannot put much emphasis on this line of reasoning. People sometimes use the present tense when they are talking about things in the past, and John may be doing just that.

He goes on to talk about a pool, but the way he locates it leaves us uncertain about his precise meaning. He says, "Now there is in Jerusalem by the Sheep—," but he does not say what goes with "Sheep." The people who read his Gospel in the first century would have understood this perfectly, and John did not need to spell it out. But we do not, so we have to guess. The most common conjecture is "gate." Hence "Now there is in Jerusalem by the Sheep Gate" is adopted by translations like the Revised Standard, the New International Version, and the Good News Bible. One objection is that no ancient writer takes it that way. (C. K. Barrett says that no one takes it

165

that way before A.D. 1283.) If it were correct, we would expect writers in antiquity to show that they understood it this way. Another suggestion is "market" (King James). There is nothing improbable about this, and it may be correct.

But on the whole the best suggestion seems to be that we should understand the word *pool* (as do most ancient writers). John is saying, then, "Now there is in Jerusalem by the Sheep Pool a pool. . . ." Somewhere near the Sheep Pool there was another pool, and it is at this other pool where the action takes place. The word used for "pool" means it was quite large; we should not think of it as a little pond. The word is connected with the verb "to swim" and means a pool big enough to swim in.

There is another problem with the name of the pool, this time due not to what John wrote, but to what the scribes did with his Gospel. The name varies in the ancient manuscripts. It seems that some of the scribes either did not understand the name or thought it was wrong, so they tried to correct it. For whatever reason, the pool is given a variety of names in the manuscripts. The name with the best support is Bethsaida (which means "house of fish" or "house of the fisher"). Another name found is Bethzatha, which appears to be a variant of Bezetha, and this, according to the Jewish historian Josephus, was the name of the part of the city where the pool was located. Belzetha, which appears in other manuscripts, is probably another variant of the same name. The name in the King James Version is Bethesda, which means "house of mercy," a beautiful and appropriate name when we think of the sick people who came there for help.

The problem is a difficult one, but it seems to have been solved for us by the Dead Sea Scrolls. One of them has references to a number of places in and around Jerusalem, one of which is "Beth Eshdatain." Now in Hebrew and Aramaic, in addition to the singular and the plural of nouns with which we are familiar, there is a form for the dual, that is to say, there is a special form of nouns that denotes two. And "Eshdatain" is dual. The ancient monastery near which the scrolls were found was destroyed in the war of A.D. 66–70, so we have here evidence contemporary with the New Testament, and its reference to the two pools seems to make it clear that we are to think of Bethesda as the correct name.

Archaeologists have found a double pool which in modern times is known as St. Anne's. There is little doubt that this is the place where the healing took place. There were five colonnades, one between the two pools and the other four around the perimeter.

People Waiting to Be Healed

John tells us that in these colonnades there was "a crowd of sick people, blind, lame, paralyzed." The true text of the Gospel does not tell us why they were there, but in some manuscripts it is made plain that they were there to try to find healing. These manuscripts go on to say that sometimes an angel went down into the pool. The waters of the pool were agitated, and whoever went into the pool first was healed. So the people were there, each hoping to be the first into the pool when the angel came, and thus be cured.

There can be no doubt that this is not part of what John wrote; it is quite out of character in the New Testament. Nowhere in Scripture do we have anything like an angel's coming and doing works of healing on a haphazard basis, with the first of a group of sick people to get into a pool being chosen and all the rest ignored, no matter how needy. It simply does not fit into the Christian way of understanding things. But there is little doubt that many people in Jerusalem believed this, and that was why the sick were there at the pool. They really thought that there was a chance of a cure if they could be first into the pool when the water was stirred.

Nobody knows what caused the disturbance of the water. Some think there was a spring that bubbled up intermittently, and this may well have been the case. There is no spring there now, but it is not impossible that there was such a spring in Jesus' day and that it dried up over the centuries. Others think that water was piped into the pool from some external source (from the temple area perhaps) and that when this happened the waters were agitated. We do not know. But there is no reason to doubt that there was something that caused the waters to move at unpredictable times, and that this was interpreted by the people of Jerusalem as meaning that an angel came and gave the sick the chance of being healed.

A Lame Man

Among them there was a man who had had some complaint for thirty-eight years. John does not tell us what the trouble was, though from verse 8 there can be little doubt that it was some form of lameness. Some exegetes draw spiritual lessons from the duration of the man's illness; they point out that it was the length of time that the Israelites wandered in the wilderness after their disobedience of God (Deut. 2:14). They see in this account a picture of the Jews paralyzed because of their lack of faith, and of Jesus giving healing to those who believed. Others think of the passage as applying generally to all those without spiritual power and not to the Jews in particular. They reason that the wilderness symbolism shows that such people have no spiritual home unless they turn to Christ. But while it may be possible to discover some edifying symbolism along such lines, it is not easy to think that this was what John had in mind. He seems rather to be

167

bringing out the fact that this lameness, being of such long-standing nature, was not going to be easy to cure. For thirty-eight years neither the healing waters not anything else had been able to make the man well.

Jesus saw the man lying there by the pool. John does not tell us how Jesus knew that the man had been there for so long; he simply says that Jesus "came to know" this. Jesus may have asked the man, or somebody may have told him. The main point is that he knew. In contrast to what happened in the case of many other healings, the man does not approach Jesus; Jesus approaches him (v. 6).

He begins by asking, "Do you want to be made well?" It may seem to us that the answer is obvious. Of course the man would want to be cured. But it is not quite so simple. A man who had been disabled for so many years had settled into a pattern. He knew what his disability allowed him to do and what it stopped him from doing. Almost certainly he was a beggar, since there was no other way he could get a living. People would know him and where to find him if they wanted to help him.

If he was to be made well, he would lose all this. He would be adventuring into an unknown life. He could no longer depend on other people, but would have to take the responsibility for his own life. He would lose all his present securities and, being no longer a beggar, would have to earn his own living. How? He had not been trained to do anything; he had no special skills. People might help a lame person, but who would help an able-bodied man? To be healed meant to enter a completely new life, a life with wonderful possibilities but also with unknown perils. What did the man really want?

What we really want is not always what we say. There is a story about a man who lost out to a rival for promotion in the organization in which they both worked. The loser felt that he ought to do the right thing, so he dictated a telegram to his secretary: "Congratulations on your success. Permit me to extend heartiest congratulations and pledge my sincere, wholehearted support." The secretary took the message down in shorthand, then said, "Shall I read it back?"

"No, no," said the man. "I couldn't stand it!"

We are left wondering whether the congratulatory message was really meant. To say a thing and to mean it deep down are not the same. We are likewise left wondering whether the lame man really wanted healing. Jesus' question concerns the man's will, deep down. Did he really want health, with all its responsibilities as well as its privileges?

William Barclay reminds us that there is a contemporary application. "The first essential towards receiving the power of Jesus," he says, "is the intense desire for it. Jesus comes to us and says: 'Do you really want to be changed?' If in our inmost hearts we are well content to stay as we are there can be no change for us. The desire for the better things must be surging in our hearts." One reason why some people have nothing to do with Christ is that they do not wish to be disturbed out of their comfortable, selfish ways. To be a Christian introduces us to a life that none who have experienced it ever want to lose. But there is a price. To enter this life means leaving the old one.

Healing

The man's thoughts are concentrated on the pool. He makes no real answer to Jesus' question, though perhaps he implies that his endeavors to get into the pool over all those long years show that he did want healing. But quite clearly he does not think of Jesus as someone who might heal him. He has his mind made up about the way healing would come and does not allow anything to disturb him from that course. John Calvin comments, "This sick man does what we nearly all do. He limits God's help to his own ideas and does not dare promise himself more than he conceives in his mind."

The sick man explained to Jesus why he had not had healing, though he had looked for it for so long. Clearly he believed firmly that the one way in which he would be healed would be by getting into the pool right after the waters moved, so that the angel's healing work would be done on him. But his infirmity made it difficult for him to move fast, and someone always beat him to it. If he had had someone to help him, he would have had more chance. But he had no one. Actually, unless he could swim, he really did need help, because the pool was quite deep and there was no shallow end.

Jesus did not discuss the pool or its alleged curative properties. He simply told the man to get up, take up his pallet, and walk (v. 8). The word I have translated "pallet" means a camp bed. Some see it as a mat, and Moulton and Milligan, who produced a Greek lexicon giving the meaning of the words of the New Testament when they occur in the papyri and inscriptions, speak of it as "the poor man's bed or mattress." It was evidently quite light and portable, as we would expect from its being by the pool. There was no absolute need for him to pick it up. The man would have been just as truly cured if he had sprung to his feet and gone around the pool, "walking and leaping and praising God" like the lame man healed in Acts 3:8. But the taking up of the poor bed on which he had lain for so long was no doubt symbolical. No longer did it carry him through the day; he carried it.

The cure was immediate. Straightaway the man was healed, and he did what Jesus told him: he took up his pallet and walked. The power of the Lord was greater than that of the lameness. With one word of

169

command, Jesus dispelled the paralysis that had lasted for thirty-eight years.

An interesting feature of this healing is that there is nothing comparable to "your faith has saved you," which we find so often in the accounts of healing miracles in the other Gospels. Not only is there no mention of faith on the part of this man, but there is no room for it. When he was asked who had healed him, this man did not know. Far from trusting Jesus, he did not even know his name. And later, though obviously the religious authorities were hostile to the man who had healed him, he did not hesitate to go and tell them who it was. He does not stand out as an attractive personality at all.

We may well reflect that while Jesus commonly acted in response to faith, this was not a necessary precondition of the power of God being at work in him. He could and sometimes did do a mighty work when, as far as we can see, there was no faith.

21

The Sabbath

Now that day was the Sabbath. The Jews therefore said to the man who had been healed, "Sabbath it is and it isn't lawful for you to carry your pallet." But he answered them, "The man who made me well, that man said to me, "Take up your pallet and walk." They asked him, "Who is the man who said to you, 'Take (it) up and walk'?" But the man who had been healed did not know who it was because Jesus had gone off, there being a crowd in the place. After this Jesus finds him in the temple and said to him, "Look, you have been made well; sin no longer, lest something worse happen to you." The man went off and told the Jews that it was Jesus who had made him well. For this reason the Jews persecuted Jesus, because he was doing these things on the Sabbath. But Jesus answered them, "My Father works right up till now and I work too." On account of this, then, the Jews tried all the more to kill him, because he was not only breaking the Sabbath, but was calling God his own Father, making himself equal to God (John 5:9–18).

The lame man had been healed on a Sabbath day, and that led to trouble. There were pernickety Jews who were more interested in the letter of the law than in deeds of mercy, and they took offense at what had happened. In verse 10 John speaks simply of "the Jews," which is a way he has of referring to the religious leaders of the nation, especially those who were hostile to Jesus. Sometimes, it is true, he uses the term in a neutral sense or even a good sense, as when he reports the words of Jesus, "Salvation is of the Jews" (4:22). But generally, as here, he does not mean the whole nation, but that section of it that was in authority and opposed what Jesus was doing.

These Jews addressed the healed man. Incidentally, John has the word *healed* in the perfect tense, which indicates that the cure was permanent. In all probability many of the "cures" that took place at the pool did not last very long. John is not talking about a sham healing, but about something that had made a permanent change in the man. He was healed and would stay healed.

But that did not matter to these Jewish leaders. They drew attention to the day and indeed put emphasis on it: "Sabbath it is," they said, "and it isn't lawful for you to carry your pallet." By putting the word *Sabbath* first, they gave it emphasis. For them what mattered was that the day was holy. They ignored the healing altogether and did not even mention it. Their precious regulations mattered to them much more than the plight of a man who had been lame for thirty-eight years!

Sabbath Regulations

The Jewish teachers made a very thoroughgoing attempt to stop all work on the Sabbath, and some of their regulations were really extraordinary. Thus in the Mishnah tractate *Shabbath* we read of thirty-nine classes of work forbidden on the Sabbath (*Shabbath* 7:2). This was not, however, a complete list: both at the beginning and the end it is insisted that these are "the main classes of work," which leaves open the possibility that other activities were prohibited as well.

And they certainly were. A man might not go out on the Sabbath wearing one sandal, unless he had a wound in his foot (*Shabbath* 6:2). The reasoning was that this would give rise to suspicion that he was carrying the other sandal under his cloak (a forbidden "work"). If he was wounded, however, nobody would think he had another sandal with him. Again, while it was quite in order to borrow wine or oil from a neighbor on the Sabbath, one must not say, "Lend me them" (*Shabbath* 23:1). To say this would imply that a transaction was being made, and a transaction might involve writing, which was one of the thirty-nine forbidden classes of work.

A man should not search his clothing on the Sabbath looking for fleas, nor should he read by lamplight (*Shabbath* 1:3). The point of this latter is that he might be engrossed in his reading and, forgetful that it was the Sabbath, might perform the work of tipping the lamp to make the oil flow into the wick so that he would have a better light. A woman was forbidden to dress her hair or paint her eyelids (*Shabbath* 10:6), for she would then be engaged in the forbidden work of building or dyeing.

One regulation that I rather like was concerned with toothache: One must not put vinegar on one's teeth in an attempt to soothe the ache (that would be a forbidden act of healing). But it was permitted to take vinegar in the ordinary course of a meal, and the rabbis added philosophically, "If he is healed he is healed" (*Shabbath* 14:4).

It is obvious from such regulations that there were many ways in which the unwary might fall into a breach of the Sabbath. But it was also the case that the knowledgeable were able to get around many of the regulations. It was stipulated that one must not carry things in either hand, in one's bosom, or on one's shoulder. These were ordinary methods of carrying things and were clearly "work." But a regulation says: "If [he took it out] on the back of his hand, or with his foot or with his mouth or with his elbow, or in his ear or in his hair or in his wallet [carried] mouth downwards, or between his wallet and his shirt, or in the hem of his shirt, or in his shoe or in his sandal, he is not culpable since he has not taken it out after the fashion of them that take out [a burden]" (*Shabbath* 10:3). None of these was a normal way of carrying things, so none was classed as work. We are reminded of Jesus' castigation of those who put heavy burdens on other people but did not lift them themselves (Matt. 23:4). Clearly anyone with a very good knowledge of the regulations would not only be able to forbid other people from doing many harmless things, but would find ways of doing most things he wanted to do himself.

"He Told Me to Do It"

It was in such an atmosphere that the healed man was interrogated. He was examined by the experts and, while he himself would not have known all the regulations, he knew that all sorts of work were forbidden on the Sabbath. He knew also that his judges were in a position to do him harm if they judged him guilty of a transgression. So he was in a difficult position.

He defended himself by saying that it wasn't his fault. The man who healed him had told him to take up his pallet and walk (v. 11). What else could he do? One of the regulations provided that if a man was carried on a couch, "he is not culpable by reason of the couch, since the couch is secondary" (*Shabbath* 10:5). But apparently a couch by itself was quite another matter. It was not secondary, and the man was therefore culpable. Our lame man presumably did not know the regulation, but his judges did. So he was in danger.

The Jews naturally asked him who it was who had told him to take up his pallet and walk (v. 12), but the man could not help them. He had not known who it was. It was enough for him that he was healed. He simply did what he was told. Nor could he point Jesus out. There was "a crowd in the place" and, human nature being what it is, the people had doubtless flocked around the healed man to see for themselves what had happened to him. Jesus would have been lost in the crowd, and the man himself would have been so taken up with his newfound health that he would not have been looking for Jesus or for anyone else. So there was no way he could answer their question.

"Sin No Longer"

It was otherwise a little time later. John tells us that Jesus found the man in the temple. He may well have gone there to offer thanks to God for the wonderful healing he had received. Jesus sometimes told people to give thanks in this way (Mark 1:44; Luke 17:14), and it is not unlikely that the man was doing something of this sort. He certainly had cause for thanksgiving.

It is plain that he was not in any sense a follower of Jesus. He had not been healed on account of his faith or anything of the sort. He was a man in need, and Jesus in his compassion simply met that need. But it was also important that the man be brought to face spiritual realities. So Jesus sought him out.

"Look, you have been made well," he said; "sin no longer, lest something worse happen to you" (v. 14). "You have been made well" is in the perfect tense, which means that the cure was permanent. He would not relapse into his former lameness. But Jesus points to his sin and urges him to abandon it. What the sin was we have no way of knowing, but it must have been real enough, and Jesus knew what it was. He does not say, "Don't begin to sin, now that you have a new life," but rather, "Stop sinning—sin no longer." The expression implies that the man had been sinning and that his sin continued. He had a new physical life. Jesus bids him start a new spiritual life.

In this Gospel it is made clear that suffering is not necessarily the result of sin. Jesus told the disciples that the man born blind had not suffered his disability because of sin (9:3). But this does not mean that suffering is never the result of sin. Thus it is possible that in the present case there was some sin that lay behind the lameness. Some have felt that the "something worse" of which Jesus spoke was a further physical disability that the man would undergo if he kept on in an evil way. This cannot be dismissed as altogether impossible, but it seems more likely that Jesus is pointing out that the eternal consequences of sin are worse than the lameness from which the man had been delivered. He had escaped from a crippling physical handicap. Let him not now live in such a way that he would incur a far worse consequence and an eternal one.

We do not always take the "something worse" seriously enough. There is a story told of Bishop Warren A. Candler that illustrates this point. He was preaching on the way Ananias and Sapphira lied to God and pointing to the seriousness of sin. "God does not strike people dead these days for lying," he said. "If he did where would I be?" A ripple of laughter went through his amused congregation. The bishop paused for a moment and then roared right back at them, "I'll tell you where I'd be. I'd be right here, preaching to an empty house!" We do not give enough contemplation to the consequence of sin. If we think about it at all, we think it will happen to someone else. We should take Jesus' words more seriously. His warning is as relevant to us as to anyone.

Persecution

The healed man was not a very nice person. When he found out that it was Jesus who had healed him, he went off to the authorities and told them. He knew that they were incensed at the healing and wanted to know who had performed it in order to take action against him. One would think that simple gratitude would have impelled the man to keep quiet. The authorities had done nothing to him; they had questioned him and let him go. Why then should he go out of his way to let them know the identity of his benefactor?

Perhaps he thought he was still in danger. We do not know what penalties were inflicted at that time on those who broke the Sabbath, but whatever they were the man was liable. The death penalty was theoretically possible, so he may have thought that he was in considerable danger. His defense at his examination had been that the man who healed him told him to carry his pallet. Now that he could name him, he could make his case. Though it meant trouble for the Healer, the man may have reasoned that it secured his own safety. It was not an admirable action.

There is an interesting difference in the way what happened is described by the authorities and by the man. They asked him who it was who told him to take up his pallet and walk (v. 12). Now he answered their question by saying that it was Jesus who had healed him (v. 15). For them it was the offense that mattered. For him the important thing was the healing. Augustine acutely commented: "They sought darkness from the Sabbath more than light from the miracle."

"For this reason the Jews persecuted Jesus, because he was doing these things on the Sabbath" (v. 16). John does not tell us exactly what they did in this persecution, but it must have been unpleasant. Note that John says that Jesus "was doing these things on the Sabbath." The verb denotes continuous action; Jesus kept on doing things like this. It seems that John is not going to tell us of a great number of activities of

175

Jesus on the Sabbath. He has apparently chosen this one as a representative action, one that enables us to see Jesus' attitude toward the Sabbath.

We should notice that according to the Jewish leaders Jesus had a totally wrong attitude toward the Sabbath. In the usual translation of their accusation, Jesus "broke" the Sabbath, but this may not be strong enough. The verb is the ordinary word for "loose"; this can be in the sense "loosen the cohesion," and thus "loosen into its component parts," that is, "destroy." It is used of destroying the temple in 2:19, and of the ship breaking up in Acts 27:41. Where physical objects are not in mind, it may be used in this way for destruction, for example, Christ's destruction of the works of the devil (1 John 3:8). It seems that it is some such meaning as this that the Jews had in mind. They thought that Jesus was not simply making a single breach of the Sabbath regulations; he was destroying the whole institution. They were concerned about what had happened on this one day, but they were more concerned because they thought that what Jesus was doing meant the end of the Sabbath. In their view, if people acted as he did, then the Sabbath was gone.

It is plain from the synoptic Gospels that Jesus' attitude toward God's day was very different from that characteristic of the Pharisees. It is interesting that people from Jerusalem went up to Galilee to oppose Jesus (Mark 3:22, etc.). That was a long way to go, and we wonder why they did it. This story may give us part of the reason. Jesus came into conflict with the authorities in Jerusalem on what they saw as a major issue. Accordingly they opposed him strongly wherever they could.

The Sabbath

Jesus' defense is interesting. He does not refer directly to the Sabbath, but to the Father: "My Father works right up till now and I work too" (v. 17). He calls God simply "My Father," which is a more intimate form of address than the Jews would use. They might call God "Father," but they would usually add something like "in heaven" to make it clear that they were not being too familiar. But Jesus does no such thing. Here and in other places he uses the ordinary language of the family when he is speaking of the heavenly Father. This is a claim to a special intimacy, and the Jews recognized it as such.

The creation story in Genesis ends with the statement: "By the seventh day God had finished the work he had been doing; so on the seventh day he rested from all his work. And God blessed the seventh day and made it holy, because on it he rested from all the work of creating that he had done" (Gen. 2:2–3). The Sabbath rest thus derives from God's resting from his creating activity. But that does not mean that God rested from everything. There might be no more creating, but unless there was a sustaining activity from God, creation could not last. He continually upholds everything.

Jesus' attitude to the Sabbath derives from that of God. As we have seen, he claims a special closeness to God. In the synoptic Gospels he justifies what he does on the Sabbath with the words: "So the Son of man is Lord even of the Sabbath" (Mark 2:28). While the wording is different, the two defenses are basically very similar. Jesus has a special relationship to the Father, a relationship that issues in his being "the Son of man" and having a special position that enables him to do what he does. And that relationship justifies him in doing on the Sabbath what God does. This close personal relationship is significant throughout the Fourth Gospel.

As we shall see in the next study, it leads to Jesus doing what God does (v. 19). We should be clear on this. When he rejected the attitude of the Jews to the Sabbath, he was not saying that they were too restrictive and that their regulations should be eased. He was saying that they had the wrong attitude altogether. They objected to his healing on the Sabbath. Why? God did not cease from works of mercy, nor should his people. If they really understood what God was doing in the world and doing all the time, they would see that deeds of compassion, like the healing of the lame man, were not simply permitted but required. That was the kind of thing God did, and therefore it was the kind of thing that God's people should be doing.

Equal with God

But the Jews were not impressed. To them it seemed that Jesus was adding another offense: not only did he continually break the Sabbath, but now he was claiming that God was his Father in a special way. They saw that as "making himself equal to God" (v. 18). On both counts he was a blasphemer.

They never seem to have asked themselves whether what he said was true. It contradicted their cherished ideas, and that was enough for them. It had to be wrong. So does prejudice blind people. The coming of the Son of God into their midst was the most wonderful thing that had ever happened to them. But they did not see what had happened. They did not recognize what God was doing. Prejudice always blinds people and robs them of their opportunity to receive the richness of God's blessings.

Right through his Gospel, John is insisting that God was in Jesus in a special way. He would have agreed with the Jews that in his claims with regard to the Sabbath and his relationship to the Father, Jesus

177

was making himself equal with God. But he would have gone on to say that those claims were justified. The error of the Jews lay not in a failure to understand Jesus' meaning, but in a failure to see that what he said was the truth.

22

The Son of the Father

*Jesus replied, "Truly, truly, I say to you, the Son can do nothing
of himself, only what he sees the Father doing; for whatever he
does, these things the Son does likewise. For the Father loves
the Son and shows him all the things that he himself does. And
greater works than these he will show him so that you will
marvel. For as the Father raises the dead and gives them life, so
also the Son gives life to whom he will. For the Father judges
no one, but he has committed all judgment to the Son so that
all may honor the Son even as they honor the Father. He who
does not honor the Son does not honor the Father who sent
him. Truly, truly, I say to you that he who hears my word and
believes him who sent me has life eternal. He does not come
into judgment, but has passed out of death into life"* (John
5:19–24).

The discourse that follows the healing of the lame man
is rather strangely neglected. It does not have striking expressions like
"the Logos," nor sustained dialogue full of human interest like the
conversation with the woman at the well. But it is critically important.
As Bishop Ryle says, "Nowhere else in the Gospels do we find our Lord
making such a formal, systematic, orderly, regular statement of His
own unity with the Father, His divine commission and authority, and
the proofs of His Messiahship, as we find in this discourse." Here we
have Jesus setting forth in orderly fashion the truth of his relationship
to the Father and something of what that means in his daily life. He

179

makes it clear also that this has consequences for his listeners. It is because of his relationship to the Father that they ought to give heed to what he says. And much of what we read elsewhere in this Gospel depends on the truths here set out. Certainly it was because of the kind of claim that he made here that his enemies finally killed him.

The discourse is a unity, but we may divide it into three sections. In the first (vv. 19–24) Jesus is concerned with his relationship to the Father, in the second (vv. 25–29) with his work of judgment, and in the third (vv. 30–47) with the witness borne to him in a variety of ways, which shows that what he claims about himself is well supported. We will consider them in order.

Doing the Same Things

John introduces this discourse in a way that shows it is important. The expression I have translated "Jesus replied" is somewhat longer and more formal in the Greek: "Therefore Jesus answered and said to them." It is followed by "Truly, truly" (which occurs again in vv. 24–25). All this is a way of emphasizing the importance of what follows. It is not a casual utterance but a considered statement of great significance.

Jesus begins by saying that he "can do nothing" other than what he sees the Father doing (v. 19). Notice the word *can*. He is not saying that he does not do things other than those the Father does, but that he cannot do them. This is reinforced with an emphatic negative. In the Greek there is a double negative, literally "cannot do nothing"; in English two negatives cancel each other out, but in Greek they strengthen each other. Jesus is saying that he can do absolutely nothing apart from the Father; he is quite helpless without the help the Father gives.

Today we more or less take it for granted that God is to be spoken of as "Father," but this was not the way it was in the first century. As we saw in an earlier study (p. 176), the Jews did sometimes call God "Father," but they kept their distance all the same. They usually added something to remove any suspicion of undue familiarity, for example, "our Father in heaven." They were sure that God had a special relationship to the Jewish nation, but they were also sure that they must take care not to presume on this relationship. One wit has complained that in modern times people tend to think of God as a celestial Grandfather rather than as the heavenly Father. First-century Jews did not make that mistake.

But Jesus often called God "Father," using the language of ordinary family life in his approach to God. Nowhere is this more apparent than in the Fourth Gospel. John has the word *Father* 137 times, of which no fewer than 122 refer to God. This is far and away the most frequent use of the term anywhere in the New Testament (Matthew comes closest with sixty-four examples of "Father"; in all the Pauline letters it is found only sixty-three times). It is to John more than anyone that we owe our use of "Father" when we think of God. He has the word fourteen times in this discourse alone. Here Jesus is concerned with his relationship to God in a very special way.

It is what the Son sees the Father doing that he himself does. Notice that he does not say that he does similar things or that he copies the Father's deeds. He does the *same* things. The Father and the Son are at work together. What the Son is doing the Father is doing, and what the Father is doing the Son is doing likewise. R. H. Lightfoot brings out this point: "The union, therefore, is absolute. It is not, for instance, as though the Son reveals the Father in certain particular ways or in certain remarkable actions; no moment of His life, and no action of His, but is the expression of the life and action of the Father." The point is important. It is easy to think of the Father as at work in the Son, say, at the moment of the healing of the lame man. But Jesus is claiming something far more than that. He is saying that in his whole life he and the Father are at one and are doing the same things. He never acts independently of the Father. The relationship between them is very close and intimate.

The Father Loves the Son

And the relationship is one of love (v. 20). The Father loves the Son, a statement that is repeated elsewhere in this Gospel (10:17; 15:9; 17:23, 24, 26; the verb is different in these passages, but they all point to a deep and constant love). Love is important throughout this Gospel, and the love that links the Father and the Son is at the basis of it all. The use of the present tense indicates a continuing love. The Father never ceases to love the Son.

Now it is of the essence of love that it gives. The gift here is one of knowledge: the Father keeps showing the Son all that he does. This "showing" on the part of the Father corresponds to the "seeing" on the part of the Son (v. 19). "All the things" indicates that there is no withholding. The love of the Father for the Son means that he opens up to him all that he himself is doing. There is full and complete mutual disclosure.

And there are greater things ahead: "greater works than these he will show him." Jesus does not explain what these greater works are; as a result, the passage has been variously understood. Some draw attention to the greater miracles that Jesus would do, miracles described by John in later chapters: the giving of sight to a man born blind (ch. 9),

181

and the raising of Lazarus from the dead (ch. 11). Others think of the spiritual resurrection involved in Jesus' gift of life to the spiritually dead, or point to what he would do through his followers in later times, the "greater works" of 14:12.

But we should surely understand "greater works" as referring to the works of which Jesus goes on to speak: his giving of life and his work in judgment. Notice that he speaks of them simply as "works." What to us is a stupendous miracle is to him no more than a work. John often uses this term for the miracles Jesus does; indeed, in this Gospel Jesus more often calls them works than anything else. John speaks of them as "signs," for they have meaning, and Jesus uses this term sometimes. But his usual word is "works."

He will do these greater works "so that you will marvel." The doing of a miracle shows that there is a power at work that we do not usually see. The point of the greater works of which Jesus is speaking is that they bring people to see something of the power of God in action. Jesus can call on people to believe "for the works' sake" (14:11). Of course, faith that rests on the works is not the highest kind of faith, but it is better than none.

Life for the Dead

Jesus points out that the Father raises people from the dead and gives them life (v. 21), a truth that his hearers would have readily accepted. There was a saying of the rabbis: "Three keys are in the hand of God and they are not given into the hand of any agent, namely that of the rain [Deut. 28:12], that of the womb [Gen. 30:22], and that of the raising of the dead [Ezek. 37:13]."

But Jesus says that the Son gives life to whomever he wills, and this was something that his hearers would have found highly offensive. Life is the gift of the Father; it is not given by any of God's agents. So this saying is something that Jesus' audience would have rejected decisively. They could not accept the fact that God was in Christ in a very special way, that what Jesus was doing was what God was doing. But it was true whether they accepted it or not, and Jesus confronts them with it.

The question arises as to whether Jesus is here speaking of the life that will be given when the dead are raised on the day of judgment, or whether he means his present gift of eternal life. There can be no doubt that a little later he is speaking of the last great day, for he refers to calling people out of their graves (vv. 28–29). But since his verbs here are in the present tense, it seems that he is referring to his present gift of life, after which he goes on to the further thought of life at the last day.

Jesus takes those who are spiritually dead, people whose whole horizon is bounded by the affairs of this life in which they are immersed, and to them he gives life. This is the great miracle of which John writes so often. It is one of the great themes of his Gospel that Jesus gives eternal life and gives it here and now. Here, in this life, we may know what it is to experience the life of the world to come.

Judgment

The thought next moves to judgment. This is apparently only a preliminary to the fuller treatment that will be given the subject a little later (vv. 25–29). But here we have what for the Jews would have been an astonishing new thought: Jesus said that the Father has "committed all judgment" to him (v. 22). It was accepted Jewish teaching that at the last day we all face judgment. There was nothing new about that.

But Jesus went on to say that the Father has committed all judgment to the Son, and this the Jews would have found very difficult to accept. They held firmly that the Judge on the last day would be God himself, that no one else would have this authority. We might think that perhaps the Messiah would be the Judge and that the Jews had simply gone astray in failing to see that Jesus was the Messiah. They did fail to see that, but there was another difficulty for them: they did not expect the Messiah, whoever he was, to be the Judge. Strack-Billerbeck, the standard authority for the writings of the rabbis, maintains that in the whole range of rabbinic literature there is no passage that says the Messiah will judge the world. This was not an accepted idea at all. Jesus was claiming that he would exercise a function that the Jews universally held belongs to God alone.

The Christians did not see Christ as in any way opposed to the Father in this matter of judging. They did not deny that the Father would be the Judge, but they held that the Father would judge the world through the One he had appointed for this task (cf. Acts 17:31). The Father gave assurance of this in that he raised him from the dead (Acts 17:31). This view sees the Father and the Son as very closely related; and that, of course, is the point of the present passage.

Judgment will be done in this way, says Jesus, "so that all may honor the Son even as they honor the Father" (v. 23). For a king is dishonored if his messengers are dishonored. There is a well-known example of this in the Old Testament (2 Sam. 10). When Nahash the king of the Ammonites died, David reflected that this man had showed him kindness, so he sent messengers to express his sympathy to the new king, Hanun the son of Nahash. But Hanun's advisers told him they were sure that there was no friendship in David; he had simply sent people spy out the land, they said, preparatory to an invasion. Convinced by this reasoning, Hanun had half of each man's beard shaved off and half of his clothing cut off. Then he sent them back. David took this insult to his messengers as an insult to himself and responded with the war that Hanun's advisers thought they were warding off.

Likewise, people who dishonored the Son dishonored the Father who sent him. To ill-treat the messenger of God is to fail to honor the God who sent him. But John is saying more than this. The passage we are considering keeps emphasizing the unity of the Father and the Son. These two do not act separately. It is what he sees the Father doing— that and nothing else—that the Son does. They do not exist separately: the Father is in the Son, and the Son is in the Father (14:10). When people do dishonor to Jesus they are not simply dishonoring a peasant from Nazareth; they are dishonoring God. What is done to the Son is done to the Father. The close unity of the two means that it is an exceedingly serious offense to do dishonor to Jesus. People are to honor the Son just as they honor the Father.

Salvation

That the Father and the Son are one is seen in the way people are saved. Jesus introduces the next saying with "Truly, truly," which is a way of drawing attention to the importance of the words. They are solemn and very significant.

Then he says, "He who hears my word and believes him who sent me has life eternal" (v. 24). He does not say, "He who hears my word and believes it." Nor does he say, "He who hears the word of God and believes it." The Father and the Son are so much a unity that Jesus speaks of hearing what he says and believing the Father. What he says is what the Father says.

We have seen in our earlier studies that John often speaks of "believing in" (e.g., 3:16). This is a way of bringing out the importance of trusting a person. It means believing in Jesus so wholeheartedly that, so to speak, we are taken out of ourselves and come to be one with him. We come to be "in" him, as Paul would put it. Here John does not use that construction, but one that means "accepting as true." He is talking about believing what God says to us, really believing it. Now if we really believe that what God says is true (not simply say we believe), then we trust him. While the two constructions draw attention to different ways of looking at faith, in the end they come to much the same. We are to believe what God says and are also to trust him. The two are inseparable.

The person who so believes, Jesus says, "has life eternal." Notice the present tense. He does not say the person "will one day have life eternal," but his words mean that the believer has it now. Of course it would be legitimate to use the future tense, because there is much more to eternal life than we can know here and now. We will enter into its fullness in the life to come. That is true. But it is not what Jesus is saying here. He is saying that the believer has eternal life and has it now. Eternal life is endless life. That is important. But what is more important is that it is life of the highest quality.

A person who is stranded on a desert island or lost in a tropical jungle might well manage to stay alive. He might manage to find food and water and even to be healthy. But such a life would be limited and impoverished when compared with the rich and full life that is possible in a civilized community. So it is with the person who is badly injured and comatose and kept alive on life-support systems. He is alive in the sense that his heart is beating, and he cannot be said to have died. But life in the sense of a rich and meaningful existence is not his.

There are different kinds of "life." Jesus is saying that the wonderfully satisfying life that is proper to the world to come, the kind of life that is lived in eternity, is made available to those who believe. That there is more to be experienced in the afterlife goes without saying. But that we enter into something of that life here and now is the wonderful gift that Christ gives his own.

No Death

For those who believe, there is no condemnation. John's word is "judgment," but here the meaning is negative judgment or condemnation. The believer need never fear that, for Jesus has delivered him. He has already passed out of death into life.

We have just seen that the person stranded on a desert island or lost in a jungle or in a coma is not experiencing a very full life. What Jesus is saying here is that people who lack faith are not really living at all. They may go through the motions, but their existence is so impoverished that compared to the life he came to bring, they are dead. They lack the peace of God. They do not know divine forgiveness. They have no experience of the dynamic of the Holy Spirit and are strangers to fellowship with God. They do not enjoy the rich and warm fellowship of the redeemed. "Life" means ever so many things of which they have no knowledge.

It is that kind of living that Jesus calls "death." It is a shallow and empty form of existence. To be limited by one's sins and unable to get free of them is a form of death. To know that in the next world one faces their consequences is a form of death. To be ignorant of the life of the world to come is another form of death. "A man wrapped up in himself makes a very small parcel," some wit has said, and it is so true. Any

185

way of living that cuts us off from God and confines us to what we are in ourselves and can achieve of ourselves is not life in the full sense, but a form of death.

The salvation Jesus comes to bring delivers us from death. We will die (unless the Lord comes back soon) in the sense that we will pass from this life. But this is a transition from one form of living to another. In the full sense of the word, the believer will never die (11:26). Already he has passed out of death and into life.

23

Life and Judgment

"Truly, truly, I tell you that an hour is coming and now is, when the dead will hear the voice of the Son of God and those who hear will live. For as the Father has life in himself, so also he has given it to the Son to have life in himself. And he has given him authority to do judgment, because he is the Son of man. Do not be astonished at this, for an hour is coming in which all who are in the tombs will hear his voice and will come out, those who have done good things to the resurrection of life and those who have done bad things to the resurrection of judgment" (John 5:25–29).

Truly, truly," shows that we are coming to another very significant saying. Jesus uses the expression to emphasize the importance of the words that follow, so there is no doubt that these words are meant to be taken with full seriousness.

But they can be taken in more ways than one, and different students of the Gospel do in fact interpret them differently. The major dispute is over whether we are to understand the judgment of which Jesus speaks as a judgment that takes place here and now, or whether he is referring to a judgment at the last day. A present judgment is certainly found in this Gospel, for example, in 3:19, where we read that to love darkness rather than the light is itself judgment. And the judgment at the end of this world is certainly in view in some passages, for example, when Jesus refers to the word he speaks as judging people "at the last day" (12:48). Both are Johannine thoughts. The question is, Which is in

187

mind in this passage? Advocates of both present and future judgment are certainly to be found.

Life

Jesus begins this section by speaking about the life he gives to the dead (v. 25). This could be understood as his calling of people from the tombs at the last day were it not for the fact that he says not only "an hour is coming," but also "and now is." The addition makes it very difficult for us to see this as a reference to the end of the world. Jesus is talking about something that happens now. We find exactly the same expression in 4:23, when Jesus is talking to the woman of Samaria about true worship. So there can be little doubt that here at any rate we should understand Jesus to be speaking about the present.

"The dead," then, are the spiritually dead, those about whom we were thinking in our last study, people who walk and talk and go through all the motions of being alive here and now, but whose spiritual lives are such that they can be spoken of only as dead. If we take this Gospel seriously, we must see that spiritual death is a grim reality. Unless people receive the life-giving touch of the Savior, they are dead where it counts.

John's use of the Greek verb *to hear* should be noticed. For the technically minded let me say that sometimes he uses the accusative case after the verb and sometimes the genitive. For those not so minded, it is enough to know that he has two ways of expressing himself. When he uses one of them (the accusative), he means that the sound is heard and that is all, like hearing the wind in 3:8 and not understanding. But when he uses the other (the genitive), at least with sounds like voices, he means that the sound is heard with understanding and appreciation, like the sheep hearing the voice of their own shepherd (10:3).

It is this second construction that John has here. When spiritually dead people hear Jesus, some of them at any rate hear with understanding and appreciation. There are, of course, others who do not give him this sort of hearing, but John is not talking about them here. Of those who hear rightly we may say that God is at work in their hearts and they do not reject the message. They take it in and are glad of it. Those who hear in this way "will live." Life is the gift of the Son of God, as we see so often in this Gospel.

Notice that Jesus refers to himself here as "the Son of God." We often use this expression when we speak about him, but he does not often use it himself. In fact, in John's Gospel he does so three times only, here and in 10:36 and 11:4. The Jews apparently took good notice, for they told Pilate that he said he was the Son of God (19:7). Towards the end of the Gospel, John tells us that he wrote it so that people may believe "that

Jesus is the Christ, the Son of God . . ." (20:31). It is interesting accordingly that he so rarely refers to Jesus as making this claim. John prefers to make his point by letting what happened speak for itself. When his readers see what Jesus did and what he taught, they will see for themselves that he was indeed the Son of God.

But here Jesus is speaking about the giving of life to the dead. In speaking of this kind of activity, it is appropriate for him to refer to his relationship to the Father. Anyone less could not do this. It is because he is the divine Son that he is able to give life. So it is that those who hear will live. This does not mean that everyone who heard him was saved. This Gospel makes it very clear that there were people who heard Jesus and yet rejected him wholeheartedly. Their response to the word of life was a preference for death. So they continued in their self-centered ways and in the end hounded Jesus to his death.

But John's interest at this point is not in those who preferred death to life, but in those who responded to Jesus. For them it was life, eternal life, the life of the coming age. They were done with the ways of death.

Life in Himself

Jesus goes on to point out that God's relation to life is not the same as that of anyone else. The Father "has life in himself" (v. 26). We have life because our parents came together and God gave them the gift of life. No one gave God the gift. Our life is a fact, but not a necessary fact. The world would have gone on without us if we had not been born. But the life of God is not like that. His life is a necessary life. It is impossible for him not to exist. If he did not exist, nothing would exist. God's life is of a different quality from ours.

Augustine, a great theologian of the ancient church, reflected on this passage. God did not "borrow" life, he thought, nor partake of a life other than his own: "The very life is to Him His very self." Augustine used a candle as an illustration. When it is night and we have a lit candle, we are not in the darkness. But if the candle is put out, we are in darkness; we have no light in ourselves. So with life. We do not have it in ourselves, but it is a gift given to us. Not so with God. His life is his own. He needs no one to give him life. With him is "the fountain of life" (Ps. 36:9); "the Lord is your life" (Deut. 30:20). We are reminded that "God gave us life eternal and this life is in his Son" (1 John 5:11).

And God has given the Son, Jesus continues, the same gift. He too has life in himself. His is a necessary life. Peter called him "the Prince of life" (Acts 3:15), which brings out the same thought from another angle. Jesus is sovereign over life, not subject, as we are, to all sorts of limitations if it is to continue. Augustine saw no difference between the kind of life the Father has and that which the Son has, except that the Father has life in himself that nobody gave him, and the Son has life in himself that the Father gave him. That the Father is the ultimate source of all life, including that of the Son, is perhaps a way of assuring us that ultimately there is but one life. We are not to think of two eternal sources of life.

It is this assurance about the nature of the Son's life that gives believers assurance about the eternal life Christ gives to them. He shares with the Father in having this life that does not depend on some external source. Since his relationship to life is sovereign, he is thus able to bestow it where he wills. The eternal life we have is the gift of the One who is in a position to make the gift because he has life "in himself."

Authority for Judgment

The thought moves on to judgment. The Father has given to the Son authority to exercise judgment "because he is the Son of man" (v. 27). Some have taken the last expression to mean "man," and understand Jesus to be saying that it is the fact that he is genuinely human that is his qualification for judging. But this is scarcely adequate, for as Chrysostom pointed out centuries ago, if that was the meaning, we would all be qualified to judge. There is a small difference between the expression used here and "the Son of man" as used elsewhere, but the difference should not be regarded as significant. Jesus is saying that it is because he is all that "the Son of man" means that he is qualified to be the Judge of us all (cf. Dan. 7:13–14).

Judgment, like life, belongs with the Father. Abraham could refer to God as "the Judge of all the earth" (Gen. 18:25), and Jephthah could speak of "the Lord, the Judge" (Judg. 11:27). As we saw in an earlier study (p. 183), the Jews grasped this truth firmly and held that in the end it is God and God only who will be our Judge. They did not even allow the possibility that the Messiah would engage in judgment. The thought that the Son of God would in the end be the Judge was a distinctively Christian thought. It did not spring from first-century Judaism, but was in fact strenuously resisted by the Jewish leaders when they heard Jesus make his claim. So we should not accept Jesus' words here as commonplace, as though he were saying something that everybody knew. He was making a great and unusual claim.

That the Father has given him the authority to judge is a way of making it clear that nothing Jesus says about himself takes away from the supreme place of the Father. We are not to think of the two as in any sort of conflict or rivalry, nor are we to think of them as acting independently of one another. Just a few verses back we saw that the Son does what the Father does and that this means not that he copies the Father, but that they are together doing the same thing. Now we have something of the same thought with regard to judgment. It is not that Jesus displaces the Father; it is rather that the Father does the judgment but does it through the Son. So it is with all the authority of the Father that the Son does his work of judging.

Resurrection

Jesus goes on to the thought of the resurrection at the last day (vv. 28–29). There are, it is true, some who hold that in this section of the discourse, as in the preceding one, we are to think of the present time rather than the end of the age. The whole is to be understood, we are told, as referring to the giving of life to the spiritually dead. That seems clearly to be the meaning in the earlier verses, but the language is against it in this part of the discourse. Jesus speaks of those in the tombs and of resurrection to judgment as well as of resurrection to life. A resurrection to judgment is certainly not the giving of spiritual life to the spiritually dead.

Jesus calls on his hearers not to be astonished at what he has just said, because there is something perhaps even more wonderful to take place in the future: he will be God's agent in bringing about the resurrection of the dead and final judgment. He speaks of those in the tombs as hearing his voice. His will be the voice that wakes the dead and ushers in the final judgment.

He goes on to speak of "those who have done good things" as called "to the resurrection of life," while "those who have done bad things" are summoned to that of "judgment." It puzzles some Christians that final judgment is linked with our deeds, when the New Testament is so insistent that our salvation is all of God's grace. But while the New Testament always regards salvation as springing from grace, it just as consistently sees judgment as proceeding on the basis of works.

We should be clear that none of us ever merits salvation. As Christians in the New Testament sense, we have come to see ourselves as sinners and yet as the objects of God's love. We are those who have been died for, and we receive God's good gift by faith. But saving faith does not leave us as we were. The saved do not go on in their sins as though nothing has happened. They repent and turn away from all evil. They live in the strength that God supplies, and their new lives are the evidence that they have been saved by grace. The lives we live are the proof of the faith we profess.

It is true that we do not always live as we should, even though we are convinced Christians. Paul deals with this problem when he tells the Corinthians that there is but one foundation, namely Jesus Christ, but that those on this foundation (and thus saved) may build with what is valuable, like gold or silver or costly stone, or on the other hand with worthless things like wood or hay or straw (1 Cor. 3:10–12). Judgment day will test our work, Paul says, "for it will be revealed in fire, and the fire will test each person's work, of what sort it is" (v. 13). He goes on to point out that the person who has built well will receive accordingly, while the person who has put in only shoddy work will suffer the loss of it, "though he himself will be saved, but so as through fire" (vv. 14–15).

This helps us to see that judgment is a reality, even though it is grace that saves us. We who are Christians are responsible people; one day we must give account of ourselves to God. The way we serve God is important, and we must never take lightly the importance of doing good works.

Condemnation

But there are others, those who have done bad things. The word I have translated "bad things" occurs in 3:20 and nowhere else in John. It is not the usual word for "evil." It means "worthless," "of no account," though we should probably not insist on the literal meaning. John often uses words with more or less the same meaning without making sharp distinctions, and this is the way we should understand this term. The Evangelist is referring to those who have rejected Christ and to the kind of lives they have lived in consequence. They have not set themselves to the service of God and of their fellows, which is the lot of every faithful believer. In one way or another they have lived lives with self at the center. The result is that in the end, when they stand before the Judge in the last great day, what they have done will be accounted worthless.

They will be raised, Jesus says, "to the resurrection of judgment." Strictly this means a resurrection at which they will undergo judgment, which theoretically might result in either condemnation or acquittal. But "judgment" may sometimes mean "adverse judgment," and that is surely the case here. Evildoers can look for no great success when they are given just judgment.

The two resurrections remind us that we are responsible people. God has set us in the world with many opportunities for helping others and generally cooperating with his purposes. We should not think it a matter of indifference whether we make use of our opportunities or not. To whom much has been given, of them will much be required. Life is a wonderfully joyous affair, but it is also wonderfully solemn. It is a one-way street; we cannot go back and do anything over again. We get just one shot at it. Let us then make the most of it.

One more thing before we leave this section of the discourse. For Jesus to speak as he did that day was a very courageous thing. He was saying things which he knew the religious people of his day would regard as blasphemy and for which they would oppose him relentlessly. But they were true and they were important, so he said them. William Barclay well says that "the man who listened to words like this had only two alternatives—the listener must either accept Jesus as the Son of God, or he must hate Him as a blasphemer and seek to destroy Him. There is hardly any passage where Jesus appeals for men's love and defies men's hatred as He does here." The sad thing is that the religious leaders simply rejected what Jesus said. There is no indication that they weighed the evidence or gave serious consideration to what Jesus was saying. They simply opposed him more strongly than ever. G. Campbell Morgan says, "On the human level, what Jesus did that day, and what He said that day cost Him His life. They never forgave Him."

24

Witness to the Son

"I can do nothing of myself. I judge as I hear and my judgment is just, because I don't seek my own will but the will of him who sent me. If I bear witness about myself, my witness is not true, but there is another who bears witness about me and I know that the witness that he witnesses about me is true. You sent to John and he bore witness to the truth; now I do not receive witness from man but I say these things so that you may be saved. That man was the light that burns and shines and you were willing to rejoice for a time in his light. But I have the witness greater than that of John; for the works which the Father has given me to do, the very works themselves that I am doing, bear witness about me that the Father has sent me. And the Father who sent me has borne witness about me. You have never heard his voice, you have never seen his form, nor do you have his word abiding in you because you do not believe him whom he sent. You search the Scriptures because you think you have eternal life in them. And it is they that bear witness about me, and yet you are not willing to come to me so that you may have life.

"I do not receive glory from men. But I know you, I know that you do not have the love of God within you. I have come in my Father's name and you don't receive me. If another should come in his own name you would receive him. How can you believe, receiving as you do glory from one another, and yet you do not seek the glory that is from the only God? Do not think that I will accuse you to the Father. It is Moses, on whom you have set your hope, who is your accuser. For if you believed Moses you would believe me, because he wrote about

me. But if you do not believe his writings how will you believe
my sayings?" (John 5:30–47).

Throughout his Gospel, John emphasizes the importance of witness. As we have seen in our earlier studies, this is noticeably more frequent in this Gospel than in any other book in the New Testament. John uses the concept in several ways, but the passage to which we now turn is noteworthy for the way in which he brings out the variety of the testimony borne to Jesus. Witness is borne to Jesus by the Father (vv. 32, 37; this is the testimony that carries conviction to Jesus), by John the Baptist (v. 33), by Jesus' works (v. 36), by Scripture (v. 39), and by Moses (v. 46). This is a very strong combination, and while it is not all the witness to Jesus that this Gospel records, it makes a powerful argument that people ought to believe in Jesus. The evidence is there.

The Witness of the Father

Jesus begins this part of his address by disclaiming that his actions are ever done independently of the Father. He uses the strong expression "can do nothing"; it is not simply that he does not act independently of God, he cannot do so (cf. 5:19). This does not, of course, mean that he is an automaton, unable to do anything unless someone from outside pulls the strings. It means that being who and what he is it is unthinkable that he should do anything that does not have the approval of the Father. We do not understand what Jesus' ministry was all about unless we see that it was the Father's work that he was doing. He came to do the Father's will and the Father's work. Precisely because of this, it was impossible for him to act independently. He always acted in the closest connection with the Father.

Jesus has just been talking about judging. He has said that it is his voice that will wake the dead and bring people from the tombs to face judgment. We saw that this is an extraordinary claim, because the Jews firmly believed that final judgment would be given by God alone. Now we see something of how and why Jesus would do this work of judgment. He is not speaking of an independent judgment which he would give and of which God might or might not approve. He cannot act independently of God. His judgment is as he hears, that is, "hears from God." He is in constant and intimate communion with the Father; this means that the judgment he gives is the judgment of God and as such is perfectly just.

He reinforces this with the firm disclaimer that his will is set to do anything other than what God wills. The present tense shows that he is referring to what happens in his life day by day. He is not referring here to final judgment. His aim throughout his life is to do the will of God. His own will is not set up in opposition to God's.

Jesus now comes to the thought of witness and points out that if he bore witness to himself, that witness would not be accepted (v. 31). There is a sense in which this is true of anyone. The law of Moses provided that there must always be two or three witnesses (Deut. 19:15). The rabbis said emphatically, "None may be believed when he testifies of himself"; and again, "None may testify of himself." Law everywhere agrees that a man's testimony to himself is not sufficient. There must be others to establish the truth.

But Jesus is saying something more than this. Several translators and commentators miss something of his point by taking the text to mean, "If I testify about myself, that testimony is not valid." But Jesus does not say "valid"; he says "true." He is not talking about the conditions under which testimony is adjudged valid. He is talking about what is true. He is making the claim that if there were nothing but his own word, it would not be true. Unless the Father supported what he said, not only would it be invalid testimony, but it would be erroneous.

William Temple has a valuable comment: "If His word stood alone, it would not be true at all. For divine revelation did not begin and end in Him, though it reached its crown and finds its criterion in Him. There must be other evidence, not only to support His own, but because the nature of His claim is such that it can only be true if all the work of God—the entire universe so far as it is not vitiated by sin—attests it."

We should be clear on this. If Jesus was what he said he was, then his claim had to be supported by other testimony. It could not stand by itself. This does not mean that there was anything lacking in it, but simply that it was a claim of such magnitude that it involved something more than himself.

And Jesus says that such testimony does exist: "there is another who bears witness about me" (v. 32). He does not say who this other is, but there is not the slightest doubt that he is referring to the Father. Notice that he uses the present tense. He says that this other "bears witness," and he speaks of "the witness that he witnesses." He is appealing to present fact. If his opponents only had eyes to see, they would discern that the Father was bearing witness in the whole life of Jesus. The things Jesus did and the things he said were done and said only because the Father was with him. This testimony is the only testimony that mattered to Jesus. It, and only it, was sufficient for him.

A little later he comes back to the thought of the Father's testimony (v. 37). He points out that his opponents do not hear the voice of God, even though they claim to be followers of Moses and Moses heard that voice (Exod. 33:11). The disciples differ from the Jews in the way they hear the words of Jesus. They not only listen to them, but they receive them and recognize Jesus' divine origin (17:8). But despite their great claims, the Jews do not recognize the voice of God when they hear it.

They have never "seen his form." Jacob saw God and his name was changed to Israel (Gen. 32:30; cf. v. 28). But though they claimed to be descendants of Israel, the Jews were not true Israelites. If they had been, they would have recognized that he who has seen Jesus has seen the Father (14:9).

Jesus also says that they did not have his word "abiding in" them (5:38). The psalmist hid God's word in his heart (Ps. 119:11). But though the Jews gave high honor to the psalmist, they did not follow his example. They professed reverence for the word of God and had a great knowledge of facts about Scripture. But it was not in their hearts. Had it been, they would have been open to receive the word of God from Jesus as the disciples did (17:14).

They did not receive him whom the Father sent (v. 38); this was both their basic error and the evidence that their high-sounding claims were false. The Father bears witness to Jesus. The Jews of the day for the most part did not recognize what God was doing. The reason they did not was their lack of will (v. 40). They willed not to come to Jesus and accordingly found all sorts of reasons for rejecting the divine witness. Let us be warned.

The Witness of John the Baptist

Immediately after introducing the thought that Jesus had another to bear witness to him (namely the Father), the Lord goes on to the witness of John the Baptist. "*You* sent to John," he says; his pronoun is emphatic (v. 33). This is not something he is bringing up of his own accord; it was the Jewish leaders' own idea that they should send to John. There is also the thought that the notion of someone's bearing witness to Jesus is not so strange. They themselves had a witness.

The Baptist bore his witness to the truth. The verb *bore witness* is in the perfect tense, which carries the suggestion of a witness that continues. Jesus is not speaking about ancient history, something of value only as a reminder of long-since-vanished events. John bore his testimony, and it continues to be of force. People remembered what he said. He bore his witness to "the truth." We would have expected that Jesus

197

would have spoken of this witness as being borne to himself. But we must keep two things in mind. The first is that Jesus himself is identified with the truth; he said, "I am . . . the truth" (14:6). It would therefore not be possible to bear witness to what this Gospel means by "the truth" without bearing witness to Jesus. In the Christian system there is no such thing as an abstract truth totally unrelated to Jesus. In the most meaningful sense of "truth" it is one with Jesus.

The other thing we must remember about "witness to the truth" is that Jesus would in due course tell Pilate that this was why he himself came into the world (18:37). The Baptist and Jesus were in a sense bearing witness to the same thing. Jesus went on to say to Pilate, "Everyone who is of the truth hears my voice." It is necessary to have a commitment to truth before one can take in what Jesus is saying. Because many of his contemporaries did not have that commitment, they rejected him and finally had him put on a cross.

Jesus gave the bearing of witness to the truth as the reason for his being born and coming into the world, and it is not without interest that the Baptist was a man "sent from God" and that he came to bear witness, in this case "to bear witness of the light" (1:6–8). Again we reflect that Jesus was "the light of the world" (8:12), so again John's witness points to Jesus. In this Gospel John the Baptist does but one thing: he bears witness to Jesus. We may see this in what is termed his bearing witness to the light or to the truth, or we may see it in John's referring to the Lamb of God or to a greater than he who would follow him or to one who would baptize in the Holy Spirit. But look at him how you will; for this Evangelist, John the Baptist was simply a witness.

Jesus goes on to say that it was not John's witness that brought conviction to himself (his "I" is emphatic). He received testimony from no man (v. 34). Since he had the testimony of the Father, why should he rely on John the Baptist? His reason for reminding them of John the Baptist was to benefit them: "so that *you* might be saved" (the emphatic pronoun again). If they had taken notice of what John was saying, they would have been started on the way that leads to salvation. That had in fact happened to some of the disciples. They had been among the followers of the Baptist and had obeyed him when he told them to go after Jesus. Why had these Jews not done the same?

When Jesus goes on to say that John was the burning lamp, he uses the past tense (v. 35). It may be that John was dead at this time or at least in prison. His ministry was in the past. Of course the lamp burns; it is consumed by shining. There may be a hint here that John's ministry was costly. He burned himself out, but he gave light to those about him.

Yet another emphatic pronoun *you* is used to draw a contrast between the Jews and the Baptist. John had such a sense of serious purpose that he gave himself wholeheartedly to his burning and shining, but they were happy to rejoice in him only "for a time" (literally, "for an hour"). They were casual merrymakers, not earnest seekers for truth. Though they had in their midst that man of whom Jesus said a greater than he had never arisen among those born of women (Matt. 11:11), they refused to take him seriously.

People often do not take the trouble to appreciate the truth when it is before them. I was reading of a woman who had trouble with her gas bill. She always paid what she saw on the bill, but some months she was told that she had underpaid, some that she had overpaid. She put this down to the inscrutable ways of the gas-company personnel, perhaps assisted by a computer or the red tape in which they were entangled. Then one day her latest check was returned along with a standardized card on which were printed various possible reasons: name of payee incorrectly entered, signature missing, and so forth. All of the usual explanations were crossed out and at the bottom was written: "You have been paying the date. *Please* pay the amount."

It was a little bit like that with the Baptist's contemporaries. They had firm ideas about the way to God and were not going to be sidetracked by a preacher like John. They were so sure that what they were doing was the right thing that they never asked whether what John was saying was true. So they missed the greatest blessing that God was offering them.

The Witness of the Works

The third form of witness is the witness of "the works" (v. 36), a witness that Jesus says is "greater than that of John." The majestic "But I" with which the verse begins sets Jesus apart from men. His "I" is emphatic again. Though John's witness was important and Jesus was happy to commend it, it was not what carried conviction to him. The works he did were evidence that God was at work in his ministry. These were works that "the Father has given me to do." God was in them.

We have seen that John in his Gospel often calls Jesus' miracles "signs," an important word, for it tells us that these are not simply works of power, but that they are meaningful. They point beyond themselves and convey spiritual truths. But John also often calls them "works," which is a more general term not confined to the miracles but covering all sorts of deeds. It indicates that the whole of Jesus' life (all his "works") mattered, for God was in it all, the nonmiraculous as well as the miraculous. It also indicates that what to us is a miracle was to Jesus no more than a work. There is no distinction between the miraculous and the more ordinary when this term is used; God is seen in it all. God is in the life Jesus lived, in his sinlessness, in his compassion, in his words of kindness, in all that he did. And because his whole life in all its variety showed forth God, it was all part of the witness borne to Jesus.

The Witness of Scripture

Jesus then referred to the attitude toward Scripture of those to whom he was speaking (v. 39). The verb I have translated "you search" might possibly be an imperative (as it is in the King James); the form of the Greek verb could be either an indicative or an imperative. We should probably take it as indicative, for Jesus was speaking about what they were doing. But is it fanciful to think of the imperative as in the background? Jesus was certainly encouraging the right attitude to the Bible.

During the early years of our era, the scribes had amassed a vast amount of curious learning about the Bible. We do not know exactly how much of this goes back to the time of Jesus, but certainly some of it does. These scribes knew how many verses and even how many letters there were in each of the books of the Bible, which verses had all the letters of the alphabet, what was the middle verse of a given book, and so on. They had compiled an incredible mass of useless information, while at the same time they failed to come to grips with what the Bible was saying.

Jesus says plainly that the Scriptures "bear witness about" him. Rightly read, the Old Testament leads to Christ. But the scribes of his day, with their wooden reverence for the letter of Scripture, failed to understand the wonderful thing it was saying and thus were quite unable to recognize him to whom the Scriptures pointed.

The fundamental trouble was that they did not want to see. Their will was set in a different direction. Jesus was in their midst, the messenger sent by God, the one who would accomplish salvation. Their tragedy was that despite the deference they paid to the Scriptures, they did not want to come to someone like Jesus. "You are not willing to come to me so that you may have life," he says (v. 40). And because they did not come, they cut themselves off from life.

The Witness of Moses

The end of the chapter includes a most unexpected line of reasoning. Jesus tells his hearers not to think that when they stand before God they will find that he is their accuser. No. Their accuser will be Moses

200

(v. 45). For the Jews, Moses was the great lawgiver, and because they so highly valued the law he gave and saw it as the law of God, they were sure that Moses would be on their side. Their attitude to the law of Moses secured his support. No matter who would be against them before God, they could surely rely on Moses, who gave the law that they made central in their thinking and living.

They had set their hope on Moses. The verb is in the perfect tense, which points to a continuing state of affairs: they had put their hope in Moses at some time in the past and there it rested. Hope in Moses was a permanent feature of religion for them.

Jesus does not say that Moses "will be" their accuser, but that he "is" their accuser. Most take this to look forward to the last day, the great day of judgment, and we should probably see this as included in the meaning. But the present tense also points to the state of affairs at the time of speaking. Moses is a standing witness against them.

The reason, says Jesus, is that Moses wrote about him (v. 46). This is in agreement with what Jesus has been saying about the witness of Scripture as a whole. What is true of the Bible generally is true of the books of Moses in particular. The Jews, however, were not holding to what Moses wrote but to what they thought he meant. Their prejudice prevented them from seeing the fulfillment of the writings of Moses when it took place before their eyes. Hoskyns wrote, "The law of Moses is not a religion of salvation, it is the categorical imperative of God by which men are accused and exposed as sinners." They are shown to need a Savior, and Jesus comes as that Savior. To read the law in the way the Jews of that day did is to miss what Moses was really saying.

So they did not really believe their great lawgiver. Jesus asks how, in view of that, they could be expected to believe what he himself says. They had put a good deal of time and energy into the study of Moses' words, words in written form which they could look at again and again and pore over in an effort to extract their meaning. And if they still did not believe what Moses had written, they would not (and they did not) believe the words that Jesus was speaking.

This section of John's Gospel makes the important point that there is adequate testimony borne to Jesus. If anyone does not believe, it is not because there is a lack of evidence. It is because of a lack of will. This sobering truth is still worth pondering.